UNWRAPPING THE EUROPEAN SOCIAL MODEL

Edited by Maria Jepsen and Amparo Serrano Pascual

First published in Great Britain in July 2006 by

The Policy Press
University of Bristol
Fourth Floor
Beacon House
Queen's Road
Bristol BS8 1QU
UK

Tel +44 (0)117 331 4054
Fax +44 (0)117 331 4093
e-mail tpp-info@bristol.ac.uk
www.policypress.org.uk

British Library Cataloguing in Publication Data
A catalogue record for this book is available from the British Library.

Library of Congress Cataloging-in-Publication Data
A catalog record for this book has been requested.

ISBN-10 1 86134 798 7 hardcover
ISBN-13 978 1 86134 798 5 hardcover

Cover design by Qube Design Associates, Bristol.
Printed and bound in Great Britain by MPG Books, Bodmin.

Contents

List of figures and tables

Figures

Tables

Acknowledgments

For the translation of certain chapters and the preparing of this book we would like to thank Kathleen Llawarne for her tremendous work. We would also like to thank the Kammer für Arbeiter und Angestellte Wien in Austria for both morally and financially supporting the research project at the European Trade Union Institute for Research, Education, Health and Safety (ETUI-REHS) on which this book is based. The ETUI-REHS is financially supported by the European Commission.

Notes on contributors

Jean-Claude Barbier is Senior Researcher (CNRS) at Modélisation Appliquée Trajectoires Institutionnelles Stratégies Socio-Économiques (MATISSE), Université Paris I – Panthéon-Sorbonne. His recent publications include: with M.T. Letablier (eds), *Social policy. Cross-national comparison: Epistemological and methodological issues*, Brussels: PIE–Pieter Lang (2005); with B. Théret, *Le nouveau système français de protection sociale*, collection Repères, Paris: La Découverte (2004); with H. Nadel, *La flessibilità del lavoro et dell'occupazione*, introduction by L. Castelluci and E. Pugliese, Rome: Donzelli (2003); with J. Gautié (eds), *Les politiques de l'emploi en Europe et aux Etats Unis*, Paris: PUF (1998); *Les politiques de l'emploi en Europe*, collection Domino, Paris: Flammarion (1997).

Jean-Michel Bonvin is Professor of Sociology at the University of Geneva. His main fields of interest are labour market policies, comparative social policy and theories of justice. Recent publications include 'What informational basis for assessing job-seekers? Capabilities vs preferences', *Review of Social Economy* (June 2005) and 'Social opportunities and individual responsibility: the capability approach and the Third Way', *Ethique économique* (2005). He is also co-editor of the quarterly review *Finance and the Common Good*.

Janine Goetschy is both a political scientist and a sociologist. She has been a senior research fellow at CNRS (attached to the University of Nanterre-IDHE, France) since 1976. She lectures at numerous French universities, business schools and *grandes écoles* in France and Europe. She is also closely connected to the Institute for European Studies at the Free University of Brussels, where she teaches on Social Europe issues, and is part of GARNET (the network of excellence on global governance and the EU). Her major subjects of interest and publications (around 95 titles) concern comparative industrial relations, organisational sociology, European integration and Social Europe. Her most recent publications focus on the European Employment Strategy and new modes of governance within the European Union.

Roy Green is Professor of Management and Dean of the Macquarie Graduate School of Management in Sydney, Australia. Previously (until 2005), he was Dean of the Commerce Faculty at the National

University of Ireland, Galway, and founding director of the Centre for Innovation and Structural Change. He has worked at universities in Australia, Ireland and the UK, and has published widely on innovation, industry and workplace analysis. He has worked on projects for the OECD, the European Union and the Australian government.

Maria Jepsen is Acting Head of the Research Department at ETUI-REHS, Belgium, and Senior Lecturer at the Free University of Brussels. Her main research interests are gender studies, comparative labour market studies and social protection systems in the European Union. Some of her most recent publications are: 'Flexicurity: an instrument for gender equality?', in *Employment policy from different angles*, Copenhagen: DJOEF (2005) and 'The wage penalty induced by part-time work: the case of Belgium', in collaboration with S. O'Dorchai, R. Plasman and F. Rycx, in *Cahiers économiques de Bruxelles* (2005).

Joel F. Handler is Richard C. Maxwell Professor of Law in the Law School at University of California, Los Angeles (UCLA), and Professor of Public Policy, UCLA. He is the author of *Social citizenship and workfare in the United States and Western Europe: The paradox of inclusion*, Cambridge University Press and, with Yeheskel Hasenfeld, *Blame welfare, ignore poverty and inequality* (forthcoming).

Maarten Keune is a senior researcher at ETUI-REHS, Belgium. His main research interests are economic sociology, neo-institutional analysis, employment policy, welfare state reform and industrial relations. He has authored numerous publications in these fields, with an emphasis on the new EU member states. Recent publications are: with A. Hemerijck and M. Rhodes, 'European welfare states: diversity, challenges and reforms', in *Developments in European politic,* Macmillan/ Palgrave (2006), and with C. Crouch, 'Changing dominant practice: Making use of institutional incongruence in Hungary and the UK', in *Change and continuity in institutional analysis: Explorations in the dynamics of advanced political economies*, Oxford (Oxford University Press, 2005).

Céline Lafoucriere has held several positions as researcher with responsibility for the European Employment Strategy and social dialogue. Recently, she joined the Foundation Centre for European Initiatives and Research in the Mediterranean (CIREM), in Madrid, Spain, as senior researcher. Her main research interests are the European Employment Strategy and its application at national level, in both member and candidate countries. Her most recent publications include: *The enlargement of Social Europe: The role of the social partners, Parts I and II.*

Lilja Mósesdóttir is Professor of Labour Market Studies at the Bifrost School of Business, Iceland, and coordinator of the EU Fifth Framework Programme project WELLKNOW (www.bifrost.is/wellknow). Her research interests include comparative labour market studies, the European Employment Strategy, gender relations and the knowledge-based society. She is the author of the book *The interplay between gender markets and the state in Sweden, Germany and the United States*, and co-editor of the books *Equal pay and gender mainstreaming the European Employment Strategy* and *Moving Europe towards the knowledge-based society and gender equality: Policies and performances.* Together with Rósa Erlingsdóttir, Lilja wrote the article 'Spreading the word across Europe. Gender mainstreaming as a political and policy project', recently published in the *International Feminist Journal of Politics.*

Robert Salais is Professor of Economics and co-director of the research centre IDHE, Ecole Normale Supérieure de Cachan, France. His main research areas include historical economics, public intervention, employment, social fairness and institutions. A selection of his recent publications are: with E. Chatel and T. Kirat, *L'action publique et ses dispositifs. Institutions, économie, politiques*, L'Harmattan (2005); with R. Villeneuve (eds), *Europe and the politics of capabilities,* Cambridge: Cambridge University Press (2005); with D.G. Mayes and J. Berghman (eds) *Social exclusion and European policy*, Cheltenham: Edward Elgar (2001); with E. Chatel and D. Rivaud-Danset (eds), *Institutions et conventions. La réflexivité de l'action économique*, Raisons Pratiques no 9, Paris: Editions de l'EHESS (1998); with N. Witheside (eds), *Governance, industry and labour markets in Britain and France,* London: Routledge (1998).

Wiemer Salverda is a director of the Amsterdam Institute for Advanced Labour Studies of the University of Amsterdam. He also coordinates the European Low-wage Employment Research Network (LoWER). Related to that network he coordinated an international research project on 'Demand patterns and employment growth'. This studied the evolution of the employment gap between the US and Europe, considering it from several angles with a particular focus on services: consumer household demand, the role of services in the structure of production, the level of low-wage service employment in relation to wage flexibility and labour market institutions, productivity and the demand for goods. The present book reflects some of the most important findings of this project. He has contributed to ETUI research previously, for example, on gender mainstreaming and youth unemployment. He was one of the editors of *Labour market inequalities: Problems and policies of low-wage employment in international perspective*, Oxford University Press (2000). He has contributed to many studies of wage inequality.

Amparo Serrano Pascual is Researcher and Lecturer in the Faculty of Political Sciences and Sociology at Complutense University, Madrid. Her main research interests are comparative employment, social and activation policies; the deconstruction of EU discourses, the political production of individuals in the European Employment Strategy, the knowledge society and the 'new social contract'. Some of her most recent publications are: (ed) *Activation policies in international perspective*, Brussels: ETUI-REHS, and, with U. Behning (eds), *L'approche intégrée du genre dans la stratégie européenne pour l'emploi*, Paris: L'Harmattan.

Introduction

Amparo Serrano Pascual and Maria Jepsen

Introduction

Social actors' political awareness of the need to reinforce the supranational dimension of social cohesion has gradually turned the concept of the European Social Model (ESM) into a key notion in political and scientific debates on social responses to globalisation. As this concept plays a key part in the articulation of the debate, a meta-analysis is required in order to avoid, often unnecessary, conceptual traps.

Use of the concept of ESM in academic and political debate is characterised by two main and interconnected features (Jepsen and Serrano Pascual, this volume): on the one hand, the usually taken-for-granted assumption of the reality status of the concept; on the other hand, its highly ambiguous and polysemous nature. The ESM is used with differing meanings in accordance with rather ambiguous definitions. A clear definition of what constitutes its essence seems to be lacking in most articles on the subject, while a review of the most important of these articles reveals that, insofar as definitions are to be found, they do not necessarily converge. When discussing whether the ESM exists and whether its various manifestations are converging or diverging, the question therefore arises of precisely what it is that is being discussed and what type of causal relationships are being brought into play. The prerequisite for answering these questions, which are basically empirical in nature, is an analytical tool; this implies analysing what we mean by the ESM and identifying its components. The polysemy surrounding the concept might well be found to reflect a lack of scientific precision in relation to its use in the debate on the European Union (EU). But this polysemy may also be understood in rhetorical terms, as a means of moving from one 'interpretative repertoire'[1] to another, for any one of a variety of purposes (for instance, to legitimise a policy proposal, to construct a sense of belonging, to turn supranational regulation into a need, and so on).

Moreover, the concept is based, to a very large extent, on a host of assumptions, most of which have not been empirically established, and the discussion is frequently built up without any serious examination of the main tools used to construct it. However, in spite of the variable ways in which the concept is used and/or constructed, the definitions do share some common assumptions, and these require discussion in order to avoid the normative character that sometimes characterises this debate. The first such assumption relates to the implicit reference to a dichotomy between the United States (US) and the European economy, on the one hand, and a distinction between two chronological phases of economic development on the other. One important feature is the concept's symbolic reliance on the US model, to which it implicitly or explicitly refers, while at the same time clearly assuming its own superiority. Implicitly, many authors and/or policy-makers take the US as a (negative) reference pole – or 'counterexample' – from which Europe is to be distinguished. These rhetorical contrasting poles – the US versus the EU and past versus the future – set the boundaries within which differences are constructed (Abélès, 2002) and trap the research within a fixed analytical framework. It is our belief that these implicit references and assumptions constitute a snare, in that they serve to inhibit further thinking on the subject.

A second common assumption relates to the interlinked nature of the economic and societal dimensions. Economic success and maintaining the social quality of Europe are presented as interrelated goals (see, for instance, Vobruba, 2001). The key question in this discussion is what type of conditions, within the analytical framework of societal change, are conducive to both economic success and the social improvement of living conditions. The arguments and claims underlying this discussion are indeed highly controversial, relating as they do to fundamental aspects such as the following: the extent to which Europe actually does share 'common' foundational features (Robbins, 1990); whether 'knowledge' is more important in the 'knowledge-based society' than in any other society; the lack of empirical evidence supporting the assertion of a real increase in global trade (Hay, 2002; Petit, 1999); the problematic description of globalisation as a non-negotiable external economic reality (Hay, 2002); the questioning of the much-touted correlation between the use of new information and communication technologies and increased productivity (Petit and Kragen, 1999); whether the 'new' economy promoted by the knowledge-based society really is all that new (Evans, 2000; Visco, 2000; Wolf, 1999); the extent to which these economic processes really do involve an increase in work-related qualifications; the real impact of these processes on organisational changes (Brödner,

2000); the need for a radical change in labour market institutions (Manning, 1998); and other questions too.

The purpose of this book is to discuss some of these assumptions and to point out how important it is to avoid taking them for granted. The relevance of this analysis is not solely to show the need for a more precise definition of the ESM and for a discussion of the assumptions underlying this concept. It is also to discuss its political status, which, in our view, is associated with the process (as well as with the project) of constructing a supranational regulation. How is it to be explained that, despite the controversial underlying conceptual assumptions and the multiple meanings attributable in some measure to the imprecise nature of the concept, this notion has acquired such hegemony in the debate about intervention paradigms? We wish to discuss the 'invention'[2] of this concept in the framework of the building and institutionalisation of supranational entities. Discourse can indeed be viewed as a social practice, underlining the 'action-oriented' nature of language use (Wetherell and Potter, 1988), and the ESM is a notion that has emerged, in the main, in the elaboration and discussion of public policy at the European level.

The first two chapters in this book deal with the conceptual definition and historical construction of the notion of the ESM. The chapter by Jepsen and Serrano Pascual (Chapter One) analyses and deconstructs the concept in order to identify the multiple meanings attributed to it in the academic and political arena. The conclusion reached is that the polysemy surrounding the concept might be explained by its rhetorical use by supranational institutions as a means of gaining and negotiating political legitimacy[3], while it is also the result of the complex status of the European arena. In Chapter Two, Goetschy presents a detailed analysis of how this ESM project has been historically built up. Describing how this historical construction is the result of multi-level tensions, she observes the concept as an evolving process, seeing it, accordingly, as the result of a *rapport de forces* between different institutional, geographical, economic and social actors. In this framework, new balances are put into place and negotiated between the various economic and social actors who take the European arena as a forum in which to reaffirm their position of hegemony.

The remainder of the book discusses some of the main assumptions behind the ESM concept. The first such assumption relates to the implicit reference to a dichotomy between the US and the European economy, on the one hand, and a substantive conception of the concept (according to which, we, as Europeans, share common values, institutions, and so on) on the other. The purpose of the remaining chapters is to discuss these assumptions and to point out how important it is to avoid taking them for granted. They set in perspective the implicit dichotomy established between the US and the European models – which underlies a definition of ESM as an *ideal type* – and deal with the question of to what extent there exists an EU model as distinct from the US one. In Chapter Three, Salverda discusses one of the main assumptions regarding what prevents the European model from becoming as competitive as the US model, namely, the idea that the regulatory tools (employment protection, wage regulation), characteristic of the ESM, result in a lack of flexibility and productivity of EU markets in comparison with the US economic model, resulting in a situation where the ESM stands in the way of employment. Salverda shows that the EU does not lack wage flexibility in comparison with the US, that the readjustment of the EU economy has taken place more rapidly in the EU than in the US – precisely because of the social institutions in place – and that this can account for a part of the employment gap observed between the EU and the US. He argues that the employment gap can be attributed to the policy of wage moderation and the fewer hours worked in the EU insofar as these factors contribute to a lower internal demand. Handler (Chapter Four), meanwhile, shows that the US and the EU share a large number of ideological assumptions and normative references behind activation policies, as well as the governance systems to implement them; however, the actors – private or public – differ to a certain extent between the two geographical areas, although some European countries are also beginning to involve private actors in the implementation of active policies (Larsen and Mailand, 2006: forthcoming; van Berkel, 2006: forthcoming).

A second assumption discussed is that which underlies the substantive conception of the ESM according to which EU countries share common values and/or common outcomes in social terms. Active policies – the fight against inactivity and social exclusion – and gender policies – the fight against discrimination and unfairness – represent the cornerstone of the ESM. Barbier (Chapter Five) calls into question this assumption, taking the specific example of activation policies. Rather than a homogeneous EU model, the values underpinning the activation measures, as well as their outcomes, vary considerably from country to country. This author concludes that no specific brand of activation associated with a homogeneous ESM emerges. Activation as a broad principle is shared across member states, but this set of broad normative orientations is compatible with a wide national diversity. This situation is further discussed by Mósesdóttir (Chapter

Six), whose arguments are based on the example of gender policies. She shows that, although supranational regulation now plays a key role in defining the problem (raising awareness of gender inequalities) and in finding common solutions (gender mainstreaming), the results of these policies vary a great deal from country to country as the idea of the dual-breadwinner model is slowly becoming a common feature. However, the rhetorical presentation of these policies, which emphasise the purpose of redressing the power relationship between the genders, has been turned into a policy of facilitating the smooth functioning of the labour market, and hence, while there seems to be some convergence between the employment participation of men and women, there does not seem to be much convergence with regard to the equal division of unpaid and paid work, which would require a regulatory power stronger than that of the European Employment Strategy (EES).

The substantialist conception of the ESM as an entity becomes even more questionable with the process of enlargement, as demonstrated by Keune (Chapter Seven). Enlargement has meant an increase in the empirical variation of social standards and regimes in the EU, with major divergence also among the new member states themselves. He also explores what influence the ESM has had on the new member states, thereby exploring its potential as a political project. The chapter argues that while no clear ESM is directly imposed upon the new member states, efforts are being made to extend the ESM as a political project to these countries.

Jepsen and Serrano Pascual, in this volume, argue that the concept of the ESM might be understood as a political project under construction. As the concept of the ESM could be understood as an instrument for elaborating a shared identity, the nucleus of this identity would be based less on an appeal to shared values or institutions than on the dissemination of cognitive frameworks to enable the construction of common formulae (intervention paradigms such as activation, gender mainstreaming) to solve the *problems* on the labour market that are institutionally constructed as shared. The policy of benchmarking and exchange of good practices, and the adoption of the political 'language' proposed by the European institutions to define the debate, forms part of this political project of constructing shared challenges and instruments.

At the very heart of the dissemination of these cognitive frameworks we find the new regulatory tool used at the supranational level, the Open Method of Coordination (OMC).[4] Benchmarking is very much at the core of the OMC. Salais (Chapter Eight) argues that the so-called harmonisation of data encouraged by Eurostat to measure these national efforts is highly misleading in view of the considerable diversity of national institutions and ways of conducting a national public policy. Reducing the complexity of the European models to a small number of indicators, which is a substantial component of the task represented by the EES, enables the political construction of common problems. Salais analyses the underpinnings of this policy of benchmarking, showing how this exercise of regulation has degenerated into a game of statistical performance, which in no way indicates whether or not the employability of citizens has actually improved.

The adoption of the 'language' proposed by the EU institutions, which is partly spread by the OMC, has had a major ideological impact on constructing the terms of the problems of unemployment and poverty in national debates, and has also influenced the demarcation of the areas of the debate (targeted audience), its major thrusts, and the manner in which the problems are described. This has been the case with the dissemination of concepts such as activation and gender mainstreaming. Bonvin (Chapter Nine) analyses the main sociological and ideological changes involved in the integration of activation policies and modernisation of the ESM as it has been defined by the EU institutions. He concludes that, while the changes do serve to prepare workers to be more adaptable and better able to respond to the new economic demands, they do not help to empower individuals to become citizens, as proposed by the ESM.

Finally, the ESM insists on the provision of common tools to solve problems that are recognised as nationally defined. One of these key tools is social partnership, so that establishing social dialogue appears as an intrinsic regulatory tool of the ESM. In this framework, the ESM should serve as a political tool to empower social partners and civil society. Lafoucriere and Green (Chapter Ten) analyse to what extent the process of integration of Eastern European countries into the EU may have positive effects in reinforcing institutions in these countries. They stress that the weak role currently played by these institutions, due to the deep legitimacy crisis suffered by the trades unions in these countries and their accession to the EU, has, rather than pushing them to empower their social institutions, actually served to weaken them even more.

ESM: a multi-level governance project

In Chapter One, Jepsen and Serrano Pascual suggest that the concept of the ESM may be understood as a set of propositions, which symbolically shape a European identity, thereby providing, at the same time, political legitimacy to EU institutions. The set of such propositions used by the European institutions for the purpose of self-representation is subject to permanent shift and constantly changing meanings, depending on how the institutions feel the need to adjust their identity, the strategies through which they seek legitimacy, or the balance of power. Construction of the political project of the ESM takes place in a complex context of tensions and search for political balances and compromises (Abélès, 2002; Goetschy, this volume) between national and supranational, and between social and economic actors, as well as between actors within the supranational institutions (for instance, between the different Directorates-General within the European Commission). Accordingly, as argued by Goetschy in this volume, the content of the ESM is the outcome of the manner in which different social, economic and institutional actors have reappropriated, for their own purposes, the different European treaties and different strategies for alliance and agreement established between them. In the supranational context characteristic of the economic challenges (discourse of globalisation and internationalisation of the economy) and the gradual calling into question of the national framework as the predominant (or even in some instances exclusive) area for demarcation of social concerns and remedies (Bauman, 1998; Muntigl et al, 2000), new balances are being put in place and negotiated between the various economic and social actors who take the European arena as a new forum in which to reaffirm their positions of hegemony.

As emerges from a reading of this volume, the most striking aspect of this political project is the paucity of precise identity marks to reinforce its social character. Rubbing shoulders in the European arena is a variety of different national models used to articulate the social question, a situation that is in stark contrast to the process of gradually institutionalised social responses that accompanied the development of industrial societies in the member countries. Institutionalisation of the national social models was the outcome of a complex process of establishing class alliances, which fostered the hegemony of a specific political culture in each European country (closer to social democratic compromises at one extreme and to neoliberal positions at the other). Such a political culture is the result of a broad and complex process of negotiation and articulation of conflict-based and/or negotiation-based cultures between different social actors that gradually come to form part of a nation's culture (Jorgensen, 2002). Historical traditions and social institutions articulate collective identities, configure values and social norms, reviving and strengthening the sense of belonging to a geographical community.

As opposed to the *economic* identity marks of the EU – for example the euro and the European Central Bank – the common *social* identity marks are few and do not shape any encompassing or integrated sphere where the ESM can be fostered and developed. The ideological position of the ESM is therefore complex, insofar as its construction is taking place in a common cultural vacuum, while one of its aims is the construction of just such a common culture. In other words, while the EU countries actually share very little in terms of common institutions and values (see contributions by Barbier, Handler, Lafoucriere and Green, Mósesdóttir, and Salverda), one important project of the European institutions is the production of a common identity (see Jepsen and Serrano Pascual, this volume). Whereas the processes whereby national identities have been built up have been based on the reaffirmation of a historical memory that reconstructs a representation of the past and a sense of belonging to the community, the specific feature of the European political project upon which European identity depends is its projection towards a reference located in the future. It is a project that resorts to an instrumental reason (search for collective solutions, efficiency of intervention mechanisms, creation of communities of thought, and so on) rather than appealing to the emotions and seeking to instil a sense of belonging.

The ambiguity of the concept of an ESM is not only the result of the battle of ideas between different social groups to gain precedence for their own particular hegemonic vision of the mission invested in the European project; it is also a reflection of the tremendous institutional and normative variety present within Europe and of the absence of any historically constructed legitimacy. Accordingly, the concept of the ESM could be understood as an instrument for elaborating a shared identity. The nucleus of this identity, still to be constructed, would be based less on an appeal to shared values than on the dissemination of cognitive frameworks to enable the construction of *common formulae* (intervention paradigms such as activation, flexicurity, and others) to solve the *problems* of the labour market (inactivity, unemployability, adaptability, eurosclerosis), which are, at the same time, institutionally constructed as shared. The policy of benchmarking and exchange of good practices, and the adoption of the political 'language' proposed by the European institutions to define the debate, form part of this political project of constructing shared challenges and instruments (see contributions by Mósesdóttir and Salais, this volume). It is thus a process of ideological construction geared to the search by the European institutions for viable areas of policy-making. These formulae and common problems are thus constituted as emblematic representations, which provide a basis for the political project proposed by the ESM.

The Open Method of Coordination: governance without government?[5]

According to the reconstruction of the evolution of the ESM, as compiled by Goetschy in this volume, the European social project has been conducted along two paths. There has been, on the one hand, an increase in the number and a broadening in the nature of the social questions tackled by the European institutions and, on the other hand, a diversification, multiplication and transformation of the modes of their regulation. Whereas at the beginning, the relatively few areas of regulation tackled at European level gave rise to legally binding instruments (European directives), gradually, while the areas of regulation are being extended, the nature of the regulation is changing, in two respects. First, it is a regulation that is procedural (dissemination of procedural routines) rather than substantive, consisting of the establishment of a series of 'rituals'[6] geared to the dissemination of epistemic paradigms structured under a set of concept headings. Second, the control mechanisms in the hands of the European institutions are undergoing diversification in such a way that complementary modes of regulation are introduced, characterised by a lack of formal sanctions. This development represents a shift from a form of regulation based exclusively on legal (for example, directives) or economic (for example, Economic and Monetary Union, EMU) sanctions to a form of coordination that appeals to the member states' preparedness to cooperate ('soft regulation'). The range of policy instruments available to the European institutions increases; alongside less use of directives, an increasing number of 'soft' methods of regulation have been introduced, such as the OMC, peer group pressure, encouragement of social dialogue at European level and the redistribution policy conducted in the context of the Structural Funds. We believe that the way in which this growing emphasis on persuasive regulation is taking place at the EU level runs the risk of depoliticising the regulation of social issues. We will develop this argument with the concrete example of the EES, which provides a good example for the analysis of the ESM as a political project and the drawing of conclusions as to the implications for Social Europe of constructing the ESM in the way this is being done at present.

Cognitive regulation by the EU institutions

The formulation of proposals in the context of the EES takes place in relation to concepts (employability, activation, gender mainstreaming, flexibility and security, and so on) rather than to methodologies or specific and concrete procedures for social intervention. These concepts, as already stated, are of a rather special nature in that they are highly ambiguous and general, enabling them to signify many different things at one and the same time. This *polysemy* reflects the particular position of the European institutions, faced as they are with the complex situation in which they have to put forward proposals compatible with the diversity of political philosophies and situations existing within the EU (see Chapter One).

This rather vague character of the concepts enables the member states to turn the drafting of National Action Plans, in which they respond to the European guidelines, into a merely formal and bureaucratic exercise that consists of translating already existing practices into the 'language' proposed by the European institutions. But this seemingly neutral and banal exercise of reclassifying existing policies to fit the conceptual framework devised in the employment guidelines is not ideologically neutral. A specific vocabulary (employability, knowledge-based society, lifelong learning, activation, gender mainstreaming, active ageing, competence-building, and so on) is gaining currency in national political discourse. This 'adoption' of the language proposed by the European institutions has had a major ideological impact on constructing the terms of the problems of unemployment and/or poverty, thus influencing the demarcation of the areas of the debate, its major thrusts and the manner in which the problems are described (see Barbier, Bonvin, Mósesdóttir and Salais, this volume). Although these concepts were not invented by the European institutions, they have, nonetheless, been popularised and disseminated by these bodies and used to polarise the political – and in many cases scientific – debate. The principal regulatory nature of these institutions thus comes to consist of proposing and disseminating a rhetoric articulated in accordance with concepts that enable construction of an interpretation of the position of our European societies (see the debate on the knowledge-based society), their challenges and problems (see the discourse on employability) and the alternatives (see the discourse on activation). As is demonstrated in this volume (in particular, see contributions by Bonvin and Salais), these concepts are not neutral and their incorporation into the political debate will entail the dissemination of normative references and social interpretations about what is to be considered problematic or not and, hence, what lends itself to revision. Many of their expressions[7] end up becoming reified as a result of continual use and repetition so that they turn into a kind of totem used to justify and revive projects and collective identities.

Accordingly, the discourse of the European institutions does in fact exert in some cases an important socio-cognitive influence and national policies are increasingly adapting themselves to the language and reference frameworks proposed by the European institutions. In this way, a European interpretative framework for an understanding of employment and social policies has been built up (Barbier, 2004; Jacobsson, 2004).

The EES has promoted new ways of thinking about and discussion of the problem of unemployment and social exclusion. Inactivity as a legitimate option is being increasingly called into question, with programmes being introduced to encourage labour market participation by groups traditionally not covered by these active policies (single mothers with young children, women, older workers, workers with temporary or permanent disability) (see Bonvin, this volume). In areas such as active ageing, equal opportunities, and others, important changes have taken place in the policy approach of member states (see Keune and Mósesdóttir, this volume). This has helped give legitimacy to new policy proposals and given additional power to certain policy decisions.

And so the employment policy debate in the national agendas has come to be increasingly focused on questions such as employability, activation, lifelong learning, as well as equal opportunities and active ageing. Meanwhile, other highly important social aspects, such as public investment in redistributive policies, organisational change, and so on, receive little or no mention in this debate.

Benchmarking policy and the construction of 'common' problems

The importance accorded to the setting of common indicators – or benchmarks – in the regulation of the EES provides further confirmation of what is being said here. Reducing the complexity of the European models to a small number of indicators, which is a substantial component of the task represented by the EES, enables the political construction of common problems (see Jepsen and Serrano Pascual, Salais and Bonvin, this volume). A series of statistical indicators[8] are to serve as benchmarks of national endeavours. As shown by Salais (this volume), the so-called harmonisation of data encouraged by Eurostat to measure these national efforts can be misleading in view of the considerable diversity of national institutions and ways of conducting national public policies.

The instruments for the measurement and monitoring of member states' compliance with the EES guidelines enable national policies to be subject to public scrutiny, facilitating explicit comparison with the other countries' results. Poor results measured by these indicators may generate considerable political debate at national level, thus representing a form of pressure on member states to achieve convergence towards these ideal goals. The sanction in this process comes to be the pressure exerted by peer group and public opinion. Even in the absence of official penalties in the event of failure to implement the strategy, this symbolic pressure can induce a high degree of compliance. Recommendations issued by the EU can place member states in uncomfortable positions.

The indicators used give precedence to quantitative rather than qualitative goals and the guidelines may be seen to be subject to economic criteria (see Salais and Bonvin, this volume, for a detailed discussion of this subject). A quantitative attitude to social problems is in this way encouraged, disregarding the need for a qualitative approach and thus tending to reproduce the problems. A high employment level may stimulate economic growth but it is far from apparent that it necessarily has positive effects on workers' quality of life. Insofar as gainful employment is viewed as the universal panacea, the main policies hinge on the achievement of four aims:

- to increase the activity rate of women;
- to encourage labour market participation of older workers;
- to adjust tax and social security systems to make them more employment-friendly;
- to remove administrative and tax obstacles to investment and employment.

The question of the quality of the jobs that are being created as a result of these policies is barely raised, in spite of the fact that this dimension has been receiving increasing attention in the European Commission's proposals. The notion that any job at all is preferable to unemployment might be justified if the jobs in question actually were a means of enabling people to improve their situation, by facilitating access to other better-quality jobs but, as shown in a recent European Commission *Employment in Europe* report (European Commission, 2003), temporary jobs do not necessarily serve as springboards towards better-quality jobs (and this is especially true in the case of low-skilled workers, older workers and women). Similarly, the number of individual action plans is a criterion for positive implementation of the policies but it is a criterion that says little about the quality of the plans in question. Accordingly, there is an urgent need for the introduction, alongside the quantitative criteria (numbers of jobs created, numbers of unemployed people), of qualitative criteria.

What is being encouraged is a construction of the problems in a manner that does not necessarily reflect the most pressing social problems but rather those that stand in the way of an optimum functioning of the economy in general. The indicators selected are thus those that best accord with the Broad Economic Policy Guidelines. In other words, social policies are being instrumentalised in the service of these guidelines (that is, financial equilibrium, labour market flexibility or employment rate).

From where do the concepts proposed by the European institutions derive?

If the main regulatory power possessed by the European institutions derives from their capacity to normalise the discourse pertaining to employment, an important question relates to the political origin and ideological inspiration of the concepts they are promoting. To answer this question it is important to remember the political status of the European institutions characterised by their nature as plural structures with multiple centres of power (see Goetschy, this volume).

A feature of most of the concepts relating to employment is the mixed political philosophies present in their various meanings. Terms deriving from discourses historically associated with highly diverse political philosophies come to be regarded as equivalent. To take one example, when referring to the need for European societies to adapt to increasingly acute global competition, the term invariably used is 'knowledge society', which connotes a political system that encourages workers' 'creative' capacities and 'autonomy' and is thus potentially emancipatory.

This makes it particularly difficult to identify the precise philosophical and political inspiration of these concepts. While numerous authors stress the neoliberal sources of this strategy (Handler, this volume), some emphasise the proposals of the Third Way as a major source of inspiration (Bonvin, this volume), and others the social democratic origin of some of the concepts (Barbier, this volume).

The complex nature of these proposals as a hotch-potch of numerous levels of compromise between diverse actors ('multi-level governance') makes it difficult to establish clear conclusions concerning their ideological origin. Even so, this so-called 'deliberative' community does not necessarily translate into the democratic reappropriation of a range of different *voices* from civil society. Given the asymmetrical power relationships between these different social actors, the hybrid and paradoxical discourse so characteristic of the institutions may, rather than reflecting a dialogue among different actors, become a monologue that simply reproduces the conventional economic wisdom.

The need to achieve ideological compromises between different groups and political philosophies also explains the terminological creativity and fertility of the European institutions and the 'expertocracy' surrounding them. One feature of this process is the proliferation of 'mixed words' (or words deriving from different levels of 'voice'), such as, for example, 'flexi-curity', 'employ-ability', 'activation', corporate social responsibility, and so on. These notions have taken on a pre-eminent position in economic and political – as well as academic – discourse. These terminological proposals are not necessarily to be interpreted as 'anglicisms' or as the transfer of concepts – and hence ideologies – deriving from the English-speaking world, for, in most cases, they did not previously exist in English (for example the concept of activation). In other cases, concepts have been directly imported from the world of economics (for example, benchmarking, contractualisation, flexibility, negotiation, involvement, partnership, peer-group pressure), which is evidence of the way in which the debate has been colonised, to a certain extent, by the concepts and discourse of the employer sector (Collignon et al, 2005; Hamzaoui, 2003; Salais, this volume) and is thus subject to a bias according to which social issues are viewed through economic spectacles.

The ambiguity of the concepts and the resulting difficulty in defining them with any precision also reflects the need for actors with very different cognitive and normative frameworks to agree on a 'solution' to a specific 'problem' (see Jepsen and Serrano Pascual, this volume). Taking the example of flexicurity, Kerstens et al (2005) demonstrate how this concept permits actors with a neoliberal cognitive and normative framework and actors with a more traditional socialist cognitive and normative framework 'to meet halfway'. They argue that the discussions and negotiations on policies that emphasise either flexibility and/or security can take place despite very different understandings of how the world functions and what the policies should attain. But this does, however, raise important questions as to the balance of power in the negotiations, the definition of what security is and what flexibility is and, even more important, how to generate a genuine 'win–win' situation; in summary, it raises questions as to what type of policy emerges from the process.

EU concepts as suppliers of strategic resources

The politically open character of the ESM, and its transformation into an arena where different actors – institutional, geographical, social and economic – struggle to gain precedence for their own policy preferences and proposals, can be explained by the important role played by concepts disseminated by the European institutions and used as strategic resources by a whole range of actors to rearticulate or affirm their own political positions and proposals.

As stressed earlier, as a result of the role of the EES in public debate and in raising awareness of topics not previously regarded as central to social and political discussion, this strategy is turning into an instrument of political mobilisation in the hands of civil society. In this framework, the European institutions are in a position to give new impetus to topics that had remained virtually absent from political analysis. This strategy may serve to raise social awareness of the situation of certain groups in society (for example, women, poor workers, the inactive population, older workers, minority ethnic communities) and to promote incorporation into the agenda of political priorities that, in spite of their importance, have remained undervalued at national level (for example the aspect of the quality of work). It may also help to stimulate political involvement in certain topics of relevance to social cohesion. Thus, this exercise may serve to raise awareness in the member states of specific labour market problems and to prompt questions about specific situations that might otherwise have remained unquestioned.

The EES has enabled some power, strategic opportunities and political resources to be granted to specific social groups insofar as it has encouraged political participation of a broad range of social actors. This applies, for example, to certain sections of the women's movement, to a lesser extent, to the trades unions, and to other pressure groups with their origins in civil society. For example, the guidelines on equal opportunities made it easier for some of these social groups to demand specific actions in this sphere (see Mósesdóttir, this volume). In this case, the National Action Plans can serve as strategic resources in the hands of these actors, enabling them to exert pressure and ensure that proposals they regard as important are placed on the policy agenda. The extent to which the different social groups are able to make these conceptual and symbolic resources their own will differ depending on their political position and the consequences of this mode of regulation will accordingly depend on the institutional context and the (im)balance of power between the social actors.

But the national actors and economic lobbies are also in a position to use these resources as political strategies. 'Europe' can be used as a political resource to legitimise politically contentious and delicate changes. This strategic resource may facilitate the implementation of unpopular policies by national governments, either concealing the national government's loss of control in certain areas or enabling it to blame the reforms on 'Europe', thereby externalising the pressure to the European institutions.

The EES and articulation of the policy paradigms for intervention

The European institutions have come to play an important role in defining not only the terms of the social debate on unemployment and social exclusion but also the strategies for seeking solutions to these problems. The nature of these strategies will be affected by the diagnosis proposed in the light of the definition of the terms of the problem but also by the hierarchical position accorded to the coordination of social questions in relation to those of European economic integration.

In the wake of the more stringent economic regulation at European level resulting from EMU, the national governments have less room for manoeuvre in adjusting the course of their economies for social policy purposes (for example, adjustment of exchange rates, currency devaluation, increasing public deficits, promotion of public employment, state aid, and so on) and conducting macroeconomic policies that would contribute to social cohesion (Scharpf, 2002). The economic criteria defined in the context of the EMU are, unlike the integration of social policies, subject to specific sanctions and close monitoring[9] by the European institutions and the peer group.

One important – albeit not always explicit – influence of European integration has been to replace a Keynesian-inspired approach of seeking to influence the *demand* for labour with employment policies that target labour *supply* factors (activation, employability, training, careers guidance, and so on). The fact that national sovereignty has been transferred to a supranational level in certain macroeconomic areas could explain why social intervention comes to be directed to areas previously perceived by the welfare state as lying outside its area of application, namely intervention to determine individual behaviour (disciplinary action) by a reaffirmation of the work and responsibility ethic. In this process of redefining the purpose of the welfare state, the European institutions are playing a central role. Three examples of intervention models (in the promotion of which the European institutions have been extremely active), deriving from different theoretical and political paradigms but featuring this common tendency to 'regulate the will', are the OMC (directed at the national governments), the practice known as 'corporate social responsibility' (directed at the world of business) and the paradigm of activation (directed at workers).

The angle of intervention having thus shifted from a focus on the demand for labour by means of Keynesian-type macroeconomic policies to an approach geared mainly to the labour supply angle (intervention in motivation and the willingness to take part in the labour market), the developments fostered by the European institutions cannot accurately be described as neoliberal strategies to *dismantle* the welfare state since the state is still expected to intervene, albeit in quite a different manner. Rather than seeking the political and institutional conditions for a redistribution of wealth, the route now taken is to assert personal responsibility, introduce incentives, and seek to strengthen the will and the determination to work. Political problems are thus turned into matters of personal motivation and will (Crespo Suárez and Serrano Pascual, 2006: forthcoming) and the management of social conflicts is *depoliticised* in the process. No mention is made of the emergence of the socio-political nature of social exclusion because the possibility of any nexus of causes involving relations of power and oppression has been removed from the equation.

Given this set of factors, the solution proposed to most of the problems (social exclusion, unequal opportunities, lack of competitiveness, and so on) is labour market participation. That strategies are focused on providing incentives for labour to become economically active is attributable to the mythical status thus accorded to gainful employment. Involvement in the economy comes to be regarded as the universal panacea.

Conclusions

With the spread of the discourse of globalisation the nature of economic challenges is shifting increasingly to the supranational level. Insofar as national governments are perceived as powerless to alter this redefinition of the rules of the game of the international economy, the question of European governance in relation to the ESM is becoming an area for the emergence of new (im)balances of power between different social actors.

Within this analytical framework it is possible to understand the construction by the European institutions of the ESM by means of which these institutions seek to acquire political legitimacy in the context of the deep ideological, political and social diversity that characterises the EU. In spite of the fact that the European countries actually share rather little in terms of values, institutions or social achievements, one of the most important functions of the ESM is the production of scientific-sounding paradigms with which to structure the discussion of social issues. The European institutions are playing a central role in the dissemination of polarising notions, which serve to structure political discussion of the social alternatives available within the new economic set-up.

The peculiar position of the European institutions, compelled as they are to seek forms of regulation applicable amid diversity, explains the ambiguous, polysemous and paradoxical nature of many of their concepts. This ambiguity reflects the range of ideological registers to be accommodated within the areas in question, as well as the strategic role played by a large number of these proposals for different social groups.

An important feature of these concepts disseminated by the European institutions is the way in which they posit a normative reformulation of the most pressing social problems and the agencies responsible for solving them. Inactivity is made to appear as the central cause of the majority of social problems (inequality, social exclusion, unemployment, pension crisis, and so on). The social problem of unemployment becomes a matter of individuals' lack of competences to manage their lives and practise 'self-government'.

This diagnosis of the problem will define, in turn, the strategies for tackling it. Increasing responsibility is placed with the individual, and the welfare state intervenes to govern behaviour in order to ensure adequate conditions for the adaptation of individuals to the market situation. This represents an attempt to provide individuals with the wherewithal – in terms of motivation, determination, and so on – to fulfil the moral obligation supposedly incumbent upon every ethical being, namely to take charge of oneself. The function of the welfare state becomes helping subjects to adapt to the new rules of the game of the current economic set-up. The market appears as the main agency of regulation, in not only economic but also social terms, and social rights thus come to be understood in terms of an ethic of allocating responsibility.

This individualistic reformulation of the social question in purely economic terms entails its depoliticisation, as a result of which the laws of the market appear to be reaffirmed more strongly than ever in company with the vision of individuals' taking upon themselves responsibility for avoidance of social exclusion. This discourse is gradually serving to deconstruct the symbolic structures whereby welfare states were consolidated in the course of industrialisation (socialisation of risk: unemployment, decommodification, market failures, and so on) in such a way that the respective roles played in this formerly prevailing structure by the individual and by the welfare state are increasingly being called into question. The only institution that is not subjected to this exercise in deconstruction is the market, which, it seems, remains unquestioned and unquestionable, 'an inevitable destiny' (Muntigl et al, 2000), such that, given this 'naturalisation' of the laws of the market[10], its political regulation appears unjustified and 'unreasonable'. This *power without authority* (in the words of Sennett, 2000, p 120) or *governance without government* (Rosenau and Czempiel, 1992), on which European political regulation is based, enables public institutions to disclaim most social responsibility. In doing so, the question arises of whether what some claim is the European way of 'doing things' is being transformed into the US way of 'doing things', thereby eroding what might have become a genuinely ESM.

The European institutions are putting in place an (a)political project of highly normative ambiguity, the ESM, which acts as a vehicle for numerous 'open' concepts subject to interpretation in each given situation. The nature of European regulation in the social and employment sphere is based, accordingly, not on constraints imposed from outside (legislation, or economic sanctions) but on pressure from inside (persuasion, indoctrination, spread of paradigms to conceive of and articulate the social question) that engenders forums in which the social question can be given a good airing and formulated anew. This model of regulation seems to be endowed with considerable power in terms of the ability to disseminate concepts; nonetheless, its room for manoeuvre is likely to be much more limited with respect to its capacity to strengthen institutions and, thus, to transform an established and unequal balance of power between actors, which it will tend rather to reproduce.

Notes

[1] Wetherell and Potter define interpretative repertoires as 'the building blocks speakers use for constructing versions of actions, cognitive processes and other phenomena' (Wetherell and Potter, 1988, p 172).

[2] In the sense proposed by Salais et al (1986).

[3] The recent Dutch and French rejection of the Constitutional Treaty has deepened the legitimacy crisis of the European institutions.

[4] The OMC is not the sole regulatory tool of the European institutions. However, as underlined by Goetschy in Chapter Two, and Hemerijk et al (2006: forthcoming), this tool has acquired a hegemonic position vis-à-vis other supranational regulatory methods, for example European directives, Structural Funds, social dialogue, and so on.

[5] This is a well-known expression coined by Rosenau and Czempiel (1992), which is used as the title of their work, but for the current volume, we would like to emphasise another sense, the risk of depoliticising the social question (see Serrano Pascual, 2006: forthcoming).

[6] This method takes place in a series of stages. First, it proposes a set of guidelines (general aims grouped under concept headings ('activation', 'employability', and so on). These guidelines are translated into national and regional policies by the member states (National Action Plans). A series of indicators – or 'benchmarks' – are then identified to enable synchronic (among countries) and diachronic (over time) comparison between developments in member states and identification of what have been called 'best practices'. Finally, a process of evaluation, revision and control is conducted by the peer group (government representatives from member states, labour market experts) and the European institutions (the Joint Annual Report on Employment).

[7] For example, the expression used by the Council of Lisbon and so frequently repeated in political and scientific documents: 'a new strategic goal for the next decade: to become the most competitive and most dynamic knowledge-based economy in the world, capable of sustainable economic growth, with more and better jobs and greater social cohesion' (European Commission, 2000, p 3).

[8] For a complete list of the indicators, see http://europa.eu.int/comm/ e m p l o y m e n t _ s o c i a l / e m p l o y m e n t _ s t r a t e g y / i n d i c / list_from_compendium_jer2002.pdf

[9] Although these instruments that represent sanctions under the Stability Pact are being reviewed and made increasingly flexible as is evident from the recent meeting of EU finance ministers (EcoFin).

[10] 'The things most important for the well-being and life prospects of its citizens are largely beyond the government's control: they are in the hands of the so-called 'market forces' – that enigmatic entity reminiscent of primeval elements, natural disasters or blind fate, rather than of well considered, purposeful and rational human decisions' (Bauman, 1998, p 5).

References

Abélès, M. (2002) 'Political anthropology of European institutions: tensions and stereotypes', in K. Liebhart, E. Menasse and H. Steinert (eds) *Fremdbilder- Feindbilder- Zerrbilder: Zur Wahrnehmung und diskursivern Konstruktion des Fremden*, Klagenfurt: Drava Verlag, pp 241-54.

Barbier, J.-C. (2004) 'Activation policies: a comparative perspective', in A. Serrano Pascual (ed) *Are activation policies converging in Europe?*, Brussels: ETUI, pp 47-85.

Bauman, Z. (1998) *Europe of strangers*, in A. Rogers (ed), Working Paper Series, Transnational Communities Programme, WPTC-98-03 (www.transcomm.ox.ac.uk/working_papers.htm)

Brödner, P. (2000) 'El futuro del trabajo en una economía basada en el conocimiento', *Economía y trabajo en la sociedad del conocimiento*, Barcelona: Fundación CIREM, pp 41-79.

Collignon, S., Dehousse, R., Gabolde, J., Jouen, M., Pochet, P., Salais, R., Sprenger, R.U. and de Sousa, H. (2005) 'The Lisbon strategy and the open method of coordination', Policy Paper No 12, *Notre Europe* (www.stefancollignon.de/PDF/Notre%20Europe%20Policypaper12-en.pdf).

Crespo Suárez, E. and Serrano Pascual, A. (2006: forthcoming) 'The paradoxes of the active subject in the discourse of the EU institutions', in R. van Berkel and B. Valkenburg (eds) *Making it personal: Individualising activation services in the EU*, Bristol: The Policy Press.

Evans, J. (2000) 'Workers in the new economy', *OECD Economic Studies*, vol 31, no 2, pp 66-8.

European Commission (2003) *Employment in Europe*, Luxembourg: Office for Official Publications of the European Communities.

Hamzaoui, M. (2003) 'La politique sociale différenciée et territorialisée: activation ou ébranlement du social? Le minimalisme social au service du marché ou la déconstruction des politiques sociales et leurs effets: analyses et comparaisons internationales', *Cahiers de Sociologie et d'Économie Régionale*, no 4, pp 11-27.

Hay, C. (2002) 'Common trajectories, variable paces, divergent outcomes? Models of European capitalism under conditions of complex economic interdependence', Paper presented at the Biannual Conference of Europeanists, Chicago, 14-16 March.

Hemerijk, A., Keune, M. and Rhodes, M. (2006: forthcoming) 'European welfare states: diversity, challenges and reforms', in P. Heywood, E. Jones, M. Rhodes and U. Sedelmeier (eds) *Developments in European politics*, Basingstoke: Palgrave Macmillan.

Jacobsson, K. (2004) 'A European politics for employability: the political discourse on employability of the EU and the OECD', in C. Garsten and K. Jacobsson (eds) *Learning to be employable: New agendas on work, responsibility and learning in a globalising world*, Basingstoke: Palgrave Macmillan, pp 42-63.

Jorgensen, H. (2002) *Consensus, cooperation and conflict: The policy making process in Denmark*, Cheltenham, UK/Northampton, MA: Edward Elgar.

Kerstens, P., Jepsen, M. and Keune, M. (2005) 'Analysing the flexibility-security nexus', mimeo, Brussels: ETUI.

Larsen, F. and Mailand, M. (2006: forthcoming) 'Danish activation policy – the role of normative foundation, the institutional set up and other drivers', in A. Serrano Pascual (ed) *Activation regimes and supranational regulation*, Brussels: ETUI.

Manning, A. (1998) 'The Third Way?', *Centrepiece*, vol 3, no 2, pp 16-18.

Muntigl, P., Weiss, G. and Wodak, R. (2000) *European Union discourses on (un)employment*, Amsterdam: John Benjamins Publishing Company.

Petit, P. (1999) 'Décoder la nouvelle économie', *Problèmes Économiques*, no 2642, pp 1-6.

Petit, J. P. and Kragen, E. (1999) 'Une décennie de croissance qui n'est pas si exceptionnelle', *Problèmes Économiques*, no 2642, pp 7-11.

Robbins, K. (1990) 'National identity and history: past, present and future', *History*, no 75, pp 369-87.

Rosenau, J. N. and Czempiel, E. (1992) *Governance without government: Change in world politics*, Cambridge: Cambridge University Press.

Salais, R., Baverez, N. and Reynaud, B. (1986) *L'invention du chômage: Histoire et transformation d'une catégorie en France des années 1890 aux années 1980*, Paris: Presses Universitaires de France.

Scharpf, F. W. (2002) 'The European social model: coping with the challenges of diversity', MPIfG Working Paper 02/8 (www.mpi-fg-koeln.mpg.de/pu/workpap/wp02-8.html).

Sennett, R. (2000) *La corrosión del carácter: Las consecuencias personales del trabajo en el nuevo capitalismo*, Barcelona: Anagrama.

Serrano Pascual, A. (2006: forthcoming) 'Expertocracy and the policies of production of identities', in M. Kuhn (ed) *The European: A new global player?*, New York, NY: Peter Lang.

van Berkel, R. (2006: forthcoming) 'Activation in the Netherlands: the gradual introduction of a paradigm shift', in A. Serrano Pascual (ed) *Activation regimes and supranational regulation*, Brussels: ETUI.

Visco, I. (2000) 'The new economy: fact or fiction?', *OECD Economic Studies*, vol 31, no 2, pp 6-10.

Vobruba, G. (2001) 'Coping with drastic social change: Europe and the US in comparison', in W. Beck, L. J. G. van der Maesen, F. Thomèse and A. Walker (eds) *Social quality: A vision for Europe*, The Hague/London/Boston: Kluwer Law International.

Wetherell, M. and Potter, J. (1988) 'Discourse analysis and interpretative repertoires', in C. Antaki (ed) *Analysing everyday explanation. A casebook of methods*, London: Sage Publications, pp 168-84.

Wolf, M. (1999) 'Une 'nouvelle économie' pas si nouvelle', *Problèmes Économiques*, no 2642, pp 15-17.

ONE

The concept of the ESM and supranational legitimacy-building [1]

Maria Jepsen and Amparo Serrano Pascual

Introduction

One of the fastest growing European catchwords at the present time – the 'European Social Model' (ESM) – is used to describe the European experience of promoting, simultaneously, sustainable economic growth and social cohesion. The concept is characterised by a high degree of ambiguity and polysemy; it is a loosely defined normative concept and, as such, is used with differing meanings in accordance with rather half-baked definitions. A clear definition of what constitutes its essence seems to be lacking in most articles on the subject, while a review of some of the most important of these articles reveals that, insofar as definitions *are* to be found, they do not necessarily converge. This chapter aims to discuss the concept of the ESM as it is understood in the academic literature and as it occurs in the discourse of the European Union (EU) institutions.[2] The concept is analysed and deconstructed in order to identify the main understandings and various dimensions of the model in question. The second section summarises, classifies and discusses the ways in which the ESM is most frequently construed and proposes a new approach to its understanding. The third section examines the concept of the ESM as a political project and argues that it is a key factor in legitimising the European institutions. The conclusions are in a fourth section.

Main conceptions

Jacques Delors was one of the first people to popularise the term 'European Social Model' in the mid-1980s by designating it as an alternative to the American pure-market form of capitalism. The basic idea of the ESM is that economic and social progress must go hand in hand; economic growth, in other words, is to be combined with social cohesion. However, after nearly 20 years of discussion of the ESM in both academic and political circles, the term remains, in the face of analytical scrutiny, sorely imprecise.

One of the first definitions of the ESM appears in the White Paper on social policy (European Commission, 1994) where it is defined as a set of common values, namely the commitment to democracy, personal freedom, social dialogue, equal opportunities for all, adequate social security and solidarity towards the weaker individuals in society. This is a definition that fits into the broad strand of literature that deals with the ESM in a normative manner.

Without exploring all the various definitions of the ESM put forward by the European Commission, the authors wish to draw attention to the wording used in the presidency conclusions of the Lisbon Summit on 23-24 March 2000 (European Council, 2000). The emphasis here was on modernising the ESM. The features stressed are the need for education and training, adaptation of skills and lifelong learning, reform of social security systems and, finally, the promotion of social inclusion. The first features are concerned with human capital and are clearly focused on the supply side of the labour market. With regard to social protection, the emphasis is on the fiscal sustainability of pensions, and on making work pay, as well as on social inclusion and promoting the capacity for participation. Hence, the focus is on enhancing individuals' capacities to deal with, and survive in, the economy; a risk that was formerly social has instead become individual.

In the literature on the ESM more generally, the term is used in many different contexts and many different definitions can, accordingly, be identified. These definitions can be grouped into the three categories to be discussed later (based on those developed in Hay et al, 1999). The categories are not mutually exclusive; hence a definition given under one heading may well also be applicable under another.

In the first cluster of definitions the ESM is considered as the model that *incorporates certain common features* (institutions, values, and so on) that are inherent in the status quo of the EU member states and are perceived as enabling a distinctive mode of regulation as well as a distinctive competition regime.

The second cluster of definitions establishes the ESM as *being enshrined* in a variety of different national models, some of which are put forward as good examples; the ESM thus becomes an ideal model in the Weberian sense.

The third way of identifying the ESM is as a *European project* and a tool for modernisation/adaptation to changing economic conditions as well as an instrument for cohesiveness with a view to enlargement.

Under this mode of apprehension, the ESM is an emerging transnational phenomenon.

The ESM as incorporating common features

The most commonly encountered definition is that which refers to the common features shared by the EU member states. Under this heading, definitions range from being quite vague to rather detailed and tend, by and large, to suggest a normative approach. The ESM is often referred to as enshrining 'common views and principles on different social issues and their importance within the EC construction' (Vaughan-Whitehead, 2003, p 4).

It is described as a specific common European aim geared to the achievement of full employment, adequate social protection, and equality. Another way of defining it is via the institutions of the welfare state and in terms of a capacity for political regulation of the market economy. Vaughan-Whitehead (2003) proposes a lengthy enumeration of components constituting the ESM. These factors encompass labour law on workers' rights, employment, equal opportunities, anti-discrimination, and so forth. He stresses that the ESM is not only a set of European Community and member-state regulations but also a range of practices aimed at promoting voluntaristic and comprehensive social policy in the EU. Scharpf (2002)[3], following a similar line of reasoning, sees the 'identity marks' of the ESM as generous welfare state transfers and services together with a social regulation of the economy. These translate into the provision of social assistance to the needy, universal provision of education (primary and secondary) and health care, a complex nexus of social insurance and social services, as well as an elaborate system of industrial relations. In Hay et al (1999) the ESM is defined as a group of welfare regimes characterised by extensive social protection, fully comprehensive and legally sanctioned labour market institutions, as well as the resolution of social conflict by consensual and democratic means. Statistically speaking, there might seem to be a grouping of identical welfare states in Europe; this is, however, as demonstrated by Esping-Andersen (1990), no more than a statistical artefact, and this author argues that European welfare capitalism encompasses different worlds of welfare state. This is a position also followed by the supporters of path-dependency theory.

The ESM as an ideal model

In the second strand of literature, specific national models are identified. The United Kingdom (UK), Sweden and Germany are put forward as paradigm cases and certain countries are pinpointed as showing the way towards an ESM that successfully combines economic efficiency with social justice. Esping-Andersen (1999) endorses this approach. Ferrera et al (2001)[4] describe – and implicitly define –the key features of the model as being extensive basic social security protection for all citizens, a high degree of interest organisation and coordinated bargaining, and a more equal wage and income distribution than in most other parts of the world. They argue that these features are institutionalised to various degrees in the EU and that the UK and Ireland are definite outliers. The Netherlands, Denmark and Austria are put forward by these authors as good examples of how generous welfare policy can accommodate economic progress. Ebbinghaus (1999) identifies four groups of welfare state, which together form what he calls the 'European social landscape'. He defines a model as a 'specific combination of institutions and social practices that govern market–society relations in a particular nation-specific combination' (Ebbinghaus, 1999, p 3).

The classification is based on the type of governance of market macroeconomic policy, labour market policy and social policy. Ebbinghaus argues that Europe is far from possessing any single best institutional design; rather, unity, in combination with diversity, is its hallmark.

The ESM as a European project

The third way of understanding the ESM has a considerable degree of overlap with the two former strands. The authors, in this strand of literature, all agree that the ESM is a dynamic and evolving model, which is affected by both national and European forces and processes. However, rather than emphasising the similarities between national systems, the focus here is on the development of a distinctive transnational model. Vaughan-Whitehead (2003)[5] may be seen as a proponent of this trend, which is also endorsed by Wilding (1997) when he points out that for one single country to conduct its own individual social policy can no longer be regarded as viable. The evolution of the varying modes of European social and economic policy regulation has led to a steady increase in the number of subjects dealt with at a supranational level.

Black (2002) seeks to demonstrate that the core of the ESM lies in industrial relations and labour market standards and policies. Its essence, in his view, is a multi-level system of regulation stemming from national as well European systems of regulation/deregulation and taking as its basis the common European values and rights set out and formally agreed in the Charter of Fundamental Social Rights. He argues that Europe has made a considerable impact on cross-national convergence within the ESM. Lönnroth (2002)[6] also states that the Charter of Fundamental Social Rights codifies the key principles of the ESM and thereby establishes the challenges that are to be met by the ESM in the future. In the background report for the International Conference of the Hellenic Presidency of the European Union on the Modernisation of the European Social Model (Amitsis et al, 2003), the ESM is described as a set of social values, principles and methods, which, in essence, may be reduced to three basic and universal principles: the recognition of social justice as a policy target; the acceptance of the productive role of social policy and its contribution to economic efficiency; and finally, the development of a high level of bargaining between the social partners. The authors argue that the ESM has not attained a normative definition at the European level and that the definition of the future ESM will depend on reactions to the changes currently affecting the economic, social and demographic structures of the EU.

Most of the authors/policy-makers who use the concept of ESM as a European project take the current situation to be a turning point between different models of advanced capitalism. The process of globalisation produces a variety of common pressures, which, in turn, expose the different parts of the world (including the US and Europe) to the same imperatives of competitiveness and internal economic integration.[7] In the face of technological, economic and social change, which are presented as inevitably and obviously 'given', the 'need' for social and institutional modernisation (structural reform, more training for new technologies, and so forth) is considered equally obvious.[8] This modernisation appears, accordingly, as the 'natural' response to economic change and globalisation. Many authors and policy-makers at the European level use the term 'knowledge-based society' to illustrate the essence of these changes. Underlying this term is the notion that, due to a variety of causes, the conditions of our production model have changed and that the ESM is geared to the framing of a response to the new economic/societal challenges. This 'naturalisation' of the process makes it appear as written into the order of things, beyond the sphere of human volition (Serrano Pascual and Crespo

Suárez, 2002).The term 'knowledge society' comes to designate mainly the technical management of change, while also leaving room for political choices; and the expression 'social model' is intended to indicate the European approach to coping with the challenges deriving from the process of social change.

But what is behind this process of change? Why does the predominant social model appear to be challenged? A first set of reasons relates to the strengthening of the economic union, in conjunction with the process of EU enlargement.[9] In the wake of the Economic and Monetary Union (EMU), a significant asymmetry between market efficiency (economic policies have been Europeanised) and policies promoting social protection (these remain at national level) has come into being, the most telling example of this asymmetry being the manner in which the European Employment Strategy is intended as a counterweight to the European EMU. Furthermore, economic integration has reduced the capacity of member states to use traditional national economic policy instruments (exchange rates, deficit spending, monetary policy, increasing labour costs) for the achievement of self-defined social policy goals (Scharpf, 2002). The balance of power between fiscal and monetary authorities has shifted (Begg, 2002, p 6). Last but not least, there is the risk of wage and social dumping (Jacobsson and Schmid, 2002; Kittel, 2002). The ability of firms to move production from one location to another might be expected to create downward pressure on the taxes, wages and social security system. These are some of the reasons why authors argue that there is a risk of downward adjustment of social standards and of an attack on collective bargaining and labour market regulation (Ferrera et al, 2000; Kittel, 2002), and hence a need for a further reinforcement of the social dimension of European integration.

A second set of reasons is based more on demographic and societal changes, instances of which include the increasing participation of women in the labour market, the ageing of the population, changing patterns of consumption, the transformation of institutions such as the family, and so forth.

Finally, a third set of reasons (socioeconomic) relates to the assumption that our economies are more internationally exposed and that, together with an increasing use of information and communication technologies, this has changed the conditions of our production model. In contrast to the principle of stability, on which industrialised societies were traditionally based, the basic characteristic of the currently emerging model is constant change and instability. In the past, in order to achieve the requisite stability, it was necessary to eliminate uncertainty by means of strict labour regulation, removal of risks and control of future events. Economic and social stability was a key requirement for this model of production. In contrast with this past situation, it is currently considered impossible to regulate events before they happen. This makes it 'necessary' to promote flexibility, so that people are able to accommodate uncertainty and adapt to rapid changes in production demands. Under this production model, the ability to cope with unforeseen and sudden changes is presented as a prerequisite for economic success; and this model of labour regulation is accompanied by the emergence of a model of social welfare regulation that sees insecurity as inevitable. According to this ideal model, rather than protecting against risk, the welfare state should concentrate on promoting the management of risk (in the form of workfare, that is, providing the instruments – in terms of employability – required by the individual in order to facilitate his or her management of the situation and the capacity of the labour market to adapt), thereby consolidating the laws of the market. The market punishes anyone who fails to adapt to its absolute laws of technological development and competitiveness. This technological determinism and tendency to see change as inevitable prompt a number of Darwinist metaphors. Likewise, the previously mentioned change in the role of the welfare state seeks justification in the portrayal of unemployment as something for which the individual is responsible. The individual is seen as being responsible for managing the risks (for example job loss) that are represented as an inevitable fact of life.

Against this background, citizenship is held to be, rather than a right, something that the individual is required to earn. As such, citizenship is described in fundamentally individualistic rather than social terms, as being determined by personal behaviour, that is, by individual choices and attitudes. The main features of this trend are summarised in the following table.

Taken together, these reasons and circumstances justify, in the view of EU institutions, the need to transform the model upon which solidarity has been built in our society. First, it is seen to be important to strengthen the supranational dimension of solidarity. Within this framework, which is also regarded as self-legitimating, the European institutions have been discussing what they call the 'European Social Model'.

In the light of the arguments previously discussed, to the three clusters of definitions earlier identified the authors would like to add a fourth understanding of the concept, namely, the ESM as a political project. This new approach involves regarding the ESM as a concept whereby,

Table 1.1: From socialisation of risk towards individualisation of risk

	Socialisation of risk	Individualisation of risk
Principles of productive and social model	Planning and pre-regulation	Rapid change and instability
Social representation of unemployment	Social risk: societal duty to tackle risk (of unemployment, poverty)	Individual risk with the help of institutions: risk is unavoidable. Individual duty to tackle the situation
Target of the institutionalisation of solidarity	Wage-earner condition implies dependence on employers	Dependency on welfare state
Social model	Protection against risk. Provides resources that guarantee security and stability	Provides tools to individual to manage risk

via the definition of a distinct policy, a common European solution may be provided to problems that are politically constructed as common to a varying degree. This definition builds on the third set of reasons for having a common European social dimension, namely the change in our production model. It promotes the idea of a productive social policy as a way forward for the social models in Europe and feeds into ideas such as flexicurity, activation, partnership, and so forth, as previously discussed. Such a concept implies attuning social policy to the need to enhance the individual's capacity to survive in the economy, rather than using it as a means of seeking to correct market forces. Instead of being a 'market-correcting' factor, social policy becomes, in the European discourse, an instrument for optimising the adjustment of social protection systems to market forces. This 'sympathetic catchword' is thus used to promote, in some countries, a quite new departure in the design of social policy. This way of defining the ESM overlaps with the third way, insofar as it is a European project. However, as will be argued later, far from being an exogenous factor, it is very much a political project aimed at building a European identity, not so much via common institutions and values as via – *precisely* – the common social policy solutions themselves.

Some key ideas driven by the concept of the ESM as a political project

Despite the diversity characterising the underlying conceptions of the ESM, the exercise of compressing the peculiarities of an economic and social region into a few features (Vobruba, 2001) can be seen as aiming towards the goal of constructing a European identity.[10] In our opinion, what underlies this discussion is the aim of restoring the political legitimacy of the European institutions after a period of crisis. To some extent, the proliferation of research dealing with the ESM in itself serves this process of constructing a European political project. In this framework, the authors believe that the concept is, rather than something external waiting to be discovered, a political project, and therefore, a social and political construct put in place by the academic and political discussion of how to deal with current socioeconomic challenges.

This discourse coincides with a process of constructing a European identity and, in particular, a process of searching for the values whereby such an identity can be given substance and shape.[11] In the course of this search it is taken for granted that the European social and economic model is ill-adapted to the new economic and social conditions. The rules of the industrial model appear inappropriate under the conditions of the new economy. This society thus requires, according to the argument, new standards, new competences (technical, methodological and moral[12]) from the worker, and also new structures to regulate the labour market institutions (procedural and flexible rather than substantive[13]).

Therefore, the concept of the ESM can be understood rather as a political project by means of which the European institutions are seeking to increase their legitimacy. As pointed out by Lord (2000), this is particularly important in the wake of the crisis of legitimacy suffered by the EU in recent years. This author mentions the three components of legitimacy in democratic societies identified by Beetham (1991): the performance of institutions; conformity with democratic values; and political identity (Beetham, cited by Lord, 2000, p 3). The legitimacy of the EU institutions, which has been built up, in the main, on its performance in previous phases, needs to be taken further and to respond to yet another two dimensions of legitimacy, namely democracy and identity. The first aspect, democracy, lies beyond the scope of this chapter (see the debate on governance), but the authors would like to focus on the second aspect, namely identity, and to argue that, in order to enhance legitimacy based on identity formation, the identification/attribution of key values plays a crucial role. The concept of the ESM can be construed as a way to identify these core values whereby a European identity might be constructed. The argument the authors would like to advance is that this constructed identity is based less on common values than on a sharing of problems and intervention solutions (policy paradigms). This demonstrates that the nature of European integration lies in the production of common notions and concepts (Abélès, 2000), despite the different institutional settings and political values across Europe. In this political production the EU institutions play a crucial role,[14] a highly relevant example here being the activation model. Despite the popularity of this model and the broad consensus to implement this intervention paradigm in different European countries, the values invoked to justify the model and the concrete policies inspired by it vary a great deal from country to country (Barbier, 2004; Serrano Pascual, 2004). Therefore, the same recipe will be translated into different modes of preparation incorporating different values among their ingredients.

Another example of this process of creating a common identity is the production of European statistics (Eurostat) or promotion of comparative projects by the EU institutions, which seek to reduce the complexity of European models into a small number of indicators, thereby creating 'common' problems.[15] This might induce a feeling of belonging to the same community and might foster the construction of a common identity. Although this European model might not be based on common values (because of the disparities between the national social models that underpin the European model), this process can encourage European countries to share common problems – by which they are 'threatened' – and to produce similar key recipes to fight against these (socially constructed) common problems. The binding tie in this situation is not so much values or cultures (as in the case of national models), but rather a common identity, which results in sharing the problems and the solutions (policy paradigms and cognitive filters through which the debate takes place). In this way, the ESM discussion and the tools associated with the concept of the ESM are contributing to the construction of common challenges for Europe and to the building of a consensus as to how these are to be faced and tackled.

In this framework, there are two main issues shaping the discussion of what the role of public action and/or institutional remedies[16] should be. First, there is the question of what tools can most appropriately be used. Second, there is the cluster of issues relating to the various alternative approaches to regulation. Regarding the first question, the main mechanisms seem to be flexibility and activation, which – translated into EU discourse – read: flexicurity[17] and employability. Both mechanisms stem from the conviction that, despite subordination to economic constraints, there is a need for an innovative and proactive adaptation to a new capitalist model. The main idea behind both concepts is that solidarity has been institutionalised in such a way that it diminishes people's willingness to adapt their behaviour to economic requirements[18] (Lindbeck, 2003). Accordingly, there is a need to shift from passive support towards activation, and to replace the old political frames for the socialisation of people's attitudes and morals with a view to persuading them to participate in the modernisation process. The role of the institutions, in this context, should become to provide the instruments (employability, flexicurity)[19] that will allow individuals to find ways of adapting to changing economic and social conditions.

As for the second question, many authors support the claim that substantive and standardised rules are ill-suited to the new conditions of production and they argue, rather than for substantive rules, in favour of post-regulatory tools – that is, those that are general, more accepting of diversity, incomplete and open-ended clauses (Sisson and Marginson, 2001) – and new forms of enforcement based on voluntary and flexible participation of the actors concerned, for example persuasion[20], in order to deal with the variety and dynamic complexity of postmodern societies. Examples of the new popularity of this type of approach are the Open Method of Coordination (OMC), which constitutes the regulatory model for the coordination of employment policies, social inclusion and pensions by the EU institutions, and the discussion on 'soft regulation' and flexible frameworks rather than 'compulsory rigid systems' as manifestations of the Europeanisation of industrial relations (Sisson and Marginson, 2001). This OMC is aimed at the harmonisation of ideas, visions and norms of action, rather than of institutions and legislation, in order to define goals that can converge towards a common political vision (Palier, 2001). In this political vision, policy changes are legitimised by reference to uncontrollable processes of globalisation and its discursive transformation into challenges (Fairclough, 2000; Crespo Suárez and Serrano Pascual, 2004). Muntigl et al (2000) show how, in the face of the new economic constraints, the discourse about globalisation rhetorically bypasses the nation state and emphasises the supranational nature of the challenges – presented in a deterministic mode – making the supranational level appear as the appropriate and 'normal' level for responding to these current threats.

In this framework, the different meanings previously identified (see second section) can be understood as belonging to different interpretative repertoires. In the light of this polysemy, the different meanings of the concept are made to appear equally valid, particular political philosophy labels being affixed in relation to differing needs. For instance, in order to show the evidence of common threats and to legitimise the need for common projects (fourth understanding of the concept), the EU institutions will appeal to the essentialist understanding of the concept ('the EU shares common values and common institutions' – first and second understanding/interpretative repertoire of the concept). From this understanding of the concept, it is concluded that common results (equality, social fairness, and so forth) are to be produced. Using this concept of the ESM as a common denominator, EU discourse can thus move from a concept of ESM as a political project (sharing policy tools) towards arguing the need for common results. And yet the same policy tool may be used to quite different effect in different countries depending on institutional setting and specific cultural values (see, for instance, the example of activation: Serrano Pascual, 2004).

Another example of this use of discourse is the way in which words are transformed to underline the 'made-in-Europe' approach to the treatment of issues. In order to emphasise that this European way of handling situations is a long way away from the US approach, concepts such as workfare are reprocessed and relabelled as 'activation', flexibility as 'flexicurity', globalisation as the 'knowledge-based society', and corporate governance as 'corporate social responsibility'. But the question with this 'conceptual metamorphosis' is to ascertain to what extent changing concepts also transform the reality/philosophy behind the concept, particularly in countries where, in comparison with the market, social and political institutions are weak. In actual fact, the creation of such concepts establishes equivalences that serve to conceal the differences between countries.

The polysemy may also result from the EU's rather peculiar position, insofar as it needs to find ways of reconciling the differing political philosophies that hold sway in the different countries of Europe. The style of governance exercised by the EU institutions of necessity bears the hallmark of a form of 'regulation amid diversity', and this diversity is also reflected in the meanings underlying or attributed to the concepts. The vagueness of the concepts used by the EU institutions might accordingly be due, in some measure, to the regulatory needs and rather fragile position of these actors, whose need is to articulate their goal of institutionalising and creating a supranational identity, while respecting, at the same time, the member states' claims to national sovereignty. This might go some way towards explaining the tendency of the EU institutions to offer political concepts with an excessively open meaning, thereby allowing national actors to infuse them with a specific meaning in accordance with national traditions.

Conclusion

The concept of the ESM has been understood as a particular set of institutions (powerful welfare state, interventionist social partners, and so forth); as a particular set of values with reference to which these institutions are built up, for instance temporary postponement of individual interests in order to achieve collective gains (Vobruba, 2001) or a commitment to minimum guaranteed resources (Begg, 2002); as a particular way to deal with common problems (policy paradigms and legitimacy rhetoric); but also in terms of the outcomes of these institutions and values (levels of poverty and inequality, individual/collective empowerment, economic performance, decommodification of society) (Vobruba, 2001).

The vagueness and polysemous nature of the concept of the ESM results not only from the lack of discussion devoted to the concept but also from a political construction of a self-styled European social policy identity by the EU institutions. In opposition to the idea of the ESM as a fact, the authors set up the concept of ESM as a politically constructed project. This concept could be understood as a way of legitimising the notion of a European social policy and feeds into concepts such as activation and flexicurity. However, it is far from being an exogenous factor but, on the contrary, very much a political project aimed at fostering a European identity.

There are, in general terms, several rather debatable aspects of these different ways of understanding the concept of the ESM. First, it is by no means clear that different European countries do actually share common values and common institutions, or that the similarities between countries are more important than the differences distinguishing them from other regions in the world. Second, the debate frequently moves from one semantic field (or interpretative repertoire) to another, so that from a discussion of the ESM as the sharing of values, for instance, it can easily shift to a conception of the ESM as built on common outcomes. Each of these ways of understanding the ESM is to some extent autonomous, which means that the link between different ways of construing it cannot be taken for granted. Third, most of this research is based on controversial assumptions concerning which the debate is taking place elsewhere.

These observations underline the need to identify and verify empirically the main assumptions on which the debate is founded, in order to avoid deterministic explanations of currently changing paths of social policy-making. Accordingly, in order to avoid a situation in which the ESM can be pulled in to help convey just about any policy proposition, be it economic or social, and to present as 'natural' what are, in fact, political options, a critical analytical reflection is required.

Notes

[1] This chapter is based on the article 'The European Social Model: an exercise in deconstruction' published by the authors in *The Journal of European Social Policy*, vol 15, no 3, pp 231-45.

[2] As has been stressed by several authors (Alonso, 1999; Boltanski and Chiapello, 1999; Muntigl et al, 2000; Crespo Suárez and Serrano Pascual, 2004; and so on), political discourse and research are intertwined. This is particularly the case with the EU institutions. On the one hand, political proposals from the European Commission are supported by research for purposes of legitimation. This technocratic exercise ('expertocracy': Muntigl et al, 2000) may be explained by the lack of clear legitimacy of supranational regulation, and by the need to make (controversial) political arguments pass for (objective) scientific conclusions. The goal of this technocratic exercise is to resort to epistemic communities in order to appear politically and ethically neutral (Boltanski and Chiapello, 1999). As Darmon (2001, p 97) underlines, 'recourse to expert opinion tends in fact to overshadow the highly political nature of the decisions being made'. On the other hand, the EU institutions, in particular the European Commission, play a key role in the circulation and dissemination of the concept and, therefore, in framing the terms of the debates on employment policies at the European level. They play an important persuasive role in providing concepts that structure the current political and scientific debates. Furthermore, their discourse is presented as being based on conclusions emanating from scientific debates, which are in reality political options.

[3] '... countries and interest groups that had come to rely on social regulation of the economy and generous welfare state transfers and services are now expecting the European Union to protect the 'European Social Model'...' (Scharpf, 2002, p 649).

[4] 'The basket of requisite policies for sustaining the European social model and ensuring an equitable trade-off between growth and social justice ought also to include, not only a minimum guarantee and health protection guarantee, but also a universal human capital guarantee, providing access to high-quality education and training. In the latter areas the Scandinavian and Continental countries do well (although adaptation to the new economy is required), but the UK and their Southern counterparts perform much less adequately' (Ferrera et al, 2001, p 180).

[5] '... there is no doubt that the construction of the European Union and the willingness of EU member states to develop coordination, cooperation, interdependence, and also common rules on social policies, have helped to maintain EU member states' commitment to social policy and have constrained 'free-riding' or 'social-dumping' in the social area' (Vaughan-Whitehead, 2003, p 5).

[6] '... there are some values, which we Europeans share, and which make our life different from what you find elsewhere in the world. These values cover the quest for economic prosperity which should be linked with democracy and participation, search for consensus, solidarity with weakest members, equal opportunities for all, respect for human and labour rights, and the conviction that earning one's living through work is the basis upon which social welfare should be built. These principles could be defined as the 'European Social Model'. The individual Member States of the Union have then a certain degree of freedom to find the means to implement this model, while its main principles are of 'common concern'' (Lönnroth, 2002, p 3).

[7] 'The European Union is confronted with a quantum shift from globalisation and the challenges of a new knowledge-driven economy. These changes are affecting every aspect of people's lives and require a radical transformation of the European economy' (European Council, 2000, p 1).

[8] 'Such modernisation is becoming urgent in the light of profound changes affecting our societies in the medium term. These include ageing of the European population, with consequences in terms of financing social protection systems and responding to the needs of an older population in terms of working conditions, health or quality of life' (European Commission, 2003a, p 5).

[9] For a summary of the current state of research concerning the welfare implications of European Monetary Union and EU enlargement, see Kittel (2002).

[10] We do not wish to discuss here to what extent we are moving toward a process of convergence or divergence in the way different European countries are dealing with common pressures (for a good discussion of the theoretical and analytical positions behind these two opposed positions, see Hay, 2002), but rather how this presumption that there is something in common is an inherent component of the political construction of the EU.

[11] 'The Union must shape these changes in a manner consistent with its values and concepts of society and also with a view to the forthcoming enlargement' (European Council, 2000, p 1).

'The modernisation of the social model means developing and adapting it to take account of the rapidly changing economy and society, and to ensure the positive mutually supportive role of economic and social policies' (European Commission, 2001, p 5).

[12] See the discussion about the concept of employability (Serrano Pascual, 2000).

[13] The regulatory nature of the Open Method of Coordination in the European Employment Strategy has been discussed by, among others, de la Porte and Pochet (2002) and Goetschy (2002).

[14] As some surveys show (Barbier, 2001; Palier, 2001; Serrano Pascual, 2003; Jacobsson, 2004), the EU institutions are playing a crucial role in providing cognitive frames and conceptual paradigms in the case of the European Employment Strategy. A certain vocabulary (employability, partnership, activation, gender mainstreaming, and so on) has spread into the national political discourses. This 'adaptation of the language' proposed by the EU institutions has had an important impact on the construction of the terms of the problem of unemployment and/or poverty, influencing the main lines along which the debate has been conducted and the way in which the problem is described. European institutions play an important role in determining the direction of the debate (socialising role), intervening in the terminological constructions employed to designate the problem of

exclusion from the labour market, and in proposing common frames of reference.

[15] 'The ageing society calls for clear strategies for ensuring the adequacy of pension systems as well as of heath care systems, while at the same time maintaining sustainability of public finances and inter-generational solidarity' (European Council, 2001, p 21).

'The European Union is confronted with a quantum shift from globalisation and the challenges of a new knowledge-driven economy. These changes are affecting every aspect of people's lives and require a radical transformation of the European economy' (European Council, 2000, p 21).

[16] 'Social policies are not simply an outcome of good economic performance and policies but are at the same time an input and a framework. In this context, the modernisation of the social model means developing and adapting it to take account of the rapidly changing economy and society, and to ensure the positive mutually supportive role of economic and social policies' (European Commission, 2001, p 5).

[17] See the discussion about the concept of flexicurity (Transfer, 2004).

[18] 'The system of financial incentives is one of the main determinants of participation in the labour market.... The balance between income from work against income in unemployment or inactivity determines the decision to enter and to remain on the labour market' (European Commission, 2003b, p 11).

[19] '... the modernisation of labour markets and labour mobility need to be encouraged to allow greater adaptability to change by breaking down existing barriers' (European Council, 2001, p 16).

'People are Europe's main asset and should be the focal point of the Union's policies. Investing in people and developing an active and dynamic WS [welfare state] will be crucial to Europe' (European Council, 2000, p 7).

'... making the right offer to the right person at the right time.... Such an approach would rely upon an early identification of the needs of each jobseeker and the design, at an early stage, of a personalised action plan, with a view to a sustainable integration in the labour market' (European Commission, 2003b, p 11).

[20] 'To replace politics with persuasion: social development is seen less as a question of institutionalised preconditions and political frames, but as a question of people's motives, goodwill and morals' (Vobruba, 2001, p 263). Although Vobruba is referring here to the American way of promoting flexibility, we consider that this is the main characteristic of the regulatory model proposed by the EU institutions (for a detailed discussion, see Crespo Suárez and Serrano Pascual, 2006: forthcoming).

References

Abélès, M. (2000) 'Virtual Europe', in I. Bellier, T. M. Wilson (eds) *An anthropology of the European Union: Building, imagining and experiencing the New Europe*, Oxford: Berg Publications, pp 31-52.

Alonso, L. E. (1999) *Trabajo y ciudadanía*, Madrid: Editorial Trotta.

Amitsis, G., Berghman, J., Hemerijck, A., Sakellaropoulos, T., Stergiou, A. and Stevens, Y. (2003) *Connecting welfare diversity within the European Social Model*, Background report for the International Conference of the Hellenic Presidency of the European Union on the Modernisation of the European Social Model, 21-22 May (www.eftrofia.gr/ Social_Model_report_en.pdf).

Barbier, J.-C. (2001) 'Europe social: l'emploi d'abord', *Centre d'Etudes de l'Emploi*, no 44 (www.cee-recherche.fr/fr/pubicationspdf/ 4p44_web.pdf)

Barbier, J.-C. (2004) 'Activation policies: a comparative perspective', in A. Serrano Pascual (ed) *Are activation policies converging in Europe?*, Brussels: ETUI, pp 47-85.

Beetham, D. (1991) *The legitimacy of power*, Basingstoke: Macmillan.

Begg, I. (2002) *EMU and employment social models in the EMU: Convergence? Co-existence? The role of economic and social actors*, Working Paper 42/02 (www.one-europe.ac.uk/pdf/w42begg.pdf).

Black, B. (2002) 'What is European in the European Social Model', mimeo, Belfast: Queen's University.

Boltanski, L. and Chiapello, E. (1999) *Le nouvel esprit du capitalisme*, Paris: Gallimard.

Crespo Suárez, E. and Serrano Pascual, A. (2004) 'The EU's concept of activation for young people: towards a new social contract?', in A. Serrano Pascual (ed) *Are activation policies converging in Europe?*, Brussels: ETUI, pp 13-47.

Crespo Suárez, E. and Serrano Pascual, A. (2006: forthcoming) 'Political production of individualised subjects in the paradoxical discourse of the EU institutions', in R. van Berkel and B. Valkenburg (eds) *Making it personal: Individualising activation services in the EU*, Bristol: The Policy Press.

Darmon, I. (2001) 'Civil dialogue, governance and the role of the social economy in civil society', in A. Serrano Pascual (ed) *Enhancing youth employability through social and civil partnership*, Brussels: ETUI, pp 93-129.

de la Porte, C. and Pochet, P. (2002) 'Supple co-ordination at EU level and the key actors involvement', in C. de la Porte and P. Pochet (eds) *Building Social Europe through the Open Method of Coordination*, Brussels: Presses Interuniversitaires Européennes – Peter Lang, pp 27-69.

Ebbinghaus, B. (1999) 'Does a European Social Model exist and can it survive?', in G. Huemer, M. Mesch and F. Traxler (eds) *The role of employer associations and labour unions in the EU*, Aldershot: Ashgate, pp 1-26.

Esping-Andersen, G. (1990) *The three worlds of welfare capitalism*, Princeton, NJ: Princeton University Press.

Esping-Andersen, G. (1999) *Social foundations of postindustrial economies*, Oxford: Oxford University Press.

European Commission (1994) *White Paper - European social policy: A way forward for the Union*, Luxembourg: Office for Official Publications of the European Commission.

European Commission (2001) *Employment and social policies: A framework for investing in quality*, COM (2001) 313 final, Luxembourg: EUR-OP.

European Commission (2003a) *Improving quality in work: A review of recent progress*, COM (2003) 728 final, Luxembourg: EUR-OP.

European Commission (2003b) *The future of the EES: A strategy for full employment and better jobs for all*, COM (2203) 6 final, Luxembourg: EUR-OP.

European Council (2000) *Presidency conclusions: Lisbon European Council 23 and 24 March 2000*, Brussels: European Council.

European Council (2001) *Presidency conclusions: Stockholm European Council 23 and 24 March 2000*, Brussels: European Council.

Fairclough, N. (2000) *New Labour, new language?*, London: Routledge.

Ferrera, M., Hemerijck, A. and Rhodes, M. (2000) *The future of Social Europe*, Lisbon: Celta Editora.

Ferrera, M., Hemerijck, A. and Rhodes, M. (2001) 'The future of the Europe 'Social Model' in the global economy', *Journal of Comparative Analysis: Research and Practice*, no 3, pp 163-90.

Goetschy, J. (2002) 'The European employment strategy, multi-level governance and policy coordination: past, present and future', in J. Zeitlin (ed) *Governing, work and welfare in a new economy: European and American experiments*, London: Blackwell/OUP, pp 59-87.

Hay, C. (2002) 'Common trajectories, variable paces, divergent outcomes? Models of European capitalism under conditions of complex economic interdependence', Paper presented at the Biannual Conference of Europeanists, Chicago, 14-16 March.

Hay, C., Watson, M. and Wincott, D. (1999) *Globalisation, European integration and the persistence of European Social Models*, Working Paper 3/99, Birmingham: POLSIS, University of Birmingham.

Jacobsson, K. (2004) 'A European politics for employability: the political discourse on employability of the EU and the OECD', in C. Garsten and K. Jacobsson (2004) (eds) *Learning to be employable: New agendas on work, responsibility and learning in a globalising world*, Hampshire: Palgrave, pp 42-63.

Jacobsson, K. and Schmid, H. (2002) 'Real integration or just formal adaptation? On the implementation of the National Action Plans for Employment', in C. de la Porte and P. Pochet (eds) *A new approach to building Social Europe: The Open Method of Co-ordination*, Brussels: PIE Peter Lang, pp 69-97.

Kittel, B. (2002) *EMU, EU enlargement and the European Social Model; trend, challenges and questions*, MPIfG Working Paper 02/1, pp 24, available at www.mpi-fg-koeln.mpg.de/pu/workpap/wp02-1.html

Lindbeck, A. (2003) *Improving the performance of the European Social Model: The welfare state over the life cycle*, IUI Working Paper 587, Stockholm: The Research Institute of Industrial Economics.

Lönnroth, J. (2002) 'The European Social Model of the future', Speech at the EU Conference organised by the Ecumenial EU – Office of Sweden, Brussels, 15 November.

Lord, C. (2000) *Legitimacy, democracy and the EU: When abstract questions become practical policy problems*, Policy Paper 03/00, available at www.one-europe.ac.uk/cgi-bin/esrc/world/db.cgi/publications.htm

Muntigl, P., Weiss, G. and Wodak, R. (2000) *European Union discourses on unemployment*, Amsterdam: John Benjamins Publishing Company.

Palier, B. (2001) 'Europeanising welfare states: from the failure of legislative and institutional harmonisation of the systems to the cognitive and normative harmonisation of the reforms', Paper presented at the conference 'Ideas, Discourse and European Integration', Center for European Studies, Harvard University, 11-12 May.

Scharpf, F.W. (2002) 'The European social model: coping with the challenges of diversity', *Journal of Common Market Studies*, vol 40, no 4, pp 645-70.

Serrano Pascual, A. (2000) 'The concept of employability: a critical assessment of the fight against youth unemployment', in E. Gabaglio and R. Hoffmann (eds) *European trade union yearbook*, Brussels: ETUI, pp 253-71.

Serrano Pascual, A. (2003) 'A contribution to evaluation of the EES', in E. Gabaglio and R. Hoffmann (eds) *European trade union yearbook*, Brussels: ETUI, pp 237-61.

Serrano Pascual, A. (2004) (ed) *Are activation policies converging in Europe?*, Brussels: ETUI.

Serrano Pascual, A. and Crespo Suárez, E. (2002) 'El discurso de las instituciones europeas sobre la sociedad del conocimiento', *Revista Española de Investigaciones Sociológicas*, no 97, pp 189-211.

Sisson, K. and Marginson, P. (2001) *'Soft regulation':Travesty of the real thing or new dimension?*, Working Paper 32(01), p 37 (www.one-europe.ac.uk/cgi-bin/esrc/world/db.cgi/publications.htm).

Transfer (2004) 'Flexicurity – conceptual issues and political implementation in Europe', *Transfer 2004/2*, Brussels: ETUI.

Vaughan-Whitehead, D. (2003) *EU enlargement versus Social Europe? The uncertain future of the European social mode*, Cheltenham: Edward Elgar.

Vobruba, G. (2001) 'Coping with drastic social change: Europe and the US in comparison', in W. Beck, L. J. G. van der Maesen, F. Thomèse and A. Walker (eds) *Social quality: A vision for Europe*, The Hague/London/Boston: Kluwer Law International, pp 251-70.

Wilding, P. (1997) 'Globalisation, regionalisation and social policy', *Social Policy and Administration*, vol 31, no 4, pp 410-28.

TWO

Taking stock of social Europe: is there such a thing as a community social model?

Janine Goetschy

Introduction

The European Social Model (ESM) is a notion that constitutes a valuable analytical tool for the academic world as well as being a term capable of mobilising political decision-makers, especially when it comes to envisaging, constructing and implementing a common social and employment policy agenda at the European level, or alternatively when some of the very foundations of the ESM come under threat and are in need of reform. It is a heuristic tool but also, increasingly, a political referent used to legitimise reforms.

Despite the many shortcomings of such a 'catch-all' concept, it has proved useful from an academic point of view for the following reasons:

- Be it at the national or European level, the model enables us to reflect cogently on the workings of the entire set of economic and social institutions and the policy crossovers between economic governance, industrial relations, social protection and employment.
- It enables us furthermore to reflect on change and the variety of forms it takes at the national level: the ESM has grown out of a particular historical context, which is bound to evolve in step with transformations in the international and European economy, sociological, demographic and political changes in our societies and the balance of power between capital and labour.
- Generally speaking, this all-encompassing term lends itself to multidisciplinary approaches and simultaneously embraces law, economics, political science and institutional history.
- It also enables researchers and practitioners to pool their ideas and facilitates transfers of knowledge between these two worlds.

In this chapter the author examines the European dimension of the ESM. Can it be said that the building of Social Europe has put in place a coherent ESM? The answer is obviously no, in that employment, social protection and industrial relations policies are still essentially matters of national responsibility. Given that there are several very different social models within the European Union (EU), what is the role and function of European Community social policy amidst all this diversity? How has European social policy been put in place over the years? Clearly, the content of Social Europe has to a large extent been fashioned by the political vicissitudes and attitudes that have presided over its development and, of course, by the history of European economic integration.

The content of the European social agenda, its expansion and results are, in this author's opinion, dependent on seven major sets of factors, some of them closely connected:

- the different phases in the building of Economic Europe (common market, internal market, monetary union) and the nature of the unresolved social policy problems caused by each new phase;
- successive enlargements and the socioeconomic level of the acceding countries;
- the scale of national repercussions of accelerating economic integration and successive enlargements taking in new member states as perceived by the national players (citizens, governments, trades unions, and so forth): in this respect there are still no large-scale studies detailing the social repercussions on each member state of ongoing European integration (economic integration and successive accessions);
- the content of the treaties, which circumscribes the potential activities of the players: the treaties lay down not only the subject areas over which the Community has competence but also the institutional rules of the game, which will affect the stakeholders' capacity to adopt social measures in a relatively effective manner;
- the political will of the national and supranational political and social players (member states, social partners, European institutions) to arrogate powers from the treaties and their individual organisational ability to do so;
- the stakeholders' institutional creativeness in inventing novel procedural solutions and methods based on a reading of past experience, either to reform the treaties or to devise solutions independent of the treaties in view of the urgency and scale of the social problems needing to be solved;

- more broadly, the impact of more general factors – such as the internationalisation of trade and economic globalisation, new economic policy paradigms, the new information technologies, demographic change and sociological lifestyle changes – likewise clearly have a bearing on the formulation of both national and European social agendas.

There are those experts who, in the early 1990s, regarded the building of a Social Europe as an impossible venture on account of the huge diversity in national social systems (industrial relations, social protection) or else because of the profoundly neoliberal make-up of the EU; others, by contrast, believed it not improbable that a pattern of industrial relations similar to that in the member states might emerge at the European level. In actual fact the course of European social history has followed other routes, ones quite different from those anticipated by these specialists.

The first section of this chapter gives an unavoidably brief overview of the principal stages in the building of Social Europe, while the second section will be devoted to a more detailed analysis of these stages based on the elements set out in this introduction.

History of European economic integration, social themes, treaty reforms

The most virulent critics of Social Europe – most notably those who view the building of Europe essentially as a neoliberal undertaking whose social dimension can (by definition) be nothing other than inadequate and symbolic, if not suspect – have often deplored the fact that more research has been devoted to procedures than to content, thereby masking the poverty of this content as well as its outright propensity for deregulation.

The corpus of themes whose content is inherently linked to the history of European economic integration and to successive treaty reforms will be analysed in the following paragraphs. Intergovernmentalism hampered by sovereignty and by the diversity of national interests, coupled with the weakness of the treaties as a legal basis, is generally invoked to explain the lack of headway made by Social Europe, whereas on the contrary the European Commission's entrepreneurial capacity and the alliances it has forged with proactive social players (trades unions, European Economic and Social Committee, European Parliament, and so on) have often been singled out as factors of progress.

Three periods have been identified in the history of the building of a Social Europe.

Market ethos at the core of Europe's first social provisions 'by definition' or 'by default' (1957 Treaty of Rome; 1986 Single European Act)

The earliest social progress in the Community derived above all from the economic and competition-based logic of European economic integration. This orientation was in line with the philosophy of the Treaty of Rome in this field, which authorised the Community to act only in certain situations and certain spheres, namely the movement of labour, vocational training and equal salary for men and women. The Treaty of Rome envisaged that the situation of working people would improve as a result of both the smooth operation of the common market and the approximation of legislative, regulatory and administrative provisions to the extent necessary for the functioning of the common market, a twofold assumption that is ambiguous, to say the least (Vogel-Polsky, 1991).

Therefore, in order to promote a European area of labour mobility and with a view to achieving the common market, a series of legal provisions were adopted in the 1960s and 1970s concerning freedom of movement for workers, equivalence of qualifications and coordination of social security systems. According to the liberal thinking of that era, it was necessary to ensure the smooth operation of the markets in goods, services and capital – but also of the labour market. Even in these market-oriented spheres, however, social progress was fairly slow and often not free of conflict. The definition of clearly targeted Community powers, few in number and governed by a market ethos, combined with the principle of unanimity voting, were serious constraints, which impacted even on the nature of the topics addressed and on their limited effectiveness in terms of results.

Some headway had nevertheless been made at the Paris Summit in 1972, which called for more vigorous social action in the Community. To this end, the Council of Ministers gave the green light for certain articles of the Treaty of Rome (ex Articles 100 and 235) to be used for social purposes. This meant that measures could now be taken in spheres not initially covered by the Treaty (including the social sphere) if they were required for the establishment and operation of the common market. While Article 100, on the approximation of legislation, as well as Article 235, which likewise enables the Council to adopt measures in situations where the power to act was not initially envisaged by the

Treaty, already appeared in the Treaty, the absence of a political consensus among member states, coupled with a literal reading of the Treaty, had prevented their use between 1958 and 1975. This made it possible to adopt the directives on collective redundancies (1975), transfers of undertakings (1977) and employer insolvency (1980), all three adopted on the basis of Article 100.

The draft directives on worker information and consultation (the draft 5th directive and the Vredeling draft) were conceived within the same rationale but fared less well, in that they were not adopted by the Council.

As for the post-1975 provisions on equal treatment for men and women, these were based on an article of the Treaty of Rome (ex Article 119), which guaranteed equal pay for both sexes so as to limit distortions of competition between countries owing to the cost of labour. On the basis of this article, the European Court of Justice (ECJ) subsequently played a very important part in extending the principle of equal treatment to other areas such as equality at work and equality in social security. The role of the ECJ on the one hand and, on the other, the consensus within the Council of Ministers on a less restrictive reading of the Treaty (in this instance having recourse to ex Article 235) explain why the first directive on equal pay for men and women (1975) was followed by two other major directives, one on access to employment (1976) and the other on social security and vocational qualifications (1979). The numerous and very real cases of social progress in this field are often lauded, but we should not overlook the significant amount of time wasted between 1958 and 1975: it would have been perfectly possible from a legal point of view to counter wage discrimination between men and women at a much earlier stage.

Health and safety at work gave rise (in the 1970s and early 1980s) to a greater number of directives than the other topics, especially following the 1986 Single European Act when this topic became subject to qualified majority voting (QMV). The fact that the Single European Act allowed for QMV in this area (whereas unanimity was retained in other areas) is attributable to a favourable set of circumstances that it is interesting to recall. Indeed, apart from the fact that these topics enjoyed greater legitimacy (they touch on health and human dignity and invalidate 'dirty competition') and the fact that technical health and safety standards could potentially act as barriers to free movement in the same way as technical standards in other spheres of the internal market, this headway made in the Single European Act can also be explained by the existence of an original approach previously put in place by the Commission. This approach had two characteristics: first, the health and safety directives were confined to laying down general requirements while specific technical standards were delegated to Community standardisation bodies; second, the Commission's proposals for directives in this field enjoyed increased legitimacy since they were based on suggestions from a tripartite body (trades unions, employers and governments) established to this end in 1974: the Advisory Committee on safety, health and protection at work (Ross, 1995). Furthermore, previous experience of directives on safety at work adopted under the EURATOM Treaty and the European Coal and Steel Treaty constituted useful points of reference for health and safety directives under the EEC Treaty.

Social progress came to a standstill in Europe during the 1980s, particularly because of the British veto and the reluctance of the other member states to adopt binding new Community legislative provisions in a social climate where the need for labour market flexibility was becoming apparent because of a rise in unemployment, especially after the two oil crises of 1974 and 1979, and also because of the change of economic policy paradigm in the member states as they abandoned Keynesianism.

So as to bring about the enlarged market, the Single European Act introduced the principle of QMV for all measures crucial to the completion of the single market and institutionalised the principle of mutual recognition. However, the provision on QMV excluded fiscal matters, freedom of movement for persons (not to be confused with that of workers) and the rights and interests of employed workers. In respect of social affairs, only decisions relating to health and safety matters – an area, moreover, where a high level of protection was advocated – could now be taken by QMV. In addition, the Single European Act instituted European social dialogue, strengthened the respective powers of the Commission and the European Parliament, and emphasised the need for economic and social cohesion (Vogel-Polsky, 1991). Whereas the Single European Act constituted an important step for accelerating European economic integration, its social counterpart was eminently poor.

In the 1970s and 1980s the proactive roles played by both the Commission and the ECJ facilitated the achievement of social progress despite the severe legal restrictions contained in the Treaty of Rome and the Single European Act.

Social ethos as part of a deliberate trade-off for progress in economic integration (1992 Maastricht Treaty)

Nevertheless, the new phase of European economic integration planned by the Delors Commission – namely the establishment of a large internal market (1992) aimed at completing the common market by abolishing the technical standards still hampering the free movement of goods and services and at accelerating freedom of movement for capital and services, which was still far from complete – was accompanied on the Commission's part by in-depth reflection about the social dimension needed in order to ensure acceptance of the advent of this enlarged market and to offset its harmful consequences (Venturini, 1988).

In 1989, 11 countries (the UK refused to sign) adopted the Community Charter of Fundamental Social Rights of Workers. The Charter comprised 12 rights and a mainly symbolic declaration with no immediate legal impact (and which in no way empowered the Commission to expand the legal bases of Community social policy as was the case in 1972). This was followed up by a Commission action programme in 1990 and, above all, prepared the ground for the adoption of the social chapter of the Maastricht Treaty in 1992 (which the UK likewise refused to ratify).

The Maastricht Treaty (and primarily the Social Policy Agreement annexed to it) represented a major leap forward since, on the one hand, it substantially extended the reach of Community social competence (with an extension of QMV in some areas, while others remained subject to unanimity) and, on the other, it opened the door to collective bargaining and the possibility of negotiating European collective agreements. This new Treaty boosted the role of the social partners in three ways: they were now able to negotiate European collective agreements; they could take responsibility for national transposition if they so wished; and they were now formally consulted by the Commission about the Community actions it envisaged.

Despite this leap forward, the Social Policy Agreement annexed to the Maastricht Treaty had several limitations. Whereas certain topics were dealt with by QMV, many other fields of Community competence were still subject to unanimity (social protection, protection for workers made redundant, representation and collective defence of workers, employment of third-country nationals, financial contributions for the promotion of employment). Certain collective labour rights (pay, the right of association, the right to strike and lock-outs) were explicitly excluded from Community competence.

This Treaty moreover delivered an ambivalent message in respect of social affairs: at the same time as extending the reach of Community competence (with QMV for some fields and unanimity for others) and diversifying the modes of social regulation, it introduced the principles of subsidiarity and proportionality. Subsidiarity – the legal translation of political recognition for the national diversity of social systems – was thereafter regularly invoked by the member states in the Social Affairs Council and by the European employers (Union of Industrial and Employers' Confederations of Europe, UNICE) to justify their refusal to adopt Community measures in these newly extended fields of competence. In short, the Maastricht Social Policy Agreement gave rise to the following paradox: while fresh potential was created for the adoption of a larger number of Community directives, the possibility of such adoption was restricted due to the simultaneous entitlement to invoke the subsidiarity principle so as to take no action or only minimal action. This is in essence a trade-off and an implicit compromise between member states' opposing interests in relation to the (wholly relative) importance to be attached to the building of Social Europe.

The Commission's entrepreneurial capacity in drawing up the Maastricht Treaty was remarkable and ingenious in several respects (Ross, 1995). It proposed a sizeable expansion of EU legislative influence in the social policy sphere, but in an incremental fashion and based on the content of previous action plans. It also proposed going further down the collective bargaining road (in the hope of circumventing those member states with reservations about social progress, in particular the UK), which created additional means of achieving social outcomes at the European level as well as modelling the methods of producing social regulations at the Community level on those prevailing nationally in most countries. The Commission skilfully built the social partners' new collective bargaining rights into a complex procedure predicated on the 'threat of legislation' so as to incite UNICE to negotiate (the Commission can return to issuing directives if negotiations between the social partners break down). It encouraged the social partners themselves to draft the part of the Treaty on European collective bargaining (October 1991), of direct concern to them. When the negotiations with the UK foundered at Maastricht over the social chapter of the new Treaty, the Commission proposed the solution of an 'opt-out' for the UK and two annexes to the Treaty, one whereby the UK permitted the other 11 countries to forge ahead without it, the other being the Maastricht Social Policy Agreement with 11 signatories.

This institutional creativity and political ingenuity nevertheless contained some shortcomings since the new regulatory mechanism proved highly complex and fragmentary. The Maastricht Treaty ushered in a dual process for the formulation of social policies: the Social Policy Agreement applying to the 11 countries; the content of the Treaty, to the 12 countries. This state of affairs moreover strengthened the Commission's own hand, since it alone was in a position to handle this complexity. However, the employers (UNICE) had been caught off guard by this overall strategy and were politically nowhere near ready for European negotiations, as subsequently became apparent from their rather feeble bargaining efforts (Falkner, 1998; Keller and Platzer, 2003).

Be that as it may, the social progress attributable to the Maastricht Social Policy Agreement and the large number of European measures that ensued should not delude us as to the quality of their content. In actual fact, even though an impressive number of directives were adopted in the wake of the Maastricht Treaty, two significant points should be noted. First, these directives were clearly minimum prescriptions. Second, applying the usual criterion of classifying directives into two categories, namely those conferring collective rights and those conferring individual rights, it emerges that the latter have been on the increase.

The Structural Funds and the Cohesion Fund represented other means – of a distributive and not regulatory nature – of preserving the balance between EU economic integration, the social policy requirements of the more longstanding member states and the specific economic and social circumstances of acceding countries.

European social and employment policy coordination and the pooling of national experiences for coping with difficult national reforms (1997 Amsterdam Treaty; 2000 Nice Treaty; 2000-10 Lisbon Strategy)

Accelerating European economic integration in the early 1990s caused new problems for the member states in the field of employment and social policy: the establishment of the internal market, monetary union and the stability pact considerably reduced the policy-making room for manoeuvre of member states and businesses alike. In the sphere of employment, for example, the policies traditionally pursued in order to tackle unemployment – such as competitive devaluation, national interest rate adjustments, public deficit strategies, recourse to state aid and mass recruitment into the public sector – were all rendered obsolete by the new rules of the European economic game. Similarly, a certain number of knock-on effects from European economic integration made themselves felt in the social policy arena (health, pensions, measures to combat exclusion). With the constraints of monetary union, the member states could no longer rely as much as previously on budget deficits to finance their social protection systems.

It was principally pressure from public opinion in the respective member states that compelled them to expand the Community agenda to include social and employment issues during the 1990s. At the time of the 1997 Amsterdam Treaty, it became obvious that the EU had to provide a response to the citizens' most pressing concerns (employment, social protection, social exclusion) if the timetable and even the very principle of monetary union were not to be jeopardised.

With the Amsterdam Treaty (especially its employment Article [Art 125] enabling policy coordination of national employment policies), and subsequently the Lisbon Strategy – a 10-year project for Europe's economic and social development – new procedural tools were tabled on an enlarged social agenda. This third phase was mainly meant to help member states undertaking and implementing very difficult social reforms at the national level in the fields of employment, pensions, health care, and social inclusion. This is why national employment and social priorities appeared on the European agenda.

For member states, there were two advantages in placing these items on the European agenda: first, it enabled them to externalise the obligation to carry out reforms that were hard to effect nationally in isolated fashion, on account of the electoral sensitivity of these subjects and the budgetary restrictions surrounding them; second, a more collective effort at the European level made these reforms more palatable as a result of national comparisons, a better knowledge of reciprocal national experiences and their success factors. The pooling of national know-how proved all the more beneficial in that it pertained to policy areas where most member states already had considerable national experience, for instance, 25 years of policies to combat unemployment and 10 years of policies designed to reform the welfare state.

The addition of items to the social agenda has gone hand in hand with a diversification of methods for regulating social affairs at the European level. The Open Method of Coordination (OMC) was grafted on to Community legislation, European collective bargaining, social dialogue and the redistributive policy of the structural funds. Naturally, even before the establishment of the European Employment Strategy (EES) and the various types of OMC, there already existed an array of Community instruments designed to promote policy cooperation among member states (Community support programmes, exchanges of good practice, and EU-backed comparative studies and analyses).

While the Lisbon European Council (2000) devised the actual term 'Open Method of Coordination' and outlined its import, the new policy-making practices it entails had previously come into being with the EES based on the 'employment' procedure as detailed in the 1997 Amsterdam Treaty. Moreover, the EES itself drew inspiration from earlier measures related to macroeconomic policy coordination and multilateral surveillance, which were introduced in the Maastricht Treaty.

The OMC represents a 'new' European method of regulation, which emphasises the non-mandatory nature of rules, their flexibility and openness to a variety of players, and their appropriateness to a growing diversity of social systems within the EU. These are rules emanating from an interplay of decision-making processes between the national/ regional and European levels, and whose implementation borrows from the tools of modern public sector management. This regulatory method contrasts with the characteristics of the classic 'Community method' in several ways. Most experts in European integration, as well as the White Paper on governance (European Commission, 2001), consider the following to be the principal elements of the 'Community method':

- a transfer of powers from member states to the EU;
- the adoption of Community policies by the institutional triangle (Council, European Commission and European Parliament), which in itself constitutes a subtle mix of intergovernmental and supranational forces;
- the central role of the European Commission, a supranational body, in formulating and implementing policies;
- the possibility of adopting decisions by qualified majority in the different specialised Councils of Ministers;
- the binding nature of Community rules;
- the crucial role of the ECJ wherever Community law is infringed.

For the time being, the OMC is applied, as well as in employment, in a dozen other fields with a view to attaining the economic and social goals of the Lisbon Strategy over a 10-year period (to be discussed later). Several OMCs are up and running in respect of social affairs: social inclusion (2000), pensions (2001), health care and more broadly the modernisation of social protection (2002), and education and training (2002). After the Lisbon European Council, which decided to promote the OMC in the aforementioned fields, the environment was added to the list at the Gothenburg European Council in 2001.

The OMC was designed as a tool for developing social measures to counterbalance the acceleration of economic integration due to monetary union; it is also expected to hasten the European countries' transition towards a knowledge-based society and make our economies more competitive. It therefore applies in a series of fields other than social affairs – enterprise policy, innovation policy, research and development, structural economic reforms in specific sectors (the so-called Cardiff process already in place since 1998) – likewise promoted in the Lisbon Council conclusions.

It has to be acknowledged, however, that the OMC processes vary tremendously from one field of application to another: they differ in their aims, operational methods and legal bases. This variety can to a large extent be explained by the member states' eagerness (or otherwise) to undertake joint actions, the diversity of practices and institutions within them and the specific nature of the matter in hand. The different OMCs may have short-, medium- or long-term objectives; they may or may not have clear quantitative or qualitative targets and be accompanied by a mandatory timetable; these objectives may be defined in detail at the European level or only at the national level. The procedures to be followed, the range of political and social players concerned (European institutions, member states, regions, social partners, non-governmental organisations) and the frequency with which their implementation is reviewed are likewise highly variable. Lastly, only two OMCs (which predated the 2000 Lisbon Council), namely the employment strategy (1997 Amsterdam Treaty) and macroeconomic policy coordination (1992 Maastricht Treaty), benefit from a legal basis. The steps forward made in this respect by the proposed Constitutional Treaty remain quite modest. For the time being it is the EES which provides the most elaborate procedure and results (Goetschy, 2005a; Zeitlin et al, 2005).

Analysis

A fragmentary corpus of Community social measures

What do we learn from comparing the content of Social Europe with that of national measures? The fabric of Community provisions is by now quite extensive. The majority of the social directives forming part of the *acquis communautaire* relate to health and safety; next comes the so-called 'labour law' on employment conditions; then there are the directives on gender equality; and finally the directives on freedom of movement of workers.

We can add to this stock of legal measures in different spheres the outcomes of the various social OMCs comprising the *acquis communautaire*, mainly in the field of employment and combating social exclusion, but also concerning pensions, health care and long-term care for older people and the modernisation of social protection. This *acquis* likewise encompasses compulsory collective agreements and the many joint opinions issued by the social partners in the context of the non-compulsory social dialogue, both cross-industry and sectoral.

Compared with the elements that normally constitute the ingredients of a given social model at the national level (well-structured social stakeholders, a corpus of social law, collective bargaining, worker representation forums, the right to strike, and social protection, redistributive and public service policies), the European state of affairs is more fragmentary, does not form a coherent entity, and is clearly somewhat meagre. It could be described in brief as follows:

- Health/safety and gender equality issues dominate the corpus of social legislation and are still being developed.
- It is proving hard to flesh out European collective bargaining despite the changes for the better in the 1992 Maastricht Social Policy Agreement as only five cross-sectoral agreements have been able to be reached.
- In this regard, Europe's employers are still extremely reluctant to engage in binding action at the European level.
- Certain topics are excluded from the field of Community competence by the treaties (pay, the right of association, the right to strike, the right to lock-outs – on these points some slight improvements are to be found in the Charter of Fundamental Rights incorporated into the proposed new constitutional Treaty).
- Even though national systems differ considerably in this respect, some directives dealing with worker information, consultation and participation have seen the light of day after many years of fruitless negotiations and a watering-down of successive drafts.
- Social protection issues – a jealously guarded aspect of national sovereignty – failed to move in their entirety from unanimity to QMV in the 2000 Nice Treaty but are discussed in the context of various OMCs (in the specific case of the modernisation of social protection systems, however, a flexibility clause or even a *passerelle*

clause is provided for; the legal basis for measures to combat social exclusion has been widened).

- Employment-related issues have gained in importance and are dealt with in a variety of legal and institutional ways (directives, collective agreements, the OMC).
- Where public services are concerned, although certain values are guaranteed in the Amsterdam Treaty and the proposed constitutional Treaty, liberalisation is proceeding apace especially due to the Lisbon Strategy.

This fragmentary set of Community social provisions obviously does not constitute a cohesive entity that could represent an overall ESM – not even a minimalist one. These results obtained at the European level, in no way negligible, are meaningful only in relation to the very numerous social achievements already made at the national level. The European body of social legislation can be regarded, above all, as complementary to national social laws, functioning as a minimum safety net whether it be in a patchy fashion in respect of certain inherently national matters or in relation to typically European matters not dealt with at the national level. The outcomes of the different (non-binding) OMCs, meanwhile, are intended to serve rather as a guide for national policy-making and conduct. As for outcomes of non-binding social dialogue (cross-industry or sectoral), this form of dialogue has still not really taken on a guiding role at the national level.

In comparison with what has been achieved nationally, one feature of the Community legislative output is its highly 'cumulative' nature – in other words, earlier outcomes are not called into question – whereas at the national level we have seen social legislation go through three decades of deregulation (be it marginal or more substantial, depending on the member state). This cumulativeness (a high degree of rigidity), and its extension to the new member states, partly explains the proliferation of more flexible OMC-type approaches in recent years. To put it plainly, at the Community level, social deregulation is becoming apparent through changes in the method of regulation (that is, over and above the method of binding legislation plenty of scope has been allotted to the OMC), whereas at the national level, social deregulation is occurring from within binding social legislation.

Change coupled with continuity: consistency and a reinterpretation of European themes

The themes dealt with in the Community's different social action programmes (health/safety at work; working conditions in a broad sense; freedom of movement; information, consultation and participation of workers; equal treatment for men and women; and latterly employment and social protection) have proved remarkably stable on the agenda. This stability is due in particular to the institutional tenacity of the European Commission (once on the agenda, even if a given theme fails temporarily, it subsequently reappears) and to the slowness and 'incrementalism' of headway made in reforming the treaties.

Against this backdrop of stability, which has lasted for over 30 years (ever since the first social action programme in 1974), certain themes have come to the fore, most notably the issues of economic and social cohesion and regional redistribution at times of successive accessions (first the UK and Ireland, then the southern countries of Greece, Spain and Portugal, and now the 10 new member states. The prime topics in the 1990s were education and training, employment, social inclusion and social protection (mainly because of national circumstances: unemployment, low employment rates and demographic change).

Directives are still being adopted in traditional fields, albeit at a lesser pace; in certain cases, the slowdown in legislative activity is largely offset by the inclusion of these fields in the OMC: this is very obvious, for example, in relation to equal treatment for men and women, contained either explicitly or under the banner of mainstreaming in the EES and the OMC on social inclusion (Rubery, 2003).

The appearance of new themes does not mean that previous ones disappear. On the contrary, the emergence of new economic and social themes can lead both to a re-ordering of thematic priorities and to a change in the significance attached to former themes. The goal of raising the employment rate and the question of the sustainability of social protection systems now cut right across a series of topics (for instance, gender equality, and education and training issues in connection with lifelong learning). The idea of the OMC is to make further adjustments and find additional complementary aspects, in relation, for example, to the normative tools, content and significance of the many and varied themes addressed. These regulatory overlaps and shifts in the significance of earlier topics are well reflected in the 2000-05 social agenda. These shifts of significance within the social sphere generally result from new pressure caused by the growth and stability pact and the member states' desire to overhaul their social systems.

With globalisation, the internal market and monetary union on the one hand, and the priority attached to employment on the other, 'information/consultation/participation' and company restructuring issues have become all the more relevant. The same applies to the various questions concerning employee mobility (recognition of diplomas and qualifications, portability of social security benefits, pensions, and so on), which returned to the agenda in no uncertain fashion at the end of the 1990s when priority was accorded to boosting employment rates, and when measures such as intra-Community mobility and lifelong learning were deemed capable of helping to this end. Employment has rendered all these themes more topical, thus acting as a lever helping to ensure that, in one way or another, they are addressed more speedily.

Additions to the European agenda: national social issues take priority

The social agenda has expanded considerably over time (albeit with soft law assuming added importance) and it no longer merely addresses items related to freedom of movement for workers or primarily transnational items, but also – and increasingly – ones that are central to national social agendas (including employment and social protection).

Indeed, at its inception, Social Europe took shape mainly around typically European themes, be it the need for markets to operate properly or transnational social problems caused by the common market and the internal market. Provisions related to free movement for workers, the coordination of social security systems and the principle of equal pay for men and women were closely linked to the requirements of economic integration of markets or else to averting distortions of competition among member states.

A little later, the themes covered also had an implicitly transnational dimension, such as the successive projects concerning employee information and consultation, which emerged during the 1970s and 1980s, and the employment directives of the late 1970s (collective redundancies, transfer of undertakings, company insolvency), which were subsequently revised and set out to approximate national legislation. The aim was to deal with the effects of economic integration on corporate strategies for managing employment and their repercussions on employees' rights. In all three employment directives, it is essentially the procedural part on information and consultation for employee representatives that underwent further development.

These themes certainly featured prominently on national agendas at the time, be it issues relating to industrial democracy in the workplace, which had cropped up in several countries during the 1970s due to the period of activism leading to demands for more power for employees and their representatives in the workplace, or issues relating to workers' rights when jobs in a company come under threat, which arose at the time of the first signs of an employment crisis following the first oil crisis. But these represented only individual elements of national social agendas, ones largely connected with European integration and its transnational dimension.

These items did not disappear from the European agenda thereafter; far from it (see previous section), as evidenced by the directive on the European Works Council (1994), that on the posting of workers (1996) and that supplementing the Statute for a European company with regard to the involvement of employees (2001), for these three directives are even more markedly transnational in nature.

The period beginning in the 1990s saw the advent of European directives impinging more substantially and more directly on national social issues, linked to aspects of labour law and employees' working conditions: contracts of employment (1991); the organisation of working time (1993); protection of young people at work (1994); part-time work (1997); and fixed-term contracts (1999). These topics saw the light of day once citizens had had time to associate certain elements in the history of economic integration (internal market, monetary union) and its rapid acceleration with the upsurge in and persistence of unemployment.

From European social legislation to European governance of national public policies

In the second half of the 1990s, the labour law perspective lost out somewhat to an approach based on establishing guidelines for national government policies and for the conduct of everyone concerned. Policy implementation, assessment and subsequent ongoing adjustment over time became essential components of this mechanism.

The move from a formerly predominantly legal perspective (headway is of course still being made on that ground, but more slowly) to a perspective of European governance of national social and employment policies may result from a feeling that the limit of what is legally necessary or desirable – or even what is politically feasible – has been reached (the 2000-05 Community social agenda is explicit on this point). From now on, quality in policy implementation is considered far more important than the adoption of new measures.

Such a shift from EU-binding rules to European governance has also been observed in the European social dialogue (Goetschy, 2005b). The increase of soft law mechanisms was also the price to pay for having an enlarged social dialogue agenda.

Promoting governance rather than compulsory regulation was supposed to enable public authorities to engage a broader plurality of actors (civil society, social partners) at the various phases of the decision-making process so as to accommodate the variety of interests, to ensure the search for common solutions and to avoid resistance to change. The need to involve a plurality of actors was compounded by the fact that the changes in question were often based on measures characterised by uncertain outcomes: job creation mechanisms or pensions reforms are two good examples of areas where uncertainty as to the dynamics unleashed by the reforms remains high.

This shift from social legislation to public policy governance has been accompanied by a concomitant development: a move from fragmentary laws to addressing entire policy areas that are better coordinated with one another. Whereas the legislative elements are fragmentary and scarcely based on a cohesive ESM in the making, the social and employment OMCs are quite different. Indeed, just like European thinking around reform of social protection and pensions, the EES and the fight against exclusion each entail analysing a wide-ranging policy area sometimes almost in its entirety, as is the case for structural reform of the EES. Reflection about policy interdependence (positive and negative externalities) constituted one of the distinguishing features of social affairs at the Community level during the 1990s in the wake of the 1993 White Paper on growth, competitiveness and employment, and developed further with the Lisbon Strategy and the OMC. Policy cooperation and coordination within each of the said fields is, moreover, a prerequisite for coordination with other economic and social policies.

Diversification and juxtaposition of the various regulatory methods: enhanced legitimacy and effectiveness?

The reasons behind the diversification of regulatory modes in the 1990s are manifold. The OMC aims at attaining several goals. It seeks to push forward the building of a Social Europe, that is, to add issues of national priority to the agenda of items addressed and to obtain results in the face of accelerating economic integration. Compared with the other existing regulatory methods, it is supposed to foster a different means of advancing Social Europe: because they pay all due respect to the diversity of national circumstances and practices, the various coordination processes deployed should enable social matters to be handled in a more in-depth, better-adjusted and more effective manner. It sets out to stimulate national reforms of social and employment policy and to facilitate the establishment of a 'new social model' with the following goals and components (Trubek and Trubek, 2003):

- a skilled and adaptable labour force with access to lifelong learning;
- higher rates of employment (especially among women and older workers);
- active employment and social policies;
- supply-side measures for job creation;
- a different type of security for people without lifetime contracts;
- the reform of state pensions;
- the reduction of social exclusion;
- the reduction of gender discrimination.

It cannot be taken for granted that these different regulatory methods will dovetail perfectly with one another. Many authors fear the harmful effects of regulatory competition between binding law (legislation or collective agreements) and the mechanisms of the non-binding OMC. Furthermore, the juxtaposition of redistributive policy through the Structural Funds with the goals of social and employment policies poses a problem: strategic declarations of intent that the Structural Funds should take up and implement the goals of the EES are in short supply. The meshing or even a hybrid combination of different regulatory methods is, however, already functioning in an effective and fairly successful manner in the fields of employment, equal treatment for men and women, and the fight against social exclusion.

Another reason for the diversification of regulatory methods was the attempt to make Community social action more legitimate and effective. The collective bargaining method (1992) and the OMC were introduced in order to enhance the legitimacy of decisions taken owing to an increase in the number of players involved in decision-making processes (social stakeholders, civil society) and an increase in the number of decision-making levels (Community, national, regional); what is more, the European Parliament's more prominent role due to the co-decision procedure deriving from the 1997 Amsterdam Treaty also helped in the search for greater legitimacy.

Nevertheless, the implications and significance of these new sources of legitimacy have been equivocal: the legitimacy acquired through the enhanced involvement of the social partners (in a neo-corporatist vein) has often been contrasted with that resulting from enhanced involvement of the European Parliament (parliamentary democracy – Falkner, 1998). Here are a few illustrations: at the time of the Maastricht Social Policy Agreement, which instituted the possibility of European collective agreements, the European Parliament deplored the downplaying of its role in this field as compared with that of the social partners. Subsequently, with the OMC and the minimal involvement of the European Parliament and national Parliaments in these processes – which now constitute a very large proportion (if not the bulk) of Community social activity – some criticise the drift of these processes into elitism, in that groups of experts take pride of place. Transparency of the compromises achieved is not facilitated by the duration of the OMC processes and the technical nature of their tools, a relative 'depoliticisation' of the issues in that they are immune from unpredictable electoral cycles, the importance of specialised committees (Employment Committee, Economic Policy Committee, Social Protection Committee) and networks of experts; the media are ill-informed and it is difficult to stimulate public debate on such a basis. The fact that the European Commission steers the majority of these new regulatory processes – given its role of initiative, coordination and evaluation – further reinforces the views of those who see these modes of governance as 'bureaucratic'. Democratic monitoring mechanisms prove all the more vital for the EES and the other OMCs, since they relate to sensitive matters connected with the future of redistributive policies and employment, which lie at the very heart of our democratic societies.

The effectiveness of Community action, for its part, can be improved by means of changes to the Community method of decision-making and to national implementation. The search for more effective decision-making has taken two main forms, namely the transition from voting by unanimity to QMV on a number of topics, introduced at times of Treaty reform (1992 Maastricht Treaty, 1997 Amsterdam Treaty, 2000 Nice Treaty), and the fact that the UK agreed to exclude itself from the Maastricht Social Policy Agreement in 1992, thus enabling Social Europe to adopt a whole series of directives that would otherwise have been out of the question (the UK ended its opt-out when the Amsterdam Treaty was adopted). The desire for greater effectiveness at the stage of national implementation has been achieved mainly through the establishment of fairly elaborate monitoring, evaluation and benchmarking procedures in the different OMCs and in the redistributive policy of the Structural Funds.

As to whether the move from hard to soft law creates a genuine risk of inefficiency or, on the contrary, engenders greater efficiency of implementation, the question remains largely unanswered. Authors and analyses diverge widely on this point. Some lawyers believe that in practice the boundary between soft law and hard law is less watertight than it is often made out to be. Community directives have become more open and flexible since the early 1990s and have conferred on the social partners a new role in implementing them nationally. For this reason, the actual quality of transposition of directives at the national level can be very variable even though they constitute hard law. By contrast, careful monitoring of OMC implementation can result in successful implementation even though this is soft law.

Better-integrated policy design: social and economic policy coordination as a 10-year European project: an ambiguous, risky approach

In a context of globalisation and rapid technological change, the Lisbon Strategy is intended as a coherent medium term project lasting 10 years and giving the EU an edge over the rest of the world. It covers a whole host of policy areas – economic, technological, social and educational – its goal being to make the EU, by 2010, 'the most competitive and dynamic knowledge-based economy in the world, capable of sustainable economic growth with more and better jobs and greater social cohesion' (Lisbon European Council, 2000).

As well as inaugurating a new mode of governance, the OMC, four different strands run through this project:

- The Lisbon Strategy strives to strengthen the EU and boost its role in the international economy. There is a manifest desire to see the EU catch up with the US and Japan in areas where it is noticeably lagging behind, such as economic growth, innovation, technological change and rates of employment.
- At the same time, the Lisbon Strategy sets out to accelerate the achievement of the internal market, which has sometimes been rather sluggish in certain respects, by eliminating obstacles to

freedom of movement for services and to financial markets, as well as by liberalising the markets in transport, postal services and energy.

- From a more political point of view, the Lisbon Strategy seeks to redress the balance between well-developed European economic integration (monetary integration, internal market) on the one hand (although there is an imbalance even within economic integration in favour of monetary integration and to the detriment of macroeconomic policy coordination), and, on the other, European social integration, which remains largely unaccomplished. The 'employment' Article in the 1997 Amsterdam Treaty was itself already motivated by this concern that the social sphere should catch up with the economic, particularly under pressure from member states such as Sweden, Denmark, Austria, the Benelux countries (Belgium, the Netherlands, Luxembourg) and France.

- The Lisbon Strategy attempted, by the same token, to assert the importance and specific nature of the ESM in the eyes of the world and in the unfolding history of globalisation and European economic integration, by creating a more viable social counterweight. But there was an additional goal, namely the 'modernisation' of that same ESM.

European policy coordination nevertheless poses a number of political and institutional difficulties. It is feared that policy coordination might in reality lead to the EES and the various social policy coordination measures being dominated by economic policies (the Broad Economic Policy Guidelines). This does seem to be the case, above all due to three sets of factors: the prevalence of centralised monetary policy over other macroeconomic policies (budgetary and fiscal); the constraints on the latter arising from the stability pact; and the ambivalent and contradictory goals of the Lisbon Strategy, which advocates, at one and the same time, an acceleration of the internal market and liberalisation policies as well as the ambitious goals of job creation, social cohesion, safeguarding and renewing the ESM – an extremely tall order. In practice, rather than genuine coordination, the functioning of the Lisbon Strategy has generated a real risk of policy areas being placed in a hierarchy, whereby priorities linked to the growth and stability pact, liberalisation policies and macroeconomic objectives upstream seem to bear down rather heavily on elements downstream in respect of employment, pension reform, health care and education systems.

Other difficulties of policy coordination are institutional in nature. The European Council is often reproached for being bogged down in policy detail whereas its role is a strategic one. The General Affairs Council, for its part, does not properly perform its function of coordinating and arbitrating between the sometimes conflicting interests of the different specialised Councils. Moreover, even within the European Commission the coordination and balancing of policies among the various Directorates-General – essential to the success of the Lisbon Strategy – leave much to be desired.

The evolving role of the European Commission

The entrepreneurial capacity of the European Commission has often been put forward as one explanation for the progress and content of Social Europe. Is this assertion still valid today? Traditionally, in order to make up for the shortfall of powers flowing from the treaties, the Commission has interpreted its powers in a broad fashion and has been very adept at using legal bases to facilitate legislative headway. In the context of the European collective bargaining process, it has influenced the content and conduct of negotiations by making the legislative option loom large; in its role of initiative and social regulator it has forged constructive alliances with certain European institutions (for example the European Parliament and the European Economic and Social Committee), certain governments and certain interest groups (European Trade Union Confederation), as well as establishing its own expert groups. The Commission's intimate knowledge of diverse national interests and of the complexity of institutional procedures, coupled with its role as guardian of the memory of matters pending – by contrast with revolving presidencies – has moreover helped to flesh out this entrepreneurial capacity. Of course, the Commission's political and strategic desire to promote social affairs probably reached its peak during Jacques Delors' terms of office, whereas subsequently, during the Santer and Prodi mandates respectively, it has been more a matter of consolidating and properly implementing the existing *acquis communautaire*.

Even though the Commission's role in monitoring the OMC is far from negligible, some wonder whether or not the introduction of this method may also reflect a lack of political will on its part. The Commission is thought to have entered a period of 'legislative abstinence' in the early 1990s, whereby it acts as a self-effacing regulator (Keller and Platzer, 2003). It has encouraged the development of a more autonomous, bipartite social dialogue between national social partners (see the social partners' own multi-annual work programme for 2003-05), and is trying to make private stakeholders, primarily large enterprises, shoulder added responsibilities. This relative withdrawal by Europe's main public player – in respect of legislation and collective bargaining – might appear worrying in as much as the goal is to strengthen the ESM and not merely to try to modernise it. The role that the Commission will play in furthering (and updating) the social dialogue and the social and employment policies of the 10 new member states, whose circumstances are highly diverse and a long way from the standards of the EU-15, will constitute a real test of its political will to safeguard a strong ESM.

Conclusion

Although we cannot speak of a coherent ESM at the Community level, it is astonishing to note the substantial range of themes contained in the 2000–05 social agenda compared with earlier action programmes. This expansion of the agenda has, however, been achieved at the cost of two types of implicit trade-off. First, within the social sphere itself, the headway made in the Maastricht Social Policy Agreement was offset by the incorporation of the subsidiarity principle into the Treaty; similarly, at the end of the 1990s, the introduction of the OMC and the fairly broad array of topics covered were counterbalanced by the non-binding nature of these measures. Second, in the 1980s and 1990s, the social progress contained in the treaties or promoted by large-scale projects (1993 White Paper; 2000 Lisbon Strategy) is clearly part of a trade-off for backing the onward march of economic integration, that is, for accepting the large internal market and Economic and Monetary Union. Previously, in the 1960s and 1970s, social measures had merely been constituent elements in the workings of the markets themselves. In practice, and especially prior to the Maastricht Social Agreement, Community social legislation was largely created 'by default', that is, above all based on an extensive and judicious reading of the successive treaties' articles in order to bypass their limitations. Since 2000, we find ourselves confronted by quite a vast Community social agenda and by a diversified set of regulatory methods. Paradoxically, the member states have given the green light to a multiplicity of social OMCs, which they do not always really take into account in their respective national policies.

The term 'European Social Model' emerged at the European level and has gradually replaced the term 'European social dimension' in two contexts. First, once regulatory methods akin to national ones (legislation and collective bargaining) became available, and once substantive national issues (employment and social protection) began to be handled at the EU level, that is, once European content and procedures had attained a certain critical mass, this comprehensive, systemic concept began to make more and more sense. Second, the notion of an ESM has increasingly been invoked (by the European Commission and the European Council) in the sense of a political trade-off when it has been a matter of pushing through new adjustments between the (neoliberal) economic system and the (traditional) social system, requiring difficult reforms. It is argued at such times that revisiting and changing certain aspects of the ESM – employment or social protection policies – are vital and unavoidable if its foundations are to be preserved in the long term.

While there is now a consensus that national diversity will persist (and perhaps even increase – see Ferrera et al, 2000), the 1990s nonetheless bore witness to a genuine Europeanisation of national policies, owing to two trends. On the one hand, the social pacts of the 1990s caused national social systems to adjust to the requirements of European economic reforms in order to qualify for the euro (a considerable body of literature now exists on this process and this period). On the other hand, the OMC made it possible to tackle national social and employment matters at the Community level. This Europeanisation operated in both directions (from European to national level and vice versa) and was accompanied in both cases by another fundamental transformation: the search for a much closer meshing of economic and social policies at both European and national levels as part of a search for a fresh equilibrium.

Even though we cannot speak of a cohesive or comprehensive ESM, Social Europe does now comprise several elements of an ESM, namely:

- social values and principles enshrined in the Charter of Fundamental Rights, which is integrated into the proposed constitutional Treaty (justice, liberty, equality, intergenerational solidarity, employment, social protection, social inclusion, non-discrimination, quality of the environment, economic and social cohesion, and so on);
- a fragmentary legislative set of directives, which constitute Community social law;
- diverse modes of regulation (legislation, collective bargaining, the OMC, redistributive Structural Funds) on which Europe's political and social players can draw whenever appropriate to solve social problems that cannot be tackled at the national level alone.

Furthermore, in a climate of globalisation and different emerging forms of European capitalism (an abundance of research is currently being conducted on this topic), the aim of the ESM is to engage in blue-skies thinking at the European level and point the way towards a 'new European Social Model' or a 'reformed ESM'. The Community level aspires to be at the forefront of this process in order to lay down its paradigms and objectives (as previously discussed – particularly through the Lisbon Strategy) and thereby to mastermind the reforms of social and employment policies currently underway in all the EU member states.

References

European Commission (1993) White Paper on growth, competitiveness and employment, COM(93), 700 final, Brussels: European Commission.

European Commission (2001) *European governance: A White Paper*, COM(2001)428, Brussels: European Commission..

European Council of Lisbon (2000) *Presidency conclusions*, 23-24 March (www.consilium.europa.eu/ueDocs/cms_Data/docs/pressData/en/ec/00100-r1.en0.htm).

Falkner, G. (1998) *EU social policy in the 1990s: Towards a corporatist policy community*, London: Routledge.

Ferrera, M., Hemerijck, A. and Rhodes, M. (2000) *The future of Social Europe: Recasting work and welfare in the new economy*, Oeiras: Celta Editore.

Goetschy, J. (2005a) 'The Open Method of Coordination and the Lisbon strategy: the difficult road from potential to results', *Transfer: European Review of Labour and Research*, vol 11, no 1, pp 64-81.

Goetschy, J. (2005b) 'The European social dialogue in the 1990s: institutional innovations and new paradigms', *Transfer: European Review of Labour and Research*, vol 11, no 3, pp 409-23.

Keller, B. and Platzer, H.W. (2003) *Industrial relations and European integration*, Aldershot: Ashgate Press.

Ross, G. (1995) 'Assessing the Delors era and social policy', in S. Leibfried and P. Pierson (eds) *European social policy: Between fragmentation and integration*, Washington, DC: Brookings Institution, pp 357-88.

Rubery, J. (2003) 'Gender equality still on the EU agenda: but for how long?', *Industrial Relations Journal*, vol 34, no 5, pp 477-97.

Trubek, D. and Trubek, L. (2003) 'Hard and soft law in the construction of social Europe: the role of the OMC', UW – Madison governance project, Working Paper, Madison, WI: University of Wisconsin.

Venturini, P. (1988) *Un espace social à l'horizon 1992*, Luxembourg: Commission of the European Communities.

Vogel-Polsky, E. (1991) *L'Europe sociale: Illusion, alibi ou réalité*, Brussels: Editions de l'Université Libre de Bruxelles.

Zeitlin, J., Pochet, P. and Magnusson, L. (2005) *The Open Method of Co-ordination in action*, Bruxelles: Peter Lang.

THREE

Employment and pay in Europe and the US: food for thought about flexibility and the European Social Model

Wiemer Salverda

Introduction

The aim of this contribution is to shed some light on the European Social Model (ESM) by approaching it from the perspective of employment, or the economy more generally, but also by comparing it to the United States (US) model. The approach raises the question of what the model stands for as well as the nature of its effects. Analysis of the latter aspect may help to improve knowledge of the former, thus serving as a heuristic device. But there is more to it than that. One cannot fully know and understand a model by looking at its institutions and taking them at face value, as international comparisons often tend to do: beyond the rules as they exist on paper, the effects too are part and parcel of a social model. A good example here is the minimum wage. The US has had this institution since the 1930s and some European countries still do *not* have it; and yet, regulatory influences on low wages may be more important in the latter. There are two issues at stake here: first the 'bite' of an institution is important and, second, other institutions or arrangements and provisions may have the same or equivalent effects. What is more, the effects are at the heart of political concerns regarding the ESM – for, after all, who would bother about a model if it had no effects? The main political concern is that the ESM would unduly restrict economic development and therefore does not serve the population well. In addition to this, a model (social or otherwise) that is considered to be linked to a geographical area (Europe in this case) may – in the view of this author at least – best be analysed in a comparative fashion. I believe, in particular – and this is where the comparative perspective comes in – that it is most important to see whether, and where, the ESM differs from the US model. The latter is usually thought to be an economic model with (negative) social consequences and, similarly, the ESM is believed to have (negative) economic consequences. Behind this is the question of whether the ESM denotes a model that really is shared by the European countries and whether perhaps it may even transcend them. Rules and regulations that are developing at the European level are discussed elsewhere in this volume. The comparative perspective can help to better identify the effects of a model and may also improve perception of what features actually are shared by existing national models in Europe. Although the latter is not the focus of this contribution, it is an issue upon which I will touch when necessary.

The concern with the ESM has arisen largely on account of the employment gap that has opened up between the European Union (EU) and the US in recent decades. The popular view is that hiring-and-firing rules, as well as wage-setting, are insufficiently flexible in the European economies to allow employers to create new jobs to the same extent as in the US. European social regulations are seen as employee-friendly, and therefore as standing in the way of 'healthy' economic change. In that sense the ESM has essentially negative connotations. For the same reason it is advisable to start out from the effects when analysing the ESM. The evolution of the employment gap and its understanding were the subject of a recent international research project on demand patterns and employment growth[1] and this contribution draws heavily on its results.

For the purposes of the comparison, the project took five European economies together: France, Germany, the Netherlands, the UK and Spain. Here we will consistently take the first four of these (denoted as EU4), leaving out Spain because both its model and stage of development deviate from the predominant trend, and also because the statistical data available were insufficient for the purposes of the analysis conducted here. Generally speaking, France, Germany and the Netherlands are considered the heartland of the ESM. The EU4 countries together account for almost 60% of the working-age population of the EU15 and for slightly over 60% of its Gross Domestic Product (GDP). Apart from this quantitative aspect the choice of these four also ensures the inclusion of low- as well as high-employment EU member countries. Using the EU4 will ease the presentation, but, beyond that, the use of the aggregate can be justified from the standpoint of a proper comparison with the US. The usual focus is on individual countries, and we all know that significant differences occur between them, but this may rest on the mistaken idea that the US is a uniform economic entity on an equal footing with individual European countries, as if the latter had not become increasingly integrated economically as a result of the EU. In actual fact, disparities within the US are comparable to within the EU4 (see Table 3.1).

In the remainder of this chapter, first, the international employment gap will be described – its size and properties – in order to provide an initial basis for understanding it. Second, attention will be focused on how it may relate to the ESM, especially in relation to social regulation, in other words, the role of pay (equality). The main conclusion is that the employment gap has little to do with a lack of flexibility on the European side: first, a very rapid restructuring of industrial employment occurred, which boosted productivity and was facilitated by the ESM; second, no proof is found that the core of the employment divergence, which is in market-provided consumer services such as retail and hotels and catering, can be linked to a compression of wages in Europe as a result of wage regulation for social purposes. Instead it relates to a strong divergence in per capita income, relating in turn to a shortening of working hours and to strong wage moderation in the European countries. If anything, these two factors may be essential defining elements of the ESM. As to the shorter working hours, it should be asked whether Europeans appreciate 'leisure' time more or whether they feel constrained with regard to the choice of working hours. Insofar as the former is the case, it may be valued as a positive feature of the ESM. The second factor, wage moderation, would seem to be

Table 3.1: Regional labour market disparities in the US and Europe (2003)

Rates to population (%)	Employment	Unemployment
US Across 50 states and Washington DC (excluding Puerto Rico), non-institutional population aged 16 and over		
lowest	51.8	3.5
highest	71.5	8.1
highest – lowest	19.7	4.6
EU4 Across 40 regions (excluding French overseas departments), population aged 15 to 64		
lowest	44.9	2.1
highest	63.4	11.9
highest – lowest	18.5	9.8

Sources: Bureau of Labour Statistics, News, 10 March 2005; Eurostat, Table LF2EMPRT, extraction from http://europa.eu.int/comm/eurostat (August 2005)

motivated by the mistaken fear that inflexible wages are responsible for the employment gap. Yet moderation seems to be, on the contrary, questionable, on account of the potential downward effect it can have on employment.

Growth and nature of the employment gap

As noted above, we focus on four EU countries: France, Germany, the Netherlands and the UK, taking this aggregate to represent 'Europe' in comparison to the US. Population growth and, in its wake, employment growth differ substantially between countries and any international comparison should be made on a per capita basis. Looking at employment (see Figure 3.1) we find that at the start of the 1970s, Europe had a higher employment rate (68%) – the ratio of employment to the population of working age between 15 and 64 years old (henceforth EPOP) – than the US (64%). The European EPOP stagnated during the 1970s while the US rate gradually climbed.

The employment crisis of the early 1980s hit Europe much more than the US and, although the evolution was basically parallel, US employment growth remained slightly faster until the mid-1990s. Thus, in the space of just a few years a substantial employment gap (indicated by the solid arrows) opened up to a maximum of 8.5%. Contrary to common views, European employment rates have developed more favourably since the mid-1990s, diminishing the gap to 6%, particularly during the most recent years. On balance, an employment gap of 10 percentage points developed between 1970 and 2003, changing from a +4% advantage to a –6% disadvantage for Europe. It can be observed

Figure 3.1: Employment-to-population (15-64) ratios, head count and hours count, US and EU4 (EPOP %) (1970-2003)

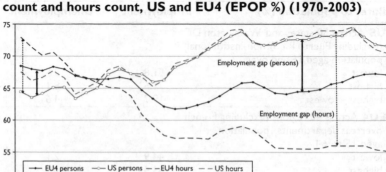

Source: Schettkat and Salverda (forthcoming), Figure 1.1

that more than one third of this increase relates to the decline in self-employment in Europe.

An estimation of the employment volume measured as hours worked per capita shows that the EU shifted from a larger advantage to a much larger disadvantage (see dotted lines and arrows in Figure 3.1).[2] This should be kept in mind in the rest of this section where all data will be on a head-count basis because proper detail on hours is lacking.

Europe may have a high rate of unemployment measured in relation to the labour force (8%) but at present this comes on top of a sustained rate of employment, while the US employment rate shows a clear decline. Consequently, the gap in unemployment rates is smaller when expressed on a per capita basis (UPOP) than on the traditional basis, which takes unemployment relative to the labour force. The difference amounts to about 1% at the present time (see Figure 3.2).

The US employment advantage looks very impressive and is often felt to be economy-wide. However, significant differences occur between the US and Europe in relation to the same individual sectors of the economy. Figure 3.3 decomposes the gap shown in Figure 3.1. In 1970 Europe had a large advantage in industry[3] and a smaller one in agriculture. The figure clearly shows how this lead dwindled very rapidly. At the end of the period, Europe still has an advantage over the US in industry, where the employment gap does not apply. The rapid decline points to a substantially faster increase in productivity in Europe until the mid-1990s up to a level that is roughly equal to the US. It also testifies to the great flexibility of the European workforce, as the process moved faster than in the US in previous years.[4] Many

Figure 3.2: Unemployment ratios to labour force (Urate) and working-age population (UPOP), US–EU4 (%) (1970-2003)

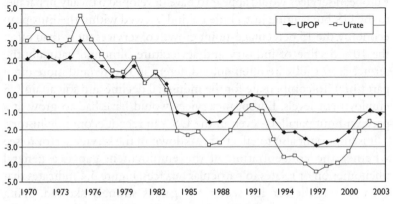

Source: Author's calculations from OECD Labour Force Survey.

Figure 3.3: Composition of the US-EU4 employment gap by major sector (EPOP %) (1970-2003)

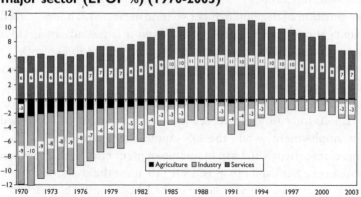

Source: Glyn et al (2005), Figure 4 updated

lost their jobs, particularly older men, but social security provided a safety net for most.

A similar development occurred in agriculture. This sector is responsible for over half of the above-mentioned contribution of declining European self-employment to the widening of the gap. Nevertheless, Europe has no employment gap for this sector.

This leaves the services sector as the sole location and cause of the employment gap. It is important to note from the figure, however, that in this sector the employment gap is a longstanding phenomenon. In 1970, US employment in services had a seven percentage-point edge over Europe. This gap then widened to some extent, subsequently declining again to 7% – only 1% more than at the outset. Over the period employment in services grew dramatically on both sides of the Atlantic, from 38 to 54% in the US and from 32 to 47% in Europe. European services would appear to have developed basically in parallel to the US, but lagging just a little behind. Viewed within the European economy, the 15 percentage-point growth of services more than offset the 10% decline of industry and agriculture, although naturally the service sector jobs are often quite different in nature (and more often part time). To compensate for the industrial decline and still attain US employment levels, European services would have had to grow at a pace without parallel – even in the US – in recent economic history.

It is important also to effect a breakdown of the service sector to see whether the concentration of the employment gap is a general phenomenon or relates to particular services. Figure 3.4 indicates that even within the service sector the gap is strongly skewed, being concentrated – almost equally – in two industries, namely, community

Figure 3.4: Composition of the US–EU4 employment gap in services by major industry (EPOP %) (1970-2001)

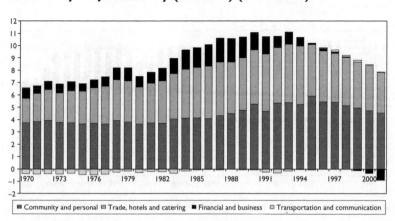

Source: Schettkat and Salverda (forthcoming), Figure 1.4.

and personal services – which include education and health care[5] – on the one hand and trade, hotels and catering on the other. These provide what can be loosely termed 'consumer services'. Again, this part of the gap is large – almost 12 percentage points in the early 1990s but also rather steady over the period, contributing 2% to the 10% increase over 1970-2001. The major part of the consumption gap was already present at the start.

By contrast, 'business services' (equally loosely defined) are provided by transportation and communication on the one hand and financial and business services proper on the other. The former industry consistently shows no gap, while the latter developed a limited gap up to a maximum of 2.5% in the late 1980s. This subsequently disappeared and was recently changed into a small European advantage.

From a slight disadvantage US women took the lead and have been contributing substantially to the employment gap (see Figure 3.5). At the time of writing women make a larger contribution to the gap than men, although the male change over the period was somewhat larger (5.4% as against 4.4%[6]), and as a whole women's employment gap grew by 4.4% (men 5.4%). However, it is important to note that this larger disadvantage of European women is not because they are less often employed within the sectors of the economy concerned. Rather, it results from the skewed composition of the economy. In services as well, as in the rest of the economy, the role of women is virtually identical between Europe and the US – although slightly larger in European consumer services (see Figure 3.6). Because the

Figure 3.5: Composition of the US–EU4 employment gap by gender (% total EPOP) (1970-2003)

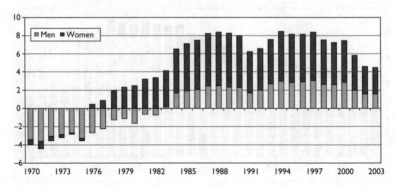

Source: Author's calculations from OECD Labour Force Survey and STAN Database.

female role is much larger in services than in the rest of the economy and the share of services is smaller in Europe, women on balance play a substantial role in the creation of the employment gap.

We have taken the four European economies together to facilitate a concise presentation. Naturally, important differences in economic development and structure do occur and the social models are by no means uniform. However, it should be added that the range of differences, economic as well as social, is limited and partly rests on complementarities that reflect the high and increasing level of economic integration. For instance, financial services naturally have a large employment share in the UK and manufacturing in Germany but the same diversity holds within the US – for example, the New York economy cannot possibly be taken to represent the US economy as a whole. For EU4 as a whole, the employment gap grew by 10 percentage points but this varied by plus or minus 2 points for Germany, France and the UK taken individually. Much of this mutual difference is attributable to the decline of German and French agriculture (and the corresponding loss of self-employment). By contrast, British industry underwent a more massive restructuring. The Netherlands had a 2% increase only – plausibly because of its part-time job growth. In spite of the mutual differences it can be concluded that the US–European employment gap is a very particular phenomenon. It looks entirely different depending on whether it is regarded from a static or a dynamic perspective, but in both cases it is strongly skewed. Statically, it does not apply to industry and agriculture, but is fully concentrated in services, and within services it is fully concentrated in two industries that mainly cater to the needs of consumer households: community

Figure 3.6: Female shares in employment in two broad sectors (% of sectoral employment) (1970-2003)

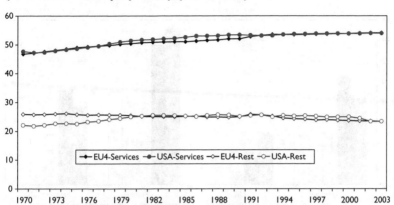

Source: Author's calculations from OECD Labour Force Survey

and personal services and trade and hotels and catering. Dynamically, however, the evolution of the employment gap is entirely attributable to European industry and agriculture: their decline served to expose the gap in consumer services, which was there from the beginning. The speed of the job restructuring behind this decline was unparalleled and it should be mentioned that its social consequences seem to have been dealt with quite adequately by social measures.

The role of the ESM

Although the gap is not universal but specific, a universal social model, that is, one that applies economy-wide, may still be responsible because it can affect sectors differently insofar as they are differently organised and/or because the model contains specific features that affect some sectors more than others. For example, a sector may be more sensitive to effects of social protection and regulation of wages because both these effects concern a particular range of (low) earnings and such earnings occur more frequently in the sector in question. This can apply, in particular, to low-paid consumer services, which may be subject to the effects of minimum wages, collective labour agreements and other constraints on wage inequality. Indeed, European countries, particularly the continental ones, have substantially less low-wage employment than the US. Figure 3.7 indicates that the total gap is virtually accounted for by a gap in low-wage employment. It shows that this also holds for low-paid services (retail trade, hotels and catering). However, before drawing over-hasty conclusions, it should

Figure 3.7: US–EU4 Employment gap by level of pay and for retail, hotels and catering (full-time equivalents) (1996)

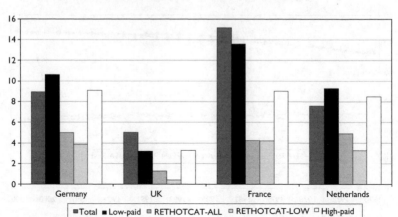

Note: RETHOTCAT-ALL = retail, hotels and catering (all); RETHOTCAT-LOW = retail, hotels and catering (low-paid).
Source: Salverda et al. (2001)

be noted that the white bars show that the total employment gap also largely overlaps with a gap in high-wage employment. In other words, a European advantage in the intermediate range of wages compensates for much of the two gaps at the low and high end.

However, by focusing on wages one may be selecting specific features of the social model while disregarding others. Employment protection is also seen as stricter in Europe than the US, but compared to the minimum wage its applicability is so universal that it seems unlikely that it would affect one sector so much more than another – be it services in the static view (let alone consumer services in comparison to business services) or industry in the dynamic view.

It is no accident that the specific wage-determining features tend to combine with specific services as the usual focus of the political debate. In general, the decline of industry and agriculture is considered a good thing, since it boosts competitiveness and productivity, and not as a failure of employment protection; on the contrary, massive dismissals have been facilitated by social safety nets.[7] The spectacular improvement of Continental European international trade balances since the early 1980s provides a strong argument of competitiveness. Scheme 1 illustrates these lines of thought.

The double-sided nature of the gap complicates the issue of how the ESM can be held responsible for the employment performance of the European countries, even more so as the static gap is in itself also two-sided, comprising as it does low-paid trade, hotels and catering on the one hand and high-paid community services on the other. In retail and hotels and catering the frequency of low pay, defined as either being in the lowest decile or below two thirds of the median of the national wage dispersion, is two or three times higher than average while in education and health the frequency is often far below average (see Table 3.2). In addition, we know that health care and education are subject to public regulation in all four countries, albeit to strongly varying degrees. This makes them difficult to compare internationally but also diminishes the potential contribution of social regulation on employment in this sector. Low-paid consumer services, by contrast, are fully market-oriented in all countries, European as well as the US. They will be the focus of the rest of this contribution.

It would appear that per capita employment in retail, hotels and catering (measured in terms of hours worked to correct for the significantly diverging incidence of part-time jobs) is far and increasingly below the US level (Figure 3.8). Around 2000, France and the Netherlands were close to just about half the US level. In France this may be to some extent attributable to a higher level of productivity,[8] but even there the decline in the employment rate that occurred since the mid-1980s was accompanied not by growing but by stagnating and ultimately declining productivity relative to the US (Figure 3.9). In contrast, the low level of demand for these services (Figure 3.10) is much more likely to aid understanding of the low employment level. Indeed, per capita demand for these consumer services is, again, not much more than half the US level. Such a demand gap is found from the outset and is consistent with the long-run employment gap for services detailed in the previous section.

The low level of demand might naturally be attributable to higher costs experienced by the sector. Although this could be true to some extent, it does not by itself signify that those higher costs result from

Table 3.2: Concentration ratios of low hourly pay to national average = 100 (1996)

| | Pay in lowest decile | | | | | Pay≤ two thirds of median wage | | | | |
	US	DE	UK	FR	NL	US	DE	UK	FR	NL
Retail	192	201	215	202	291	178	201	204	197	277
Hotels and catering	323	485	420	357	260	237	413	307	394	239
Education	78	58	39	79	14	73	49	49	85	17
Health care	96	129	67	99	58	103	145	89	105	69

Source: Salverda et al (2001), table 58.

Figure 3.8: Trade, hotels and catering, hours worked per capita (age 15-64), US=1 (1970-2000)

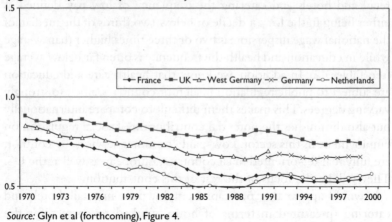

Source: Glyn et al (forthcoming), Figure 4.

Figure 3.9: Trade, hotels and catering, labour productivity per hour worked, US=1 (1970-99)

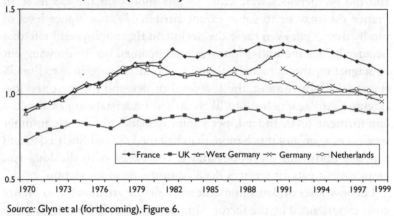

Source: Glyn et al (forthcoming), Figure 6.

Figure 3.10: Goods consumption volume per capita, US=1 (1970-2000)

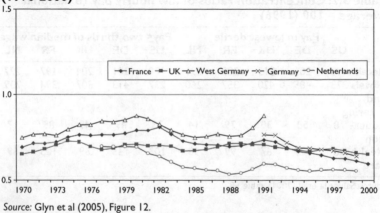

Source: Glyn et al (2005), Figure 12.

the need to pay higher wages because of social regulation. Other factors may be responsible, such as indirect taxes, but these are not commonly perceived as part of the social model even though, somewhat ironically, they *are* a common feature of the European countries.

If wages are high relative to other wages in the economy, it will be more costly to the general public to buy these services. To verify the potential effect of wages it is important to consider the structure of wages in the low-pay sector compared to the rest of the economy, this means to establish whether people – personal characteristics of age, gender and education, as well as type of job, being equal – receive a penalty or premium for working in this sector rather than elsewhere. Table 3.3, panel A, shows the results of estimating these penalties for the retail industry at three different levels of the wage distribution – from down at the second decile (20% of workers earn less) to up at the eighth decile (20% earn more). The general finding is that substantial penalties do occur but also that they are more important higher up the distribution than at the lower end. Notably, the US second-decile penalty does not exceed the European (except for France), while for higher wages it tends to do so. No convincing evidence is found that, compared to the US, Europe is substantially lacking flexibility in the structure of individual wages. Statutory minimum wages or minimum collectively agreed rates appear not to stand in the way.

The right-hand panel B of the Table 3.3[9] takes the argument one step further. In addition to rewards effects (pay penalties or premiums), composition effects are shown here. They indicate the effects, in terms

Scheme 3.1: Employment gap and the social model

			Employment gap	
			Static	**Dynamic**
			Skewed to consumer services	Decline of industry and agriculture
	General	Employment protection	No skewed effects to be expected	
Social model	**Specific**	Minimum wage, collective agreements, social benefits	Combined effect of low pay in the sector and effects of social model on low earnings	Effects of economic change aiming to increase productivity, socially enabled by benefits

Table 3.3: Structure of hourly wages in retailing relative to the rest of the economy*

A. Pay penalties (%) by decile level of the wage distribution				B. Rewards and composition effects in pay penalties at median wage**			
	End-1970s	End-1980s	Mid-1990s		Rewards	Composition	Total
US	*1979*	*1990*	*1997*	**US**			
Decile 2	-0.083	-0.154	-0.125	1997	-0.22	-0.23	-0.43
Decile 5	-0.125	-0.179	-0.180	part-time	-0.03	-0.15	-0.20
Decile 8	-0.132	-0.181	-0.192				
West Germany	*1979*	*1990*	*1997*	**West Germany**			
Decile 2	-0.168	-0.144	-0.117	1997	-0.13	-0.17	-0.29
Decile 5	-0.167	-0.147	-0.128	part-time	-0.00	-0.11	-0.12
Decile 8	-0.150	-0.151	-0.150				
UK		*1989/90*	*1998/2001*	**UK**			
Decile 2		-0.138	-0.138	1998/2001	-0.17	-0.43	-0.56
Decile 5		-0.197	-0.194	part-time	0.00	-0.25	-0.24
Decile 8		-0.217	-0.235				
FR	*1982*	*1991*	*1995*	**FR**			
Decile 2	-0.079	-0.088	-0.076	1995	-0.13	-0.12	-0.24
Decile 5	-0.118	-0.114	-0.123	part-time	-0.02	0.00	0.01
Decile 8	-0.138	-0.111	-0.143				
NL	*1979*	*1989*	*1996*	**NL**			
Decile 2	-0.121	-0.144	-0.187	1996	-0.16	-0.38	-0.55
Decile 5	-0.143	-0.156	-0.178	part-time	-0.02	-0.16	-0.20
Decile 8	-0.159	-0.148	-0.162				

* Excluding hotels and catering

** Interaction effects not shown; they are generally small.

of pay structures and the resulting wage costs, of a different composition of the workforce between sectors. It can be seen how the pay bill in retail is reduced by hiring a higher proportion of workers with 'low-pay characteristics' compared to the rest of the economy. The composition contribution to the inter-industry difference in wages appears to be quantitatively more important than that of the rewards, especially in the US, the UK and the Netherlands. The rationale of the distinction between rewards and composition is that enterprises, given the wage structures they face, can adapt the composition of their workforce to obtain lower wages compared to other sectors. In this respect, panel B also indicates the role of part-time workers. Generally, their pay penalty compared to full-time workers is rather slight but, by contrast, their role in the composition effects is highly significant. Their presence or absence largely explains the international differences in composition effects as well as in the total wage effect, for example, between France and the US. The limited role of part-time employment in France and Germany, compared to the other countries, is a different matter, one that relates perhaps more to general views on paid labour and labour market participation (especially of women) than to social provisions, on the supply side, and to the way employers like to organise the work, for example, in the large stores ('*hypermarchés*') in France, on the demand side. The fact that in this sector European women are equally represented, as compared with men, seems to point more to a lack of opportunities than to a lack of supply.

These issues are not at the core of the ESM. A more general implication is that firms are not necessarily constrained by individual wage (in)flexibility. If a country has a tighter dispersion of wages, there can still be room for manoeuvre by adapting the composition of the workforce.

The conclusion as to the relation between the US–European employment gap and the ESM is that, even where one would expect the ESM to have the strongest effect, namely in low-wage market-provided consumer services, there is no proof that the employment gap relates to social provisions.

Concluding observations

The author has argued that the US–European employment gap provides an important test for the presence and effects of the ESM. First, it was shown that the employment gap is strongly skewed, being fully concentrated in consumer services, while agriculture and industry and notably also business services in Europe fully match the situation in the US. This particular gap, which comprises trade, hotels and catering, personal services and community services such as health care and education, is of a long standing but became exposed as a consequence of the drastic decline in employment in European industry in recent decades that negated a large European employment advance in industry and agriculture – to the benefit of European productivity that was lifted to the US level and competitiveness in international trade that exceeds the US level. Generally speaking, European services grew at a similar speed as those in the US but not enough to compensate for the decline in other sectors. The skewed nature of the gap points away from a role of inflexible wages and employment protection – with economy-wide effects – as a potential explanation. If anything, it points in the opposite direction. The ESM's employment protection and social benefits supported a very drastic restructuring of industry, at a faster speed than witnessed in the US in the preceding period and without much social upheaval.

While the ESM's regulation of low wages may play an explanatory role, further scrutiny of that issue, focused on low-wage market-provided consumer services where the bite of such regulation should be most severe, showed no lack of wage flexibility for low pay compared to the rest of the economy in Europe relative to the US. Low-wage institutions are not the explanation – there is sufficient wage flexibility in the structure of individual rewards. Beyond this, firms can also adapt the composition of their workforce (especially by means of part-time employment) to achieve lower wage costs; this they have done to differing extents across the European countries. If the ESM is equated with stricter, inflexible regulation of low wages and employment protection compared to the US, it is clear that the ESM cannot explain the lagging behind of European employment, irrespective of mutual differences between the four European countries – Germany, France, UK and the Netherlands –which were taken here as *pars pro toto* for Europe.

This finding naturally raises the question of what *can* then explain the employment gap. We have seen that consumer demand for services is lacking in Europe. Such demand is mainly generated in the rest of the economy and what happened there seems important for a proper understanding. This brings us to general wage restraint, which may, in actual fact, be an important feature of the ESM to the extent that it is shared by the Continental European countries. Figure 3.11 shows the strong parallel between the evolution of the share of wages in GDP

Figure 3.11: US–EU4 gaps in the shares of wages and individual consumption in GDP (percentage points) (1970-2003)

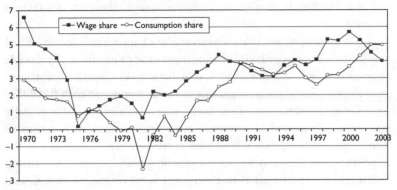

Source: OECD, National Accounts

and that of individual consumption, in comparison with corresponding trends in the US. Clearly the two gaps have grown substantially since the early 1980s. The European wage share fell while in the US it remained roughly constant; the US consumption share grew strongly while in Europe it remained roughly constant. A fall in the wage share comes about when the increase of real wages lags behind productivity growth, a development illustrated by Figure 3.12. The Netherlands started this type of wage moderation – even before it was laid down in the Wassenaar Accord of 1982 – and was followed later by other countries, especially France and to a lesser extent Germany.[10] The wage restraint in these countries was significantly stronger than in the

Figure 3.12: Real hourly wages to hourly productivity, 1979=100 (1970-2003)

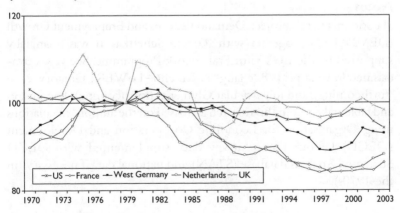

Source: OECD, National Accounts

89

US, while the UK presents a mixed picture. It would appear that aggregate wage flexibility in Europe has also been substantial – but not as a free lunch, as it seems to have come at the cost of a lack of demand.

The conclusions are that, whatever the characteristics of the ESM may be, they are not inflexible hiring and firing or insufficiently flexible aggregate wages and low wages; that firm-level wage flexibility can go well beyond the social regulation of wages; and that such flexibility – read wage moderation – can carry a cost and does not automatically guarantee job growth. Europe is more flexible than many seem to think. By contrast, the US model convincingly demonstrates the importance of demand for employment growth, during the strong 1980s and 1990s as well as in the recent years of jobless growth and the Wal-Mart-type restructuring of low-wage consumer services.

The downward effects of wage restraint have been reinforced by the shortening of working hours in Europe. This is yet another feature of the ESM and one that – with the vast array of working hours on which employers and employees can nowadays conclude agreements – can hardly be said to testify to a lack of labour market flexibility. It is imperative to ascertain, by means of further research, whether the shortening of working hours and the expansion of part-time employment– notably advocated by the Kok report of 2003 to bring EU employment growth back on the track of the Lisbon Strategy[11] – reflect genuine preferences or whether they represent constraints on labour supply and demand. If Europeans do indeed value leisure more than US citizens, this should be appropriately regarded as an economic achievement and accepted as a trade-off against lower employment rates.

Notes

[1] I coordinated this project, Demand Patterns and Employment Growth (DEMPATEM), together with Ronald Schettkat. It was financially supported by the EU's Fifth Framework Programme. See www.uva-aias.net/lower.asp?id=82&lang=en&menu=LoWER; Gregory et al (forthcoming); and in particular Glyn et al (forthcoming). The figures and tables taken from this research are based on the authors' calculations using Organisation for Economic Co-operation and Development (OECD) Labour Force Survey data, supplemented with OECD Structural Analysis database (STAN) and national data if necessary (in the 1970s).

[2] Measured against a full-time equivalent working-age population of 52 weeks times 35 hours annually. Use was made of the OECD's annual hours database. These hours data must be used with caution.

[3] Manufacturing, utilities, construction and mining.

[4] See Glyn and Erdem (2000).

[5] The government sector is also included with exception of the armed forces.

[6] Compared to the initial level the female change contributed more than that of men.

[7] The UK with supposedly poorer social provision saw an increase in self-employment in the 1980s, against the trend, followed by a stronger decline than elsewhere in the 1990s. Notably it was also the only country witnessing a decline in employee EPOPs between 1970 and 2001.

[8] Measured as the volume of goods, normalised across countries with the help of purchasing power parities in 1999, over hours worked in the sector (see Glyn et al, forthcoming).

[9] A different estimation technique explains that the rewards effects deviate from those shown for decile 5 in panel A of Table 3.3.

[10] Productivity equals the volume of GDP divided by all hours worked including self-employed hours. The wage share in GDP is closely related; it shows a less favourable evolution for wages in recent years than shown here.

[11] Compare Salverda (2005) for a critical appraisal of the report.

References

Glyn, A. and Erdem, E. (2000) 'Employment growth, structural change and capital accumulation', in T. ten Raa and R. Schettkat (eds) *Services: High costs, strong demand*, Cheltenham: Edward Elgar.

Glyn, A., Moeller, J., Salverda, W., Schmitt, J. and Sollogoub, M. (forthcoming) 'Employment differences in consumer services: low pay and the retail sector', in Gregory et al (forthcoming).

Gregory, M., Salverda, W. and Schettkat, R. (eds) (forthcoming) *Service included? Services and the European–American employment gap*, Princeton, NJ: Princeton University Press.

Salverda, W. (2005), 'Low pay and wage flexibility: what does the Taskforce offer?', *Beiträge zur Arbeitsmarkt-und Berufsforschung*, no 239, pp 35-50.

Salverda, W., Nolan, B., Maitre, B. and Mühlau, P. (2001) 'Benchmarking low-wage and high-wage employment in Europe and the United States', Report to the European Commission DG Employment and Social Affairs (http://ec.europa.eu/employment_social/docs/study.pdf).

Glyn, A., Salverda, W., Moeller, J., Schmitt, J. and Sollogoub, M. (2005) 'Employment differences in services: the role of wages, productivity and demand', Working Paper no 12, DEMPATEM project (www.uva-aias.net/files/lower/working_papers/WP12-revised.pdf).

Schettkat, R. and Salverda, W. (forthcoming) 'The US–European gap in service demand and employment: the research agenda', in Gregory et al, (forthcoming).

FOUR

Activation policies and the European Social Model

Joel F. Handler

Introduction

In their introduction to this volume, Jepsen and Serrano Pascual posit that the concept of the European Social Model (ESM) can be understood as a political project to legitimise European institutions. The goal of this political project is to build a common European identity, which is based more on creating common social policy solutions than on identifying institutions and values shared by Western European nations. One of the most widely accepted policy ideas throughout Western Europe is that welfare programmes for the working-age poor need to be changed from passive to active. Activation was needed, according to the central banks, the Organisation for Economic Co-operation and Development (OECD), employers' associations, and some think-tanks, because the existing welfare state discouraged job expansion by encouraging people to stay on benefits instead of working. Furthermore, these changes would not only help the economy but would help the social assistance recipients to re-enter society as citizens. Thus, active labour policies, otherwise called workfare, were justified as a means to promote, simultaneously, both economic growth and social cohesion. These same goals are used to describe the ESM. Although workfare programmes have been adopted by most Western European nations, it is important to note that not all of the countries adopted workfare programmes for the same reasons. While some countries have adopted workfare programmes in response to a perceived welfare crisis, other countries without welfare crises, including Denmark and Norway, have also started implementing the programmes.

Is there a common European policy of activation? Barbier (this volume) posits that there is not, as the concept cannot be defined when compared with the United States (US) model. To make his argument, he compares the activation policies in the United Kingdom (UK) with those in the US. This chapter will address the question using a different approach. It will concentrate its analysis on welfare programmes targeting the socially excluded – the long-term unemployed, youth unemployed, lone parents, immigrants, and some other groups – in Western Europe and on single mothers with children in the US. The discussion is limited not in order to divert attention from other important welfare policies, but because focusing on this one set of programmes allows a clear comparison between the US and Western Europe. It is true that each country in Western Europe has its own version of a workfare programme. However, it is also important to note that there are significant variations between state welfare-to-work programmes in the US. Narrowing the discussion to programmes providing services to the socially excluded in Western Europe and to single mothers and their children in the US will lead to a fruitful discussion of the similarities and differences in programmes. Although workfare policies in Western Europe differ from nation to nation and from the US, many of the bureaucratic practices and the assumptions behind them are strikingly similar.

This chapter starts with a discussion of the factors leading to welfare reform in the US, including the moral and economic crises perceived by both liberal and conservative lawmakers. The next section will include information on the outcomes of welfare reform in the US. As well as presenting information on the overall effects of welfare reform on recipients, the effects of time limits and sanctions, as well as how agencies have adapted to administer workfare programmes, will also be addressed. Specifically, the effects of privatisation on the provision of services to clients will be discussed. In the next section, the development of active labour policies in Western Europe will be traced. The last section of the chapter will describe the Western European experience, including the administration of workfare programmes and effects on clients. It will be shown that programmes in the US and Western Europe suffer from many of the same administrative problems. Both are driven by their own version of myth and ceremony – the positive aspects of welfare changes are touted while ignoring some of the problems resulting from policy changes. Privatisation of social services will also lead to a process of myth and ceremony around its ability to increase efficiency and improve services for clients and will make the concept of social citizenship only more problematic.

Ending welfare as we know it

US welfare policy has always focused on sorting the 'deserving' from the 'undeserving' poor. While the 'deserving' poor were eligible for government aid, the 'undeserving' poor were expected to work. Although poor single mothers and their children were originally classified as 'undeserving' and were compelled to work, in the 19th century, children began to be distinguished as a separate category of 'deserving' poor. States started enacting mothers' pension programmes to ensure that poor children could be cared for in their homes, as long as the mother was otherwise 'fit and proper' (Bell, 1965). The first federal programme was the Aid to Dependent Children programme (ADC), which was created in 1935 (subsequently changed to Aid to Families with Dependent Children, AFDC). In practice, ADC was primarily for 'worthy' white widows. All others, including African Americans, immigrants (especially Southern Europeans), Catholics, divorced, deserted, and unmarried women were, for the most part, considered 'unfit' and excluded from the programme, and were thus still dependent on the paid labour market (Gordon, 1988). The process of excluding black and minority ethnic recipients from the welfare rolls remained until the 1950s and 1960s when the composition of welfare recipients changed dramatically. The migration of African Americans to northern urban centres with high poverty rates, the civil rights movement, and an orchestrated 'welfare rights' movement, led to previously excluded women being added to the welfare rolls (Piven and Cloward, 1977). Over the next three decades, the number of welfare recipients increased from 2 million to about 13 million. Expenditures increased from $500 million to $23 billion (Handler and Hasenfeld, 1991). AFDC emerged from the shadows of welfare policy to centre stage, where it has remained ever since.

As the welfare rolls expanded, and increasingly consisted of unwed African American mothers, the reaction against AFDC began to grow. In the 1960s, there was an increase in urban crime, and serious race riots in over 20 cities. The War on Poverty was considered a failure. Then, President Reagan introduced the term the 'welfare queen' – the young African American unwed mother, having children in order to get and stay on welfare. She fails to properly socialise her children, who then grow up and repeat the same behaviours, as well as engage in crime, delinquency and substance abuse. In other words, the welfare system was creating a new underclass, if not a criminal class. Conservatives adopted the 'welfare queen' myth as their justification for the need for strict work requirements in welfare policies. They asserted that welfare policy had to be changed in order to control the spread of the new underclass. Conservatives emphasised that the US could not continue to be an 'entitlement state' because there are responsibilities as well as rights in the social contract. Welfare mothers needed to learn that they had a social responsibility to work.

At first, liberals opposed work requirements. They argued that it was punitive and unfair to impose work requirements on single, poor mothers when non-welfare mothers were not required to work. However, in the late 1980s, liberals started to emphasise that welfare recipients should be expected to work. They presented two reasons. First, social norms around female labour had changed. Now, most non-welfare mothers were in the paid labour market, and it was therefore reasonable to expect poor mothers to work. Second, research was showing that families were better off, both materially and socially, when the adults were gainfully employed instead of 'dependent on welfare' (Garfinkel and McLanahan, 1986; Ellwood, 1988).

The views of both conservatives and liberals were behind President's Clinton's pledge to 'end welfare as we know it', which he accomplished with the passage of the 1996 Personal Responsibility and Work Opportunity Reconciliation Act (PRWORA). The 1996 legislation replaced the AFDC programme with Temporary Aid for Needy Families (TANF), which consisted of block grants to states. The legislation specifically stated that welfare was no longer an entitlement for poor women and children; instead, women were now expected to fulfil requirements in order to get aid. The provisions of the PRWORA are a combination of trying to get mothers to work and seeking to change other behaviours targeted by conservatives. In terms of motivating women to work, the 1996 legislation imposed requirements on the states and recipients. States were required to move an increasing percentage of welfare recipients into the workforce over the next six years. The federal government did not explicitly tell states how to move these recipients into work. As for recipients, TANF imposed stiff work requirements and, for the first time in welfare history, time limits on aid. Cash assistance is limited to a maximum of two consecutive years with a five-year lifetime limit on aid. Furthermore, if recipients do not meet their work requirements, states are required to sanction the recipients by reducing their cash aid.

Although states were given broad flexibility to administer their welfare programmes, most have used this flexibility to enact punishments and requirements stricter than mandated by TANF. In 37 states, the entire family loses its cash aid if the adult violates work or other requirements – called full-family sanctions. Six states have chosen to eliminate only the adult portion of the grant for non-compliance while allowing the family to keep the child's portion, called a partial sanction. In the remaining eight states, the amount of the sanction can be increased over the adult's portion, but the family will not lose its entire grant (Pavetti and Bloom, 2001). States have also enacted stricter time limits than required by the federal government. Although TANF sets a cumulative lifetime limit of five years, at least 20 states have time limits that are less than five years. In 10 of these states, the time limit is only two years (DeParle, 1997). As for designing their welfare-to-work programmes, most states embraced a strong 'work first' strategy, which discourages education and training in favour of encouraging recipients to take any available job, even a low-wage job, in order to receive benefits. The idea is to move not only current recipients, but also applicants, into the labour market as quickly as possible rather than place them in long-term and costly training or education programmes.

In addition to adopting the 'work first' strategy, many states also significantly expanded contracting with private agencies to administer at least some part of their welfare programme. Although states had some experience implementing work programmes under previous welfare policy, welfare reform mandated that they meet rapidly rising quotas of recipients involved in work activities. To meet these new requirements, many states contracted with private firms to provide some services. After the passage of welfare reform, over 30 states entered into contracts for various services (Handler, 2004). However, as Brodkin et al (2002) state, there was a general trend towards contracting to provide services, but there was considerable diversity between states about what parts of welfare services were contracted. The state of Florida and Los Angeles County contracted with for-profit firms to provide both income maintenance and employment services. Mississippi initially adopted a broad privatisation effort, but returned to public provision after encountering difficulty monitoring the performance of the contractors. Illinois and other states limited contracting to specialised services and maintained a strong public agency role in other aspects of services delivery. Although it contracted out only limited services, the number of organisations receiving contracts nearly doubled and the amount of public funding going to contractors increased eightfold. The increase in contracting has also led to the creation and growth of private firms specialising in providing welfare services, including Maximus, Inc. and Lockheed Martin, which has been involved in the defence industry.

Outcomes of welfare reform in the US

Since TANF was enacted in 1996, the welfare rolls have fallen from 12.2 million people to approximately 5.3 million (Greenberg, 2004). White people left the welfare rolls faster than African Americans and Latinos; declines have also been slower in urban areas (Katz, 2001). In 2000, nearly one third of parents still on assistance were working – a threefold increase from four years earlier (Healy, 2000). As mentioned earlier, states were given the same amount of money, as long as they met specific work quotas. With the rapid decline of welfare caseloads, states used billions of dollars in federal block-grant money to expand child care, to provide services for other low-income families, and to substitute state funding for other programmes (Greenberg, 2004).

Given these results, welfare reform has been declared a 'success'. However, there are doubts about how much of the reduction of the welfare rolls and increasing employment of welfare recipients is due to TANF. Academics point to other factors to explain these remarkable changes, such as the overall national economic growth, the rapid expansion of the low-wage labour market, the broadening of health care coverage, and the expansion of the Earned Income Tax Credit.

This section will examine the 'success' of welfare reform by presenting its effects on several important areas. First research focusing on the effects of welfare reform on the employment and earnings of welfare recipients will be presented. The section then presents recent research on the effects of sanctions and time limits. Lastly, it will discuss how public and private welfare offices have adapted to implementing work programmes. Although public and private agencies face similar pressures in terms of meeting participation requirements and establishing individualised work plans, private agencies also have to meet the additional goals of increasing profits and expanding their business. The section also explores whether contracting with private agencies increased efficiency and customer satisfaction, as assumed by state governments.

Effects of welfare reform on employment and earnings

When determining whether welfare reform was successful, one can start by considering whether welfare reform met its stated goals of 'making work pay' for welfare recipients. Studies of welfare-to-work programmes reveal that the programmes are not having their intended results. In a study of 20 welfare-to-work programmes, Manpower Demonstration Research Corporation found that the programmes increased the earnings of participants by only about $500 a year more than controls. Welfare payments were reduced by nearly $400 and food stamps by $100 per person, thus resulting in welfare savings for the government if the expenses of other supportive services are not included in the analysis (Michalopoulos and Schwartz, 2000). The study also found that the programmes increased the earnings of the most disadvantaged groups (long-term recipients, those lacking a high school diploma, those with three or more children, and those with no recent work experience), but the earnings of these workers were still far below the earnings of the more advantaged earners. In summary, despite the political claims for success, the income gains for welfare recipients are very modest, and often fail to account for the added costs of working, such as transportation and child care. In fact, most former recipients remain in poverty.

Programmes that emphasise education and training show similar results to programmes adopting a 'work first' strategy. A national evaluation of welfare-to-work strategies in 11 US locations revealed that 81% of participants showed a significant increase in employment and earnings that were equal to or exceeded the results of work–first programmes. Still, these programmes were not able to lift participants out of poverty. Even though most of the programmes helped families rely on their own earnings rather than welfare checks, the resulting reductions in welfare, food stamps, and other benefits outweighed the increase in earnings. The researchers concluded that education-focused programmes do not produce added economic gains relative to programmes adopting a 'work first' philosophy. Moreover, programmes that emphasised quick entry into the workforce were cheaper to operate and moved welfare recipients into jobs more quickly than education-focused programmes (Hamilton, 2002). However, neither job-search-focused nor education-focused programmes have typically been successful in helping welfare recipients and other low-income parents work steadily or obtain higher-paying jobs (Brauner and Loprest, 1999; Strawn et al, 2001). Thus, mandated work programmes, in general, have demonstrated little effect on income since they often result in a decline in welfare benefits. Although such programmes did decrease poverty somewhat, they did so only for families with incomes just below the poverty line (Grogger et al, 2002).

All of the studies presented thus far analysed the effects of welfare-to-work programmes on women still on the welfare rolls. Researchers have also started to consider the effects of these programmes on welfare recipients who leave the rolls – referred to as leavers. These studies show that between half and two thirds of former recipients find employment shortly after leaving welfare. Most of the jobs are in sales, food preparation, clerical support, and other service industry jobs. Despite their relatively high number of work hours, former recipients still have significant periods of unemployment (Hamilton, 2002). Former recipients earn between $5.57 and $8.42 per hour, and the average reported annual earnings range from $8,000 to $16,600, thus leaving many families in poverty (Grogger et al, 2002). The increases in earnings obtained by former welfare recipients are due more to increasing work hours than to a growth in their wages. Most employed leavers do not receive employer-provided health insurance, paid sick leave, or vacation leave. Employment loss is a significant problem (Strawn et al, 2001). In addition, there were sharp declines in Medicaid and food stamps (Grogger et al, 2002). Lastly, most former welfare recipients do not receive child care subsidies despite the fact that the lack of affordable child care has been identified as a substantial barrier to obtaining and keeping employment (Pavetti, 1999).

A recent study of the employment and earnings of 600 women with a history of welfare receipt living in Miami, Florida revealed that these women are far from self-sufficient after leaving the welfare rolls. In 2001, 29% of women in the study were not working or were on welfare. Furthermore, 35% of survey respondents held three or more jobs and only 27% reported having a job that was full time, paid at least $7.50 per hour, and offered medical benefits (Brock et al, 2004). Overall, studies of leavers reveal that welfare reform successfully pushed families off the welfare caseloads, but did not lift them out of poverty.

Effects of sanctions and time limits

As mentioned earlier, one of the most significant changes made to welfare policy in 1996 was creating stricter sanction policies. Sanctioning was supposed to ensure compliance with welfare-to-work requirements by causing increased financial hardship among families. Although the number of sanctioned families varies from state to state, studies have demonstrated that high numbers of families are sanctioned at any given time. A General Accounting Office study (1997) found that an average of 135,800 families each month (4.5% of the national TANF caseload) received a full or partial sanction. Partial sanctions were used more frequently than full sanctions but, still, an average of 16,000 families lost their benefits completely. One study estimated that 540,000 families in California lost benefits due to full-family sanctions from 1997 to 1999, and that 370,000 remained off assistance at the end of 1999 (Hasenfeld et al, 2004). Cohort studies of state programmes have shown that sanction rates are quite high: one quarter to one half of families subject to work requirements is sanctioned over a 12- to 24-month period. When New York City adopted a more stringent welfare programme, over 400,000 people were dropped from the rolls (Brito, 2000).

It is important to note that many families are sanctioned due to bureaucratic errors, not because they do not comply with welfare regulations. If the computer fails to record a required appointment, then the recipient is automatically sanctioned (Diller, 2000). In their study of welfare recipients, Lindhorst et al (2000) found that about 8% of sanctioned recipients did not know why their benefits had been reduced. A qualitative study of sanctioned recipients in Northern California revealed that recipients felt that workers were applying sanctions arbitrarily; thus, even if they complied with work requirements, they could still be sanctioned (Rainford, 2004).

Who gets sanctioned? Several studies have shown that recipients who may be least able to succeed in the labour market are the most likely to be sanctioned. Sanctioned recipients have been shown to have multiple employment barriers, including cognitive and health-related barriers, and difficult aspects of home life (for example, lack of transportation, three or more children, child care problems, domestic violence) (Pavetti and Bloom, 2001; Hasenfeld et al, 2004). According to a General Accounting Office report, sanctioned families had less education, more limited work experience, and longer welfare receipt than non-sanctioned families. In Tennessee, 60% of sanctioned recipients lacked a high school diploma or General Educational Development test, compared to 40% who left welfare for work. In South Carolina, 36% of high school dropouts were sanctioned, compared to 22% of high school graduates. Studies in Arizona and Minnesota report that more than half of the families receiving full sanctions had an adult with less than a high school education. In Maryland, 41% of sanctioned families had no employment history, compared to 31% who left welfare for other reasons (Hasenfeld et al, 2004). Many sanctioned families also experience personal and family challenges at a higher rate than other recipients, including chemical dependency, physical and mental health problems and domestic violence. These studies have been replicated in Utah, Connecticut, Minnesota and Wisconsin (Hasenfeld et al, 2004; Wu et al, 2004).

Despite the extensive use of sanctions, the evidence is contradictory as to whether sanctions are effective in encouraging compliance with welfare programmes or encouraging recipients to work. Many agency staff firmly believe that sanctions 'work' – they communicate the seriousness of the requirements. Some studies show that neither the threat of sanctions nor the imposition of sanctions changes behaviour. Other studies show that severe sanctions are no more or less effective than moderate sanctions (Kaplan, 1999). However, a recent study conducted among welfare recipients in Wisconsin shows that most sanction spells are short and that most recipients obtain their full benefits after facing a full-family sanction. The authors believe this shows some evidence that sanctions have their desired effect of increasing compliance with programme requirements (Wu et al, 2004). However, the authors contend that it is still important to consider whether the imposition of sanctions led to significant hardship among families. Taken as a whole, studies suggest that sanctions influence the behaviours of many TANF recipients but not others, even with the loss of all assistance (Pavetti and Bloom, 2001).

The second major policy change made by the PRWORA was the imposition of strict time limits on aid. As stated, federal law restricts using TANF money for assistance for the ongoing needs of most families for more than 60 months. Furthermore, families are allowed to receive aid for no more than two consecutive years. The clock starts with the enactment of the state's TANF programme. The federal five-year time limit was reached on 1 October 2001. Even before the federal time limit was reached, approximately 60,000 families reached the time limits in seven states with shorter periods. Most of these families reside in three states: Connecticut, Massachusetts and Louisiana (Pavetti and Bloom, 2001). Families that reach time limits, like families who are sanctioned, face more barriers to obtaining and keeping employment – including persistent maternal and child health problems, persistent domestic violence, persistent drug use, lack of a partner, low levels of education, and increases in the number of children – than families on welfare for shorter periods of time (Seefeldt and Orzol, 2004). Even though most observers thought that states would somehow extend benefits, most have in fact not done so and benefits have been terminated. Many of the families whose benefits were terminated were working, but many were not (Haskins and Blank, 2001).

Effects on welfare offices

When the welfare rolls exploded in the 1960s, one of the charges was that the welfare programme was wracked with 'waste, fraud, and abuse'. Both the federal government and the states imposed strict quality control measures. The result was a change in mission of the offices to a concentration on minimising eligibility errors by requiring extensive documentation, including frequent reporting of income and assets, birth records, social security numbers, and other eligibility data. Caseworkers became eligibility clerks. When the 1996 welfare reform was enacted, some of its proponents recognised the changes that would have to be made in the offices to develop welfare-to-work plans, monitor progress and impose sanctions. The 'culture' of the office had to be changed from being solely concerned with eligibility and compliance to individual, service-oriented, intensive casework.

Culture in government welfare agencies

In a study of 11 local public welfare offices, changes appear to have been made or at least attempted. In Texas, case managers are now called Texas Work Advisors; in Michigan, Assistance Payment Workers are now Family Independence Specialists. Sometimes, jobs actually changed as well. Still, at the front line, the central tasks of eligibility determination and compliance with rules remained – getting the work done in a timely fashion, and eliminating fraud (Gais et al, 2001). Rather than changing welfare office culture of eligibility and compliance, the work programme was instead added to it. Adding this component has made the already complicated process of applying for and maintaining benefits even more complicated. Welfare-to-work programmes require recipients to accept offers of suitable employment or participate in various kinds of pre-employment activities (for example, job search, job preparedness classes, and so on); if, without cause, they fail to do so, they are subject to sanctions. Within these seemingly simple requirements, lie volumes of rules, regulations, standards and interpretations. There are scores of regulations attempting to spell out every element in the programme, from what determines inability to work to whether a recipient should be sanctioned for missing an appointment. There is an enormous amount of paperwork; everything has to be documented. Despite the quantity of rules, *a great many of the most crucial decisions require judgment or discretion on the part of field-level workers.*

There is a rich literature on the attitudes of welfare workers towards recipients. The workers practise what Yeheskel Hasenfeld has described as *moral typification*. The core activity of welfare agencies is to process or change people (Hasenfeld, 1983). The very nature of selecting, processing, and changing people conveys a judgment as to the *moral* worth of the person. However rule-bound the decision, somewhere along the line a value judgment has been made about the client. Cultural beliefs determine what values are legitimate and appropriate in working with clients. The welfare agency will attempt to select those clients who fit organisational needs and compartmentalise clients into 'normal' service categories. Other client problems will be considered irrelevant. Welfare agencies punish those who do not or cannot comply. Many workers see themselves as but a short step away from welfare themselves; yet, they work hard, 'play by the rules', and no one is giving them benefits and favours. Workers trained, socialised and supervised in this manner will apply rules strictly, impose sanctions, avoid errors and get through the day as quickly and painlessly as possible. Requests for change or required change consume scarce administrative time and run the risk of error. Clients with problems become problems (Hasenfeld, 1983).

The culture of welfare offices and values of workers even influence decisions over which the client should have at least some influence, including the creation of their work contract. In theory, a contract should be drawn up between the welfare recipient and the agency that spells out the mutual obligations of both and makes them accountable to the terms of the contract. However, as demonstrated in a study by Brodkin (1997), the state stacks the cards in such a way that the clients have few opportunities to influence the terms of the contract. The caseworkers use their discretionary power to force the clients to comply with their interpretation of the contract. The workers construct their own conception of the welfare contract, which, in this case, 'excluded a client's right to help in job-finding and denied a state obligation to assure that decent job opportunities existed or could be found' (Brodkin, 1995, p 15). During assessment of the clients' needs, the workers fitted the clients into available slots, ignoring information about service needs to which they could not respond. Not infrequently, caseworkers sent clients on job searches even though the clients did not meet the required level of education or literacy proficiency.

These findings by Brodkin are not surprising and are replicated in many other instances. Yet, it is disturbing that current welfare reformers seem to learn so little from history. As Schorr (1987) reminds us, social contracts were the social work strategy of the 1950s and 1960s. They did not work then primarily because of the bureaucratisation of the office, the de-professionalisation of the staff and the pressure of managing accurately a complex income-maintenance programme – in short, for the same administrative reasons that Brodkin decries 40 years later. For the average worker, the pressures are 'to cream' – to deal with those clients who more easily fulfil the programme's requirements, and, above all, who will not cause any problems. This means concentrating on the most readily employable. In the past, the workers would deflect the most troublesome cases. Now, they are sanctioned.

Contracting welfare services with private agencies

Given many of the limitations of public welfare programmes trying to administer welfare-to-work programmes, it becomes evident why many lawmakers thought that contracting with private agencies would increase efficiency and customer satisfaction. Contracting for services is extremely common in the US. In the 1960s and 1970s, confidence in the government was shaken by urban riots, Vietnam, the persistence of poverty and the urban fiscal crisis. The reputation of the government and of the welfare state was tarnished by charges of corruption and inefficiency. At the same time, studies of contracting by local governments claimed to show that services could be delivered more efficiently in a competitive environment. The principal justification for contracting was and still is efficiency. The theory is that the same or similar services or goods can be provided by the private sector at less cost than government can furnish them. Contracting can also be viewed in terms of effectiveness, equity, accountability and legitimacy, as well as other criteria (Gormley, 1991). The ideological justifications for contracting emphasise client autonomy. Large bureaucracies, it is claimed, are unresponsive to clients, consumers and workers. The private sector, in contrast, has to compete for consumers. Efficiency depends upon satisfied clients. Therefore, contracting, by breaking the public monopoly and increasing private sector competition, should enhance consumer autonomy.

In order to assess whether contracting leads to these results, Donahue (1989) examined studies of a variety of organisations. He discovered that the assumptions made about contracting are true only under specific conditions. Donahue evaluated the effects of contracting on two specific outcomes – efficiency and accountability. Reviewing the evidence on efficiency from a variety of sources – military support services, office cleaning firms, fire-fighting organisations, the transportation industry, water and power utilities – Donahue concluded that profit-seeking firms are potentially more efficient under certain circumstances. The determining factor is the presence of competition in the market. Without a credible prospect of replacement, it is difficult to control private firms. Moreover, it is hard to maintain competition. Private firms with contracts develop inside information, expertise and special relationships with government officials. Without meaningful specifications or competition, the primary drive for private organisations becomes the profit drive.

The issues raised by Donahue give rise to a number of concerns about contracting, especially in the case of human services, including asymmetric information, the difficulty of defining the costs of services and measuring quality, which often result in cost-plus contracts. In this sector, both the availability and continuity of contractors will be problematic. Particularly as programmes get under way, there will be considerable pressure to contract with those organisations that best meet the needs of the government agency, and this does not necessarily mean efficiency. In many instances, government will have to, in effect, create suppliers. In other instances, there will be an irresistible need to favour those suppliers who can best meet the demand for an acceptable level of continuous service, thus avoiding repeated bidding as well as the bureaucratic red tape that accompanies the dispersal of public funds. This means favouring large entrepreneurial firms, whether for-profit or non-profit. Thus, it is claimed that both for-profits and non-profits will come to resemble government itself – large, bureaucratic, concerned with organisational maintenance, with process and paperwork, with stability of funding, and not necessarily with service. The result will be goal displacement, a focus on funding strategies that will be decoupled from service (Kramer, 1994). These conditions will not lead to increased support for clients. For them, it will just be the replacement of one large bureaucratic structure by another large bureaucratic structure.

When making the case for contracting welfare-to-work services, government officials did not consider these factors. They ignored the fact that private agencies must cope with many of the same obstacles as public welfare offices, while also meeting agency goals of increasing profit and expanding their business. They must manage the cases of a large number of clients by balancing client needs with agency requirements. The state requires private agencies to meet performance measures, which set the specific percentage of clients that need contracts and must participate in work activities. At the same time, caseworkers are told to tailor plans to the individual needs of clients. In a study of private agencies administering work programmes in Chicago, Brodkin et al (2002) found that these agencies suffer from many of the same faults as public agencies, such as creaming and goal displacement. In interviews and field research, Brodkin et al found that caseworkers would use informal strategies to encourage enrolment among recipients who were most likely to meet agency goals, while discouraging enrolment among applicants with multiple employment barriers. They also found that Chicago's performance-based contracts 'set the stage for a numbers game in which intermediaries are rewarded for obtaining placement targets at the lowest marginal cost and in which investments in building capacity for service quality are rewarded only indirectly if at all' (p 2). In other words, workers placed clients to meet their performance goals, instead of in accordance with client needs.

When examining private agencies administering Milwaukee's welfare-to-work programme, called W-2, DeParle found more significant problems. The private agencies in Milwaukee were also evaluated based on the number of clients with employability contracts and on whether recipients were assigned to 'a full slate' of activities. To meet these goals, caseworkers employed a variety of methods from creating and mailing employability contracts to clients without consulting them to simply inputting the information on the computer. A state evaluation of all of the private agencies demonstrated that they all had dismal results at first. Although all clients were supposed to be involved in some sort of work activity, paid or community service, 67% of clients at Maximus, Inc. did not have a work assignment (DeParle, 2004).

However, instead of taking away their contracts, the state instead ignored initial results of agency failure. As Donahue (1989) predicted, state officials had developed close relationships with the private agencies. More fundamentally, the success of the private agencies was also a reflection of the success of the politicians at reforming welfare. Even though state officials knew the programme was performing dismally at first, it pushed for its welfare-to-work programme to win the prestigious Innovations in American Government Award. The purported success of the W-2 programme was highlighted on several news shows, including *Nightline*. Throughout the country, and in Western Europe, W-2 was considered to be the 'showpiece' of welfare reform's success (Graser, 2003). The Governor of Wisconsin, Tommy Thompson, also had a stake in W-2's success; he wanted to use the programme as a means to gain support for a possible presidential campaign.

From these examples, it becomes evident that private welfare agencies suffer from many of the failures associated with public welfare offices. In addition, private agencies providing services also have unique goals that distinguish them from public service providers – increasing profit and expanding business. After the passage of welfare reform, some private agencies earned contracts where the agency receives a fixed sum to serve the needs of a geographic area. This arrangement is supposed to encourage private agencies to make successful job placements, which would keep recipients off welfare. The more an agency reduced its caseload, the more profits it would make (DeParle, 2004). When welfare reform was passed, a significant number of recipients dropped off the rolls before states fully implemented their welfare-to-work programmes. The result was that private agencies had considerable money to spend on fewer clients than the state had originally anticipated. For example, in Wisconsin, the state had budgeted to provide services to 50,000 cases, but when W-2 began, only 23,000 people were left on the rolls (DeParle, 2004). Instead of investing these profits to improve services, some agencies used the money to win contracts in other states or to advertise their agency. In Milwaukee, DeParle found that Maximus, Inc. spent $1.1 million of welfare money on billboards, television advertisements, backpacks, coffee mugs, and golf balls to improve the company's image, despite the fact that caseworkers were assigned almost double the number of cases allowed by its state contract. A Goodwill subsidiary, Employment Solutions, Inc., spent more than $270,000 of welfare-to-work programme funds to win a welfare contract in Arizona. Although Maximus, Inc. is a for-profit agency, Goodwill is a non-profit agency. Thus, both non-profit and for-profit agencies used state funds in an effort to expand their business to other states and non-profits were not more likely to provide improved services to clients.

The data presented thus far do not show that private agencies are any more efficient or responsive to client needs than public welfare agencies. It does not seem that increased responsiveness to client needs is a priority with the current financial and contractual arrangements. Agencies providing contracted services have at least two sets of stakeholders: clients and the government agencies that fund them. Due to the power imbalance between these stakeholders, agencies will often tailor their services to meet the needs of the government agency mandates, not necessarily to meet the needs of clients. Furthermore, they have a goal of making a profit and expanding their business, unlike public agencies. The privatised welfare-to-work services are an example of myth and ceremony (Meyer and Rowan, 1977). As mentioned, the myth is that contracting services will lead to increased efficiency and customer satisfaction. The private agencies and state governments validate this myth through ceremonies showing that their welfare-to-work programmes are effective. However, the ceremony does not have to be based in reality. The examples mentioned earlier show that private agencies suffer from many of the same pressures as public agencies. Furthermore, they are driven by pressures to increase profits and expand business. The clients are not emphasised in these decisions.

From the right to aid to the right to work in Western Europe

In the decades following the Second World War, during a period of full employment (now referred to as the 'Golden Age'), the Western European welfare states were created or consolidated. While there were considerable differences among the various countries, the defining characteristic of welfare states was the extension of social rights. The core idea was 'social citizenship'. Social rights, including protection when faced with hardships such as unemployment, sickness, and old age, were granted 'the legal and practical status of property rights' (Esping-Andersen, 1990, p 3). In theory, benefits were universal and solidaristic; they were not based on previous earnings or work performance.

Starting in the 1970s, the economies of Western Europe began to unravel. There were dramatic changes in international trade and finance, the consolidation of the European Union free trade market, and the monetary union pursuant to which member states agreed to reduce their budgetary deficits. This also reduced their capacity to manage their own fiscal policies. There have been significant changes in the labour market, which both increased opportunities for some while creating employment barriers for the low-skilled and under-educated, as well as creating low wages and employment insecurity, especially for women and youth (European Council, 2001). For more than two decades, most countries have been struggling with sluggish economies and persistent long-term unemployment (Huber and Stevens, 2001).

The Western European welfare states have been placed under great stress from two different directions. First, populations have been ageing and birth rates have declined. To combat unemployment, most countries encouraged early retirement and introduced liberal disability policies. Consequently, more people are drawing welfare state benefits, while fewer people are working and contributing. At the same time as costs are rising for pensions, disability, and health care, governments are constrained in meeting these expenses since there is resistance to raising taxes and the monetary union is resisting deficit financing. Second, there is deep concern about long-term unemployment among vulnerable populations – unskilled or low-skilled youth and immigrants, lone parents – variously lumped together as the 'socially excluded'.

Much of the economic establishment – the central banks, the OECD, employers' associations, as well as many think-tanks – argue that the major villain behind the sluggish economies is the welfare state. Europe has to create many different types of jobs, but primarily, lower-skilled service work. However, they argue that the welfare state discourages job expansion by encouraging people to stay on benefits instead of working. In order to encourage employment, labour has to be made more 'flexible' and the welfare state has to be changed from 'passive' to 'active'. The disincentives to work must be changed to incentives. This means discouraging early retirement and disability, reducing unemployment benefits, and imposing work requirements on the long-term unemployed. These changes are called 'active labour market policies' or 'workfare'. As Jepsen and Serrano Pascual (this volume) state, this overall argument has been used by the governments of Western European nations as a justification to enact social policy that focuses on the need to enhance an individual's capacity to participate in the changing market, instead of using social policy to correct market forces.

Until now, the voters in most countries have joined the Social Democrats and resisted most of the changes proposed by the Conservatives. The basic welfare programmes – pensions, disability, and health care – are intact, although some modifications have been made. The biggest changes have occurred for the unemployed and those at the bottom, such as the long-term unemployed and the social assistance recipients. Here, the Left and the Centre, with popular support, agree with the Conservatives. They assert that these claimants cannot collect benefits indefinitely. Benefits should be tied to 'active labour market participation'. There are two reasons behind this development, both with long welfare histories. One is deterrence, also sometimes called 'compassion fatigue'. The other is rehabilitation, which is based on a deep concern for the poor. According to this view, the surest way to bring the socially excluded back into society is through the paid labour market. Rosanvallon (2000), a leading intellectual in the 'second left', states that men fought 'for the right to live from their labor.... Thus, progress demands reinventing the idea of the right to work, rather than shaping a right to income' (Rosanvallon, 2000, p 68).

Almost all of the political parties, including the Social Democrats, have adopted the 'right to work' ideology as a way out of the impasse between the neoliberals who want to dismantle the welfare state and those who defend the status quo. Consequently, workfare policies have come increasingly to dominate the welfare state in Western Europe. Moreover, workfare has spread to countries without a welfare crisis. Compulsory activation is increasing even in countries with low unemployment, such as Denmark, on the basis of the principle that 'everyone with at least some capacity to work should work' (Fafo, 2001, 46). Norway too has adopted workfare, which according to Lødemel andTrickey (2001) is not the result of a Conservative backlash, but rather a reflection of Social Democratic policy shifts in other countries towards workfare.

Unlike in the US where work requirements have always been a part of the welfare system, in Western Europe workfare represents a fundamental change in both the meaning of social citizenship and the administration of social welfare. Under the welfare state of the golden age, social benefits were rights applied by virtue of the status of citizenship. Under the new workfare regime, benefits become conditional. Rights apply only if *obligations* are fulfilled. Social citizenship changes from status to contract.

Outcomes of workfare in Western Europe

The purpose of workfare is not simply to get the socially excluded to work, but to restore their right to work. Workfare is supposed to be an empowering process for clients because it should be based on contracts of inclusion. In these contracts, social assistance recipients have a right to be included in the workforce and the state is obligated to provide opportunities for inclusion. As well as making welfare policies 'active' for social assistance recipients, governments in Western Europe agreed to make the labour market more 'flexible' so that employers would be willing to hire more workers.

The record so far of active labour market policies in Western Europe is mixed. With few exceptions, the empirical evidence at the field level is uneven. A recent report by the Fafo Institute for Applied Social Science, evaluating workfare in Denmark, France, Germany, the Netherlands, Norway and the UK, concluded that many studies show that workfare programmes have had positive effects on employment, as measured by earnings (Fafo, 2001, pp 73-4). However, in France, only about 25% leave the workfare programme due to employment. The net employment effect of the Dutch workfare programme is claimed to be about 18%, but this figure is uncertain. In Germany, there is no evidence as to whether participants are more likely to find a job as a result of participation. With the Norwegian compulsory programmes, neither the employment nor earnings of programme participants significantly improved. Overall, those who benefit the most from workfare programmes tend to be younger, with better education, and fewer social problems – or those who would have been most likely to find jobs on their own. This was true for Denmark, France, the Netherlands (including non-immigrants) and the UK.

The flexibilisation of employment has increased the jobs and income for many, especially those who prefer part-time work. In some of the countries, comparable benefits and extensive labour rights now apply to part-time and temporary work (Svensson, 1999). In other countries, flexible labour policies have led to an increase in job discontinuity (Supiot, 2000). Countries vary as to how they treat discontinuous employment. In general, protection against dismissal and safeguarding of existing jobs has eased, but there is variation (Supiot, 2000). Many working part time would prefer full-time employment. Many workers, such as those in Germany, are now considered to be in precarious jobs. In some countries, such as Ireland and the UK, there is considerable income inequality. In Denmark and the Netherlands, despite the impressive employment gains, considerable numbers of people remain inactive or marginally employed.

Governments have also tried to increase the employment of the socially excluded by providing subsidies to private employers to hire disadvantaged workers (Supiot, 2000). While the number of subsidised jobs has increased significantly in most countries, the importance of subsidies and the number of people who benefit vary considerably. So far, subsidised jobs are less effective in creating additional job opportunities. Usually, there is one new job for every five subsidised jobs. There were complaints that subsidy programmes to provide employment for disadvantaged workers produced windfall profits and were 'effective' only when firms were going to expand anyway. The consensus was that overall employment did not improve. Most countries now rely on tightening unemployment benefits (McFate, 1995). Another key component of active labour policies is supposed to be public employment services – to both reduce frictional unemployment and help disadvantaged workers gain skills and access. With the exception of Sweden, however, few job openings actually come through these offices.

Effects of sanctioning

While all the workfare programmes have sanctions, their use varies depending on worker discretion, staff attitudes towards clients, and the extent to which paperwork would be increased, not on whether sanctions would make any difference in shaping client behaviour or make matters worse. In the UK, there has been a marked increase in the use of sanctions, and 'the most socially excluded are more likely to experience sanctions ... [despite the fact that] previous research has provided no evidence that the experience of sanctions has any positive influence on behaviour, whether of the person being sanctioned or other jobseekers' (Training and Employment Network, 1999). Clients have a right to appeal against sanctions, but clients do not have the understanding or the resources to pursue this right (Fafo, 2001, p 65). In Germany, several local authorities are still not inclined to use sanctions, especially for the more experienced, older workers. On the other hand, in the Netherlands, it is claimed that sanctions are used on the basis of officer-perceived negative social background characteristics (Spies and van Berkel, 2001, pp 124-7).

Administrative practices in workfare offices

As mentioned, workfare is supposed to reintegrate the socially excluded into the labour market. Instead of simply pushing the socially excluded into the labour market, welfare offices are supposed to create individualised 'contracts of inclusion' with social assistance recipients. Thus, the process is supposed to empower clients. What have been the results so far? There is considerable evidence that Western European programmes are exhibiting some of the same administrative patterns as found in the US. Because of high workloads and bureaucratic regulations, communication between workers and clients in workfare offices tends to focus on meeting bureaucratic targets and placing clients in options without much discussion about client needs. The workers pick from a variety of options of which clients are generally unaware. In their evaluation of workfare programmes, Fafo (2001) found that in France a majority of workfare participants did not have a contract, even though it is a legal requirement. In Sweden and the UK, agencies merely provided brief sessions, with the officers restricting the options offered and beneficiaries agreeing in order to receive the benefits. Instead of matching client needs to placements, workers rank clients to match the desirability of options. 'Intuition seems to play an important role among the street-level bureaucrats; categorisation of clients, with bureaucrats selecting the 'best' clients for the 'best' options, leaving the rest for the least desirable options' (Fafo, 2001, p 67). There are suggestions of similar practices in other countries as well (Roche, 2000). The main trend has been to push more people into means-tested and behaviour-tested social assistance (Standing, 1992; Behrendt, 2000).

Once placed, there is little contact between the recipient and his/her worker. Clients are sensitive to this kind of treatment, which they consider disrespectful (Fafo, 2001, p 67). In some countries (the Netherlands, Norway and the UK), clients feel they are placed in 'second-rate jobs', while workers view these jobs as 'stepping stones'. Although most participants expressed satisfaction with the workfare programmes, a significant proportion found them to be a waste of time. Satisfaction was quite low in the Netherlands and there was evidence that the programme was harmful to the most vulnerable. In the UK, the more disadvantaged tended to have negative attitudes (Fafo, 2001, pp 71-3).

The results from evaluations of workfare policies in Western Europe have led some scholars to posit that they are having the opposite effect of what was intended. While there is considerable variation in the design and implementation of workfare programmes, they seem to all be related to the perceived characteristics of the targeted groups. The selection of options available to clients mirrors the selectivity of the regular labour market. This leads not only to creaming, but also to exclusion trajectories or low-level, dead-end jobs where clients are perpetually recycled. Thus, programmes may simply ignore most of the disadvantaged who live in areas of low labour market demand. Trickey argues that, under some conditions, compulsory programmes can be more damaging for those who fail and may face additional social exclusion (Trickey, 2001, pp 287-8). In the Netherlands, there has been an increase in marginalisation and social exclusion (Trickey, 2001). Over time, as some recipients obtain employment, a marginalised 'hard-core' will remain in the programmes (Roche, 2000, p 43).

The triumph of myth and ceremony

In the US, there is no pretence of rights in welfare-to-work programmes. Although there was a brief period when the law said that welfare was an entitlement, that notion was eliminated with the passage of the PRWORA in 1996. Instead, in line with the history of welfare in the US, the emphasis is on work requirements. The way in which welfare-to-work services are provided in the US is based on two sets of myth and ceremony. The first myth of welfare reform was that it was time to get serious about making welfare recipients work. Despite research revealing that welfare recipients are usually adults, receive welfare for a relatively short period of time, find jobs on their own, and that previous welfare-to-work programmes were only marginally effective, most states chose an aggressive 'work first' strategy. However, from time to time, a programme will help recipients obtain jobs and get off welfare. This creates the ceremony that validates the myth. An example in the current welfare reform was a programme in Riverside, California. Despite the fact that the programme had modest results – at the end of the programme, half of the participants were not working and of those who worked most remained in poverty – it was hailed as a great success and became the model for the 'work first' strategy adopted by state governments across the US. In a sense, the actual results from the programme did not matter. The country was determined to 'end welfare as we know it'. The 'work first' strategy was clear, effectively communicated, and validated commonly held assumptions about welfare recipients. The programme affirmed the US values of hard work and proper moral conduct. It made the general public feel better by punishing the victim. The pronouncements of success allowed the public to ignore the fact that most families who leave welfare remain in poverty and suffer a great deal of hardship.

The second myth of welfare reform was that contracting with private agencies to provide welfare-to-work services would increase efficiency and improve customer service. As mentioned earlier, this myth has been firmly established in the US since the 1960s and 1970s. The W-2 programme in Milwaukee, Wisconsin was touted as support for this myth. In its own ceremony validating the myth, W-2 received prestigious awards and was portrayed by the media as being an effective programme. The reputation of W-2's effectiveness has spread all the way to Germany and New Zealand where government officials have proposed reform based on the W-2 programme. However, as we have seen, the ceremony was not justified by the programme's actual performance. The assumption that private markets will lead to competition for services ignores many of the characteristics of human service agencies. As Donahue (1989) states, when contracting human services, both the availability and continuity of contractors will be problematic. The state may be forced to provide incentives to increase competition. Another possibility is that state agencies will simply develop close relationships with and support agencies currently getting government contracts. This leads to private agencies that focus on meeting performance measures over serving client needs. More importantly, the success of programmes becomes a common goal of both state government officials and the private agencies. Therefore, both only want to supply information that supports the effectiveness of the welfare-to-work programmes. The client's needs and satisfaction no longer enter the calculations of success.

Western Europe seems to be moving toward its own version of myth and ceremony. Although workfare programmes vary from nation to nation, they are all based on the assumption that the welfare state needed to be changed from passive to active. For the unemployed, governments needed to provide incentives to work instead of remaining in welfare. Making the socially excluded work will help them re-enter society. To put a human face on the changes in welfare programmes, the entire argument is put in terms of rights, contracts and empowerment. The socially excluded have a right to re-enter society and the government has an obligation to help them through contracts based on their individual needs. This is the myth of workfare. In some cases, it does take place and validates the myth. However, there is disturbing evidence that contracts are not based on client needs. Rather, worker–client interviews are perfunctory and workers place clients based on favourable characteristics and the availability of options. Thus, the most vulnerable are still being excluded. If these trends continue, the face of workfare becomes a mask that hides the reality of continuing hardship and exclusion.

There is also an increasing trend in Western Europe to privatise and decentralise government services. Research about recent shifts in governance in Western Europe has stressed that 'governments should focus more on steering and less on rowing in the provision of services' (Peters and Pierre, 1998, p 231). In other words, governments should set the priorities and goals, but allow organisations to decide how to reach those goals. As in the US, proponents of privatisation assert that it will increase efficiency, increase customer satisfaction, and decrease the size of inefficient bureaucratic government. Although Western European governments have not specifically proposed privatising their workfare programmes, they have based their programmes on the welfare-to-work programmes in the US, which are increasingly privatised. Also, the shift to privatising other services may mark a trend in this direction. However, before privatising services, Western European governments should consider the effects they will have on recipients. Based on the US experience, it does not seem that privatising services will lead to an increased ability to help the socially excluded re-enter society.

As Barbier asserts in this volume, workfare programmes are only one component of active labour market policies. Workfare programmes were designed for the socially excluded. Although this is a relatively small population, it is very diverse and includes the long-term unemployed, unemployed youth, lone parents and immigrants. The similarity in the assumptions underlying workfare programmes throughout Western Europe is striking. The initial evaluations of these programmes are also consistent – the excluded remain excluded, especially the hardest to employ.

References

Behrendt, C. (2000) 'Do means-tested benefits alleviate poverty? Evidence on Germany, Sweden, and the United Kingdom from the Luxembourg Income Study', *Journal of European Social Policy*, vol 10, pp 30-6.

Bell, W. (1965) *Aid to dependent children*, New York, NY: Columbia University Press.

Brauner, S. and Loprest, P. (1999) *Where are they now? What states' studies of people who left welfare tell us*, Urban Institute, available at www.urban.org/url.cfm?ID=309065

Brito, T. (2000) 'The welfarisiation of family law', *Kansas Law Review*, vol 48, no 2, pp 229-83.

Brock, T., Kwakye, I., Plyne, J., Richburg-Hays, L., Seith, D., Stepick, A. and Spetick, C. (2004) *Welfare reform in Miami: Implementation, effects, and experiences of poor families and neighborhoods*, MDRC, available at www.mdrc.org/publications/387/overview.html

Brodkin, E. (1995) 'The state side of the "welfare contract": discretion and accountability on policy delivery' , Working Paper 6, Chicago: University of Chicage, School of Social Service Administration.

Brodkin, E., Fuqua, C. and Thoren, K. (2002) *Contracting welfare reform: Uncertainties of capacity-building within disjointed federalism*, Joint Center for Poverty Research, (available at www.jcpr.org/wp/WPprofile.cfm?ID=338).

DeParle, J. (1997) 'Lessons learned: welfare reform's first months – a special report: success, frustration, as welfare rules change', *New York Times*, 30 December, p A16.

DeParle, J. (2004) *American dream: Three women, ten kids, and a nation's drive to end welfare*, New York, NY: Penguin Books.

Diller, M. (2000) 'The revolution in welfare administration: rules, discretion, and entrepreneurial government', *New York University Law Review*, vol 75, no 5, pp 1121-1220.

Donahue, J. (1989) *The privatization decision: Public ends, private means*, New York, NY: Basic Books.

Ellwood, D. (1988) *Poor support: Poverty in the American family*, New York, NY: Basic Books.

Esping-Andersen, G. (1990) *The three worlds of welfare capitalism*, Princeton, NJ: Princeton University Press.

European Council (2001) *Joint report on social exclusion*, Europa – the European Union online, (available at http://europa.eu.int/comm/employment_social/soc-prot/soc-incl/joint_rep_en.htm).

Fafo (2001) *Workfare in six European nations: findings and evaluation recommendations for future development*, Oslo : Fafo Institute for Applied Social Science– the Norwegian Ministry of Health and Social Affairs.

Gais, T., Nathan, R., Lurie, I. and Kaplan, T. (2001) 'The implementation of the Personal Responsibility Act of 1996: commonalities, variations, and the challenge of complexity', Paper presented at the conference 'The new world of welfare: shaping a post-TANF agenda for policy', Washington, DC, 1-2 February.

Garfinkel, I. and McLanahan, S. (1986) *Single mothers and their children: A new American dilemma*, Washington, DC: Urban Institute Press.

General Accounting Office (1997) *Poverty measurement: Issues in revising and updating the official definition*, GAO/HEHS-97-38, Washington, DC: General Accounting Office.

Gordon, L. (1988) *Heroes of their own lives: The politics and history of family violence, Boston 1880-1960*, New York, NY: Penguin.

Gormley, W. (1991) *Privatization and its alternatives*, Madison, WI: University of Wisconsin Press.

Graser, A. (2003) 'From the hammock to the trampoline: workfare policies in the US and their reception in Germany', *German Law Journal*, vol 4, no 3, pp 1-18.

Greenberg, M. (2004) 'Welfare reform, phase two: doing less with less', *American Prospect Online*, vol 15, no 9, (www.prospect.org/web/printfriendly-view.ww?id=8358).

Grogger, J., Karoly, L. and Klerman, A. (2002) *Consequences of welfare reform: A research synthesis*, RAND, (available at www.rand.org/child/bib/26.html).

Hamilton, G. (2002) *Moving people from welfare to work: Lessons from the national evaluation of welfare-to-work strategies*, MDRC, available at www.mdrc.org/publications/52/summary.html

Handler, J. (2004) *Social citizenship and workfare in the United States and Western Europe: The paradox of inclusion*, Cambridge: Cambridge University Press.

Handler, J. and Hasenfeld, Y. (1991) *The moral construction of poverty: Welfare reform in America*, Newbury Park, CA: Sage Publications.

Hasenfeld, Y. (1983) *Human service organizations*, Upper Saddle River, NJ: Prentice Hall.

Hasenfeld, Y., Ghose, T. and Hillesland-Larson, K. (2004) 'The logic of sanctioning welfare recipients: an empirical assessment', *Social Service Review*, vol 78, pp 304-19.

Haskins, R. and Blank, R. (2001) *The new world of welfare*, Washington, DC: Brookings Institution Press.

Healy, M. (2000) 'Welfare rolls fall to half of '96 numbers', *Los Angeles Times*, 23 August, p A12.

Huber, E. and Stevens, J. (2001) *Development and crisis of the welfare state: Parties and policies in global markets*, Chicago, IL: University of Chicago Press.

Kaplan, J. (1999) 'The use of sanctions under TANF', *Welfare Information Network Issue Notes*, vol 3, no 3, Welfare Information Network, available at www.financeproject.org/Publications/sanctionissuenote.htm

Katz, M. (2001) *The price of citizenship: Redefining the American welfare state*, New York, NY: Henry Holt and Company, LLC.

Kramer, R. (1994) 'Voluntary agencies and contract culture: dream or nightmare?', *Social Service Review*, vol 68, pp 33-60.

Lindhorst, T., Mancoske, R. and Kemp, A. (2000) 'Is welfare reform working? A study of the effects of sanctions on families receiving Temporary Assistance to Needy Families', *Journal of Sociology and Social Welfare*, vol 27, no 4, pp 185-201.

Lødemel, I. and Trickey, H. (2001) 'National objectives and local implementation of workfare in Norway', in I. Lødemel and H. Trickey (eds) *'An offer you can't refuse': Workfare in international perspective*, Bristol: The Policy Press, pp 1-39.

McFate, K. (1995) 'Introduction: western states in the new world order', in K. McFate, R. Lawson and W. Wilson (eds) *Poverty, inequality, and the future of social policy*, New York, NY: Russell Sage Foundation, pp 1-26.

Meyer, J. and Rowan, B. (1977) 'Institutional organizations: formal structure as myth and ceremony', *American Journal of Sociology*, vol 83, pp 273-88.

Michalopoulos, C. and Schwartz, C. (2000) *National evaluation of welfare-to-work strategies: What works best for whom: Impacts of 20 welfare-to-work programs by subgroup*, US Department of Health and Human Services, available at http://aspe.hhs.gov/hsp/NEWWS/synthesis-es00/

Pavetti, L. (1999) 'How much more can welfare mothers work?', *Focus*, vol 20, no 2, pp 16-19.

Pavetti, L. and Bloom, D. (2001) 'Sanctions and time limits: state policies, their implementation, and outcomes for families', Paper presented at the conference 'The new world of welfare: shaping a post-TANF agenda for policy', Washington, DC, 1-2 February.

Peters, B. and Pierre, J. (1998) 'Governance without government? Rethinking public administration', *Journal of Public Administration Research and Theory*, vol 8, no 2, pp 223-43.

Piven, F. and Cloward, R. (1977) *Poor people's movements: Why they succeed, how they fail*, New York, NY: Pantheon Books.

Rainford, W. (2004) 'Paternalistic regulation of women: exploring punitive sanctions in Temporary Assistance to Needy Families', *Affilia*, vol 19, no 3, pp 289-304.

Roche, M. (2000) *Comparative social inclusion policies and citizenship in Europe: Towards a new ESM, final report*, Political Economy Research Centre, (available at www.shef.ac.uk/escus/papers/papersreports/socialmodel.html).

Rosanvallon, P. (2000) *The new social question: Rethinking the welfare state*, Princeton, NJ: Princeton University Press.

Schorr, A. (1987) 'Welfare reform, once (or twice) again', *Tikkun*, vol 18, pp 15-18, 85-8.

Seefeldt, K. and Orzol, S. (2004) *Watching the clock tick: factors associated with TANF accumulation*, National Poverty Center Working Paper Series, (available at www.npc.umich.edu/publications/workingpaper04/paper9/).

Spies, H. and van Berkel, R. (2001) 'Workfare in the Netherlands – young unemployed people and the Jobseeker's Employment Act', in I. Lødomel and H. Trickey (eds) *'An offer you can't refuse': Workfare in international perspective*, Bristol: The Policy Press, pp 105-32.

Standing, G. (1992) 'The need for a new social consensus', in P. van Parijs (ed) *Arguing for basic income: Ethical foundations for radical reform*, London: Verso, pp 47-60.

Strawn, J., Greenber, M. and Savner, S. (2001) *Improving employment outcomes under TANF*, Washington, DC: Brookings Institution Press.

Supiot, A. (2000) 'The dogmatic foundations of the market', *Industrial Law Review*, vol 29, pp 321-45.

Svensson, M. (1999) *Do staff rental agencies create a dual labour market in Sweden?*, Unpublished typescript.

Training and Employment Network (1999) 'Unemployment unit and youthaid', *Weekly Briefing*, 71.

Trickey, H. (2001) 'Comparing welfare programmes – features and implications', in I. Lødemel and H. Trickey (eds) *'An offer you can't refuse': Workfare in international perspective*, Bristol: The Policy Press, pp 249-94.

Wu, C., Cancian, M., Meyer, D. and Wallace, G. (2004) *How do welfare sanctions work?*, Discussion paper, Madison, WI: Institute for Research on Poverty, pp 1-35 (available at www.irp.wisc.edu/publications/dps/pdfs/dp128204.pdf).

FIVE

Has the European Social Model a distinctive activation touch?

Jean-Claude Barbier

Introduction

Is there any connection between what is fuzzily named 'activation' and what is equally fuzzily named the 'European Social Model – ESM'? At first sight the answer might be considered obvious: social policies at the European Union (EU) level are commonly framed in terms of 'activation', a term that has now become very commonplace in political texts. Yet, to address the question more seriously one needs, first, a robust notion of what the ESM is/could be – not only as a mobilising motto, but as an existing entity – and, second, a firm conceptualisation of 'activation' and of the forms it actually takes across various EU member states.

This chapter intends to show that the activation component in the existing ESM certainly offers no clear means of distinguishing it from other social 'models' in the world.

At the EU level, where most of the talk about the ESM is taking place, it is perhaps a paradox that existing coordinating processes (Open Methods of Coordination – OMCs) have so far had little substantive impact on this question. On the other hand, both 'activation policies' and the ESM are broad concepts able to accommodate not only many different patterns, but also changing ones. The inclusion of the new member states will certainly not make convergence easier.

The notion of an ESM, between normative and analytical

The notion of an ESM is one with which it is particularly difficult to come objectively to grips, because it is so much a part of the current political discourse and international policy debate. Even so, we will argue here that, provided certain precautions are taken, the concept may also be taken seriously as an analytical tool.

A highly normative notion, the 'mobilising ESM'

It has been shown that the notion is extensively polysemous and ambiguous. According to Jepsen and Serrano Pascual (this volume), the expression 'European Social Model' was first used during Jacques Delors' presidency of the European Commission. It is indeed quite fitting that the concept should have been promoted during an era when competition between the United States (US) and Europe unleashed debates among international and especially European elites. Accordingly, the first steps of the European Employment Strategy (EES) (1992-97), the adoption of the Lisbon Strategy (2000) and the subsequent introduction of various OMCs have also been set in a wider ESM perspective and, more often than not, situated in the context of competition with the 'US model'. Interviews with European Commission officials confirm the supposition that, when devising the EES, DG Employment (ex-DG V) was explicitly comparing key features of the ESM to the US model (Barbier, 2004a; Barbier and Sylla, 2002). As is often the case with notions promoted and disseminated in EU forums and arenas, the ESM also comprises, more or less explicitly, a set of assumptions as to how the European economy and the European 'social dimension' are interlinked and operate in relation to one another.

To some extent, the notion of an ESM bears similarities, in this respect, with the German concept of '*soziale Marktwirtschaft*', which has been, at one and the same time, an economic doctrine founded by German economists like A. Müller-Armack, *and* the political project of the Erhard government, *but also* a more extensive reference within and beyond Germany. The normative ESM – if its existence as a common model were to be established – would probably also bear more affinities with what is sometimes described as the 'Rhineland' model or, alternatively, the 'coordinated market economy' (Hall and Soskice, 2001). It should also be stressed that the draft Constitution of the EU contained only a reference to the 'social market economy', alongside the objective of achieving 'a high level of social protection' (Article I-3). No mention of the ESM has yet been incorporated into the draft treaty.

Looking for the existing ESM

In order to contrast a possible analytical concept of an ESM with other existing models, especially the US one, we suggest two steps: first, to adopt a very broad notion of 'system of social protection' (Barbier and Théret, 2004) and, second, to link it to a set of 'social performances'.

If the ESM comprised such a first component, then it would consist of an aggregation of the existing national systems in the 25 member states, plus an EU-level component. Within the broad notion tentatively used here, 'social protection' would include traditional sets of institutions and policies pertaining to the welfare systems, including the areas of health, pensions, education and training, and so forth. These systems would also include various sets of actors. Institutions would comprise labour law and employment rights, as well as the various norms governing employment relationships (including informal ones). National systems of industrial relations would, of course, figure in the overall 'system of social protection' as defined here, although they might, alternatively, be considered as a separate element.

As for the second component, a tentative definition should aim at capturing social phenomena ('performances') measured by indicators (for instance, poverty, income inequality, demographic patterns, employment, and so forth). In the comparative literature, 'models' (and countries) are commonly compared according to their institutions, actors, systems, or even 'societal coherence' and a standard research approach is the effort to establish causal relations between, on the one hand, institutions and systems and, on the other, 'outcomes'. The focus on performances does not, however, automatically imply establishing causal links, but simply seeks to describe the co-existence of certain institutions and systems and of existing social situations measured by cross-national indicators. Economists, undeniably, are better at such 'reductionist' exercises (Fitoussi and Passet, 2000; Freeman, 2000). With such a definition in hand, it would be possible to systematically compare the US model with the ESM. However, since such a systemic comparison remains to be made, the scope here will be limited to a single sector of the existing ESM and will refer only to the 15 'older' members, for which an abundant cross-national literature exists.[1]

Third, in no country can the social protection system be fully understood without capturing its structural links with the economy and, especially, with economic policies. In the case of the ESM, regarded as a mix of national systems and a quasi-federal layer of institutions and policies, this means that to understand the model the complex interaction of four types of policy must be taken into account (Barbier, 2004a, pp 36-42): (i) EU-level economic and monetary policies; (ii) national economic policies; (iii) EU-level social policies; and (iv) national social policies. Were such a model to be documented through empirical research along the lines described here, comparing an existing ESM with the US model would lead to an additional question: has the set of empirical relationships existing between the four types of policy any similarity with the US model? It becomes all the more important to explore this question when considering that much comparative literature on social policies in Europe has tended to contend that the very existence of the (normatively defined) ESM is jeopardised by the economic and monetary policies enforced at the EU level, often labelled 'neoliberal', albeit without precise definition of the distinguishing features of this identity.[2] It is also important to take such a factor into consideration because a key systemic feature of present societies has been – oversimplifying somewhat – the 'capacity' of macroeconomic policies to 'deliver' a situation of 'full employment'; indeed, the relative 'capacities' of the ESM and the US model in this regard seem to have remained very significantly different for the last 20 years.

Finally, some authors have surmised the existence of two conflicting ESMs, one promoted by 'economically oriented actors' and the other by 'socially oriented actors' (Guillén and Palier, 2004).

Convergence and Europeanisation

This reflection brings to the fore a two-pronged question that an analytical perspective to the ESM cannot elude, that is, whether national systems are currently Europeanised, and whether they are converging. Both questions are implicit in any comparison of the European and the US models.

First, to state that, when compared with the US, 15 or 25 EU member states display common features, in no way implies that they are currently converging, because convergence is different from the question of common features. This chapter will go on to document the possible empirical convergence in the area of 'activation', while showing that it is important to establish what sort of convergence is meant. As with research on the changes brought by the various OMCs (Barbier, 2004b), we will contrast the convergence documented in *procedural* changes, in broad common representations and ideas, with the convergence of the *substance* of social programmes and their eventual outcomes.

Second, 'Europeanisation' should also be documented empirically and the question 'Europeanisation of what?' ought to be raised (Radaelli, 2000a). Indeed, here, the cognitive dimension of Europeanisation is important. Additionally, Europeanisation as a process could be seen as one of many possible channels contributing to the emergence, consolidation, or – at the other extreme – degradation, or even dissolution, of an existing ESM. Again, in this respect, empirical data and analyses are certainly more abundant with regard to the 'old' member states than to the 'new' entrants where one is bound to rely on scenarios rather than draw insights from existing research, so that reflection tends to be somewhat more prospective and conjectural.

If the previous developments are considered, the task of identifying an existing (and the least normative possible) ESM is rather clearly defined. This chapter intends to show that, with regard to one specific area and aspect of social protection – namely the tendency towards its 'activation' observed in the last decades, and most particularly in the 1990s – an 'activating ESM' *sui generis*, one that would stand in clear contrast with the US activation model, has yet to come into being, should it ever do so, which, on the basis of past experience, could be seriously doubted.

When social protection is activated

Given that 'activation' is simultaneously a normative *and* an analytical concept, before addressing the question 'Does an 'activation ESM' exist?', the first step is to present what is considered an analytical definition of activation.

Activating systems

In the 1990s, following the reforms in Denmark and the New Deal strategy in the UK, 'activation' became an internationally fashionable policy label. The Organisation for Economic Co-operation and Development (OECD), for instance, was happy to popularise the Danish '*aktivering*' programmes. Overall, as shown elsewhere (Barbier, 2002a, 2004c, 2004d, 2004e), an activation rationale has increasingly informed not only labour market policies, but more broadly the reforms of the national social protection systems. Accordingly, the demand for activation has consistently figured very high on the EES agenda.

As an analytical concept, activation can indeed be constructed as the description of an actually observable *tendency* in the transformation of all national systems, one that has covered an extremely broad scope. Our contention, as such, is that it is inadequate to focus the analysis of 'active strategies' on labour market or assistance policies alone. Additionally, and all too frequently, activation is seen as linked to a process of 're-commodification', but this is not the only angle to be considered.

Activation is the introduction (or reinforcement) of an explicit linkage between, on the one hand, social protection and, on the other, labour market participation. Redesigning the social protection systems has led, in many national cases, to enhancing, in increasingly compulsory forms, the various social functions of 'paid work' and labour force participation. The areas of social protection that, in practice, lend themselves to activation certainly go beyond traditional active labour market policies or French-style '*insertion*' policies (Barbier and Théret, 2001). They comprise:

- benefit programmes – unemployment insurance and various 'assistance' schemes for working-age groups (including disability and some other family-related benefits);
- pension systems and, most particularly, early retirement programmes;
- employment and training (active labour market) programmes; education policies should also be included here; but also,
- policies that aim at reforming the 'tax and benefits systems', as the European Commission discourse would have it; such reforms may aim to strengthen the demand for labour or 'incentivise' job-taking and labour supply.

Overall, in the comparative literature covering activation as defined here, two types of programme stand out. In political documents these are generally termed 'welfare-to-work' programmes and 'making-work-pay' policies.

From *the individuals' point of view*, activation programmes are deemed to provide incentives or sanctions, but also, in some cases, a wide array of offers of services (for instance, counselling, job search, training); they may also – indirectly or directly – extend individuals' choices by increasing the supply of jobs on the conventional market (especially where wage subsidies are available to employers). On the other hand, from *a system perspective*, social protection is activated in the sense that the delivery of services and benefits mainly targets *working-age people* in some sort of work activities. It is also activated in the sense that funding mechanisms and the allocation of resources are designed in order to *foster and increase job creation* or, to put it differently, to be 'employment-friendly'. That reforms are introduced to enhance job creation is certainly not alien to the quality of citizenship if considering that equal access to jobs can be seen as one dimension of such citizenship.

Awareness of historical legacies leads to the realisation that activation is no new phenomenon: in the Scandinavian countries, as well as in Austria or Germany for instance, an important dimension of social policy has long been devoted to vocational training, an active policy tool par excellence (Barbier and Ludwig-Mayerhofer, 2004; Jensen and Halvorsen, 2004; Ludwig-Mayerhofer and Wroblewsky, 2004). Moreover, the policy goal of *full employment* was always historically deeply integrated into the social protection rationale in the Nordic countries (especially Norway and Sweden), where it was also linked to a very strong commitment to work. 'Activation of social protection' should also be analytically distinguished from the efforts implemented in many countries – mostly in the continental cluster of welfare regimes – to make labour markets more flexible by introducing de-regulation measures and new forms of employment relationship, differing from the 'standard' one. Here the Italian example is a case in point: the extensive measures introduced to increase labour market flexibility created, among other things, a category of 'employees' – namely the *parasubordinati* – who suffer from broken and patchy occupational careers and have access to only second-rate social and employment protection entitlements (Barbier and Fargion, 2004). Such flexibilisation strategies provided no new link with existing social protection, but simply altered, indirectly, the mainstream terms of employment.

Activation and economic policies

As briefly mentioned earlier, in the presentation of the ESM concept, any analysis that from the outset omits to consider the essential relationship between social protection system and economic policies will be inherently unsound. This obviously applies to the study of activation as seen in this chapter.

What was shown by Hall's influential paper (1993, p 284) was that 'monetarism' replaced 'Keynesianism' as a fundamental 'conception of how the economy itself worked'. Similarly, and quite convincingly, Jobert (1994, pp 16-23) has argued that 'pragmatic neoliberalism' (*le néo-libéralisme gestionnaire*), which he opposed to 'doctrinal neoliberalism' (*le néo-libéralisme doctrinaire*), had become the mainstream ideational reference of European elites. It is in no way audacious to assume that this common cognitive and normative framework is very consensually shared in the Brussels arenas, by the 'social' actors as well as the 'economic' actors, and it has been documented that the general substantive content of the EES was consistent with mainstream economic views (Barbier, 2002a).

Yet, this supplies no more than a very general outline because (a) the cognitive and normative framework does not magically translate into actual policies (social and economic) and (b) within the cognitive boundaries of the EES discourse, at the EU level, actors fight against each other, Directorate-General against Directorate-General, member state against member state, and actors against other actors in the same country. Consequently, in matters of activation as in other areas, one is to find that substantively different national arrangements are certainly compatible with a common Europeanised discourse and cognitive framework.

The case of Sweden (Barbier, 2004a, pp 51-82) is very interesting in this respect: it shows that shared reference to the same EES discourse is certainly not incompatible with an extreme variety of domestic economic and social policies, which can be globally correlated to very different social outcomes, in terms of redistribution, wellbeing and inequality, even in a context where monetary norms are prominent in the global international economy (Barbier and Nadel, 2000) and where Sweden has steadily implemented orthodox economic policies. But this will be explored more precisely and empirically when detailing the 'actual' activation strategies existing across the EU.[3]

Looking for an activation ESM as compared with the US model

Two ideal types and no substantive convergence

Drawing mainly upon the analysis of assistance/labour market policies, it has been shown that activation strategies across Europe could be captured and stylised in accordance with two 'ideal types'. We believe, however, that these types can also apply to other areas of social protection that lend themselves to activation. Despite some exceptions (Gilbert, 2002; Handler, 2003; to a certain extent Lødemel and Trickey, 2000), the literature devoted to activation has generally admitted that the contrasting strategies result not in any substantive but only in an essentially 'procedural' type of convergence (Barbier and Ludwig-Mayerhofer, 2004; Goul Andersen et al, 2002; Jørgensen, 2002; Morel, 2000; Schmid and Gazier, 2002; Serrano Pascual, 2004; Torfing, 1999; van Berkel and Møller, 2002; Wood, 2001). *So far*, convergence has indeed been documented mainly in *processes* and *procedures* and not in the actual substance or in substantive outcomes of the policies implemented. Historically, both ideal types emerged in Beveridgean systems: the universal, 'generous' Scandinavian version, as well as the liberal or residual, 'poor' 'safety net' British version.

The *liberal type* chiefly stresses relationships with the labour market. Active labour market policies, as well as social policies, thus take on a limited role, restricted to inciting individuals to seek work, providing quick information and matching services, as well as investing in short-term vocational training. Individuals are also the target of 'tax credits' or 'in-work' benefits to 'make work pay'. Additionally, activation includes measures inciting people to be as active as possible across their lifecourse, including pension reforms that dispense with any fixed age for retirement. Having a job on the market becomes the standard way of accessing protection (private and social) from risks, and work systematically tends to replace socialised support. Here, activation entails both the re-commodification of the system (already highly commodified in comparative terms) and efforts to reduce social expenditure. Activation reforms are implemented in the areas of disability, early retirement, pensions, and all sorts of 'assistance' programmes. Characterisation of the liberal type of activation was sometimes restricted to the notion of workfare: however, this author has shown that this was a misnomer, not only because workfare has remained embedded in the particular US tradition, but more importantly because the term applies to only a small area of social protection (activating benefit recipients) (see later).

On the other hand, the *universalistic type* not only caters for the provision of complex and extended services to *all citizens*, but simultaneously guarantees relatively high standards of living for those on assistance benefits, and, for the lower-paid sections of the labour force, benefit levels amounting to a generous proportion of minimum wages. Hence the role of the market is not unilaterally prevalent. Activation applies to all citizens in a relatively egalitarian manner and the 'negotiation' between the individual's and society's demands appears much more balanced than in the other ideal type. A fully active society seems to be able to yield employment opportunities tailored to a variety of needs and capabilities. Activation applies to an already highly active population employed in a context of relatively good-quality jobs. It also entails cost containment and reforms of income compensation mechanisms, but the use of tax credits and subsidies plays a limited role, if any.

Certainly, the nature of the relationship of activation to full employment represents an important difference between the two ideal types. The universalistic type is more structurally linked to high labour market participation. Moreover, since the early 1990s, in the universalistic type, new forms of activation have seen the state taking on the role of an 'employer of last resort', when the market failed to deliver jobs. This has not been the case in the liberal ideal type, where the quality of the numerous jobs created is not comparable to that prevailing during the full employment of the 1960s.

No third fully-fledged ideal type yet

We have discussed the possibility of a third ideal type of activation. True, identifying three types of activation would nicely fit the now traditional tripartite classification of welfare regimes. However, a third type is not a feature of the European countries. France has shown mixed elements, exhibiting features associated with both liberal and universalistic types, as a result, to some extent at least, of its hybrid legacy of Beveridgism and Bismarckism (Barbier and Théret, 2003, 2004). Italy, on the other hand, seems to oscillate between the two types. Some of the measures recently implemented in Germany show that it has much in common with France. However, so far, as already mentioned, no clear third ideal type has emerged that would capture common features of the 'continental' family of countries. Consequently, two clear models for far-reaching activation strategies can be identified, which are consistent with two classical welfare regimes. How do these compare with the US model? The universalistic ideal type is clearly different from it. Further analysis is necessary, however, when it comes to the liberal model.

The US and the UK display similarities and key differences

The UK is obviously the European country that comes closest to the 'liberal' ideal type. However, the recent turn to activation in the US and the UK certainly reveals many empirical differences between the two countries, both of which now rely extensively on the implementation of tax credits and welfare-to-work programmes. The UK has learned from the US on this subject, as shown by Deacon (1999), and talk of the 'Wisconsinization' of the British welfare state has been heard. The two key elements of the activation strategy documented in the US, that is, the coupling of the federal Earned Income Tax Credit[4] (EITC) and the Clintonian welfare reform implemented from 1996, are echoed by key elements of the New Labour activation strategy launched in 1997. However, the two cases are different because of the existence in the UK of a large sector of assistance benefits, which has no counterpart in the US.

In the US, where a welfare state in the European tradition has never existed, *proper workfare* (historically, and more recently, 'welfare-to-work') strategies have constituted a US brand of activation for a rather long time, even before the term activation came into use (Rodgers, 1981). Yet these strategies actually play a marginal role within the US social protection system.[5] They have mainly targeted Aid to Families with Dependent Children (AFDC) recipients (subsequently Temporary Aid for Needy Families, TANF), most of whom are young lone mothers.

Figures indicate that, after the 1996 Clinton welfare reform, there was a dramatic decline in the number of people receiving benefits (and Food Stamps). From a peak of 5.5 million families in 1994, the AFDC/TANF caseload had dropped to 2.1 million families by March 2001 (about 2.1% of the population) (Greenberg et al, 2001, p 1) and remained roughly stable into 2002 (Office of Family Assistance, 2003). Whatever the debated explanations for that decline,[6] in the meantime, EITC, notwithstanding its tax nature, has emerged as a major *de facto social policy programme*. Its recipients (also a majority of families with children) now constitute about one in six of US households (21 million families and individuals, as of 2002), accounting for an expenditure of roughly 30 billion US$, while TANF payments amount to about 25 billion US$ (Office of Family Assistance, 2003).[7]

Leaving aside the question of how so-called 'underclass' single mothers 'living on welfare' have entered the labour market as a consequence of TANF, it should be stressed that AFDC has also represented, as convincingly documented by Morel (2000), the particularly US brand of family policy. Significantly, present TANF evaluation reports to the Congress analyse indicators concerning the evolution of teenage birth rates, out-of-wedlock births and marital behaviour, as outcomes attributable to welfare reform (Office of Family Assistance, 2000).[8] Comparing TANF (ex-AFDC) and EITC, in terms of numbers of participants (also more recently in financial terms), clearly indicates that EITC has been the main US 'in-work' programme to alleviate poverty, whereas workfare has targeted a considerably smaller number of people. On top of this, when not directed to ordinary jobs, workfare participants remain assisted (versus accessing employee status), whereas the bulk of the poor are working EITC recipients (the working poor).

In that context and notwithstanding its important symbolic and rhetorical function, workfare emerges as *marginal* to the US system. Most 'ordinary' poor and the unemployed, who enjoy limited access to unemployment compensation, have to look for jobs on the market (including 'bad' jobs). Ordinary labour market jobs and tax credits play the prominent role, in the context of government policies that foster full employment through traditional monetary and fiscal policies. Income and wealth inequalities are also a very well-documented feature of the US and the latest statistics indicate that the number and percentage of Americans living below the poverty line increased for the third consecutive year in 2003 (CBPP, 2004, p 1).[9]

Although its ideological inspiration is today very American (Deacon, 1999), the *UK reform* is very dissimilar. True, the UK and US labour market policy approaches have been close to each other for a long time (King, 1995), but common ideological inspiration does not translate automatically into similar policies and social protection system rationales. UK Conservatives resisted the introduction of proper workfare schemes for a long time. Not until 1996, just before Labour came to power, did John Major's government launch his short-lived 'project work' for the long-term unemployed in 10 pilot areas (Finn, 1998). Why the 'Thatcherites' doggedly opposed such schemes is no mystery: they were acutely wary of the danger that the state, at the end of the day, would emerge as an 'employer of last resort'.

The UK approach to activation has to be considered in the wider context of a genuinely existing and wide-ranging UK welfare state, the main elements of which include (a) a universal health care system – the National Health Service – combined with (b) a universal safety net. Income Support is the key benefit for the assisted people. It somehow constitutes the standard reference, the universal welfare basis for the *out-of-work* poor. Separate unemployment insurance benefits were de facto merged with traditional assistance benefits. Moreover, under different benefit names, a dramatically expanding number of disabled people – that is, Sickness/Disability Benefit recipients – have been catered for. The disabled caseload has now come to represent one of the main social protection items on Labour's agenda, along with state pensioners, who earn similar levels of benefit on a universal flat-rate basis.

Key benefits mainly include Job Seeker's Allowance (JSA), three benefits for disabled people, and Income Support. These are all benefits for people of working age. Family Credit (FC), later transformed into Working Families' Tax Credit (WFTC) and then into Working Tax Credit (WTC),[10] should be added to this group of benefits. The overall number of claimants of all benefits and credits fell from about 6.5 million people in February 1997 to 6.14 million in February 2000 but then increased to 6.18 million in August 2001 (DWP, 2002).

Because of the changes to the programmes, the group on 'key benefits' and group on 'tax credits' should now be considered separately. The key benefits group amounted to 5.85 million in February 1997 and was 4.95 million in February 2004 (DWP, 2004, p 22). The FC and then WFTC were served to around 800,000 recipients in November 1997 and to 1.48 million in February 2003. Hence the global population eligible for either key benefits or in-work benefits appears stable, due to an increase in tax benefits and a decrease in key benefits. About 14% of the working-age population is presently eligible to one of the key benefits, a very considerable figure if compared with the small proportion of the US population on TANF. This is one of the *key differences* between the UK and the US.

Over the most recent period, the proportion and numbers of assistance benefit claimants who are considered disabled have increased tremendously. Sick and disabled people now account for roughly 60% of the working-age population on key benefits. Contrary to unemployed people claiming JSA, the number of people on any of the sickness and disability benefits continued to grow from February 1997 to February 2004 (from 2.80 to 3.08 million) (DWP, 2004, p 29), while the number of unemployed claimants decreased by nearly 900,000 over the same period. This obviously constitutes an important challenge on the agenda of the third term of Tony Blair's Labour government.

The Economist (1999) acknowledged that 'employment and activity rates for men of all ages are several percentage points lower than they were at the start of this decade [the 1990s]'. The British activation problem is thus of a thoroughly different nature from that of the US, with its full employment achievement. Like France, Germany and Italy, whatever their huge prima facie differences in terms of unemployment rates, the UK also experiences some form of underemployment. From October 1999, the Labour administration has engaged in the transformation and extension of the existing tax credits. The new WFTC/WTC is bound to extend further and Child Credits have been reformed separately. Present developments from 1997 nevertheless show that the extension of tax credits inspired by the US approach has not resulted in a significant decrease of the large caseload of benefit recipients who are not 'activated'. *Before* the introduction of the new credits, substantial evidence also showed that there was a considerable gap between the politicians' rhetoric and the *actual* effects of welfare reforms on patterns of labour market participation and activity, at least with regard to lone parents (Bradshaw et al, 2000).

All in all, despite common moral and political inspirations, activation strategies in the UK and the US have retained significantly different features and circumstances. However, the UK, with regard to activation, stands out of the pack of EU countries (Wright et al, 2004), a fact that would make it difficult to identify any common '*existing* ESM' in matters of activation. Many elements – including the 2005 approach by the British presidency to the ESM – suggest that this contrast will not be bridged easily.

A marginal role for the OMCs in the area of activation?

Given this persisting diversity, might it be the case that the OMCs introduced at the EU level could rapidly favour convergence and 'Europeanisation'? OMCs indeed appear as one of the key channels for such influence, especially the EES and the OMC/inclusion (Barbier, 2004c).

Certainly OMCs should not be seen simply in the context of one-way effects from the European to the national level. There are various reasons for this:

(i)   Cross-influences should be considered.
(ii) Interacting with national policy systems, OMCs should be envisaged as embedded in much larger transformations of the social protection systems.
(iii) Effective transformations should be separated from potential ones and documented, some being more 'procedural' than 'substantive'.[11]

Research findings today seem to establish rather firmly that the new administrative and political activities sparked off by the OMCs have modified national systems, also creating new rules and institutions at the EU level; that a common discourse has been invented (here, activation certainly features prominently); and that previous systems of actors have been modified from various perspectives. While it may also occur at other levels, the dissemination of ideas has been documented only at that of the small elites who are direct actors in the EES and particularly in the Brussels arena (Barbier, 2004a). Concerning public management, empirical data point to substantive changes and, in some new member states, the construction of new institutional capacities is favoured (Guillén and Palier, 2004). Yet, as regards the actual substance and distinctive features (and outcomes) of policies and programmes in the social areas, the literature has, so far, produced no convincing elements. Even less have the more far-reaching consequences been documented.

Consequently, apart from the creation and transformation of activities and their formal institutionalisation, three main mechanisms seem to be at stake: the socialisation of actors (with learning processes and competition between conceptions); the creation and transformation of resources for actors in power games at the EU level and at national levels; and the introduction of new actors in policy processes.

Rather than effects or impacts of the EES, we prefer the term 'transformation', in the sense that observed transformations are less explicitly meant to be causally linked to a particular OMC. Table 5.1 lists the transformations documented so far in the activation tendency; of course, they form only a part of wider transformations (Barbier, 2004b). Separating transformations observable at national levels into the procedural and the substantive, we suggest ordering them hierarchically into three types.[12]

Whereas Type 1 transformations are limited to the discourse, the other two categories entail more significant change. Type 2 groups transformations of policy methods, administrative organisations and principles, as well as modifications in the systems of actors involved in national policy and their internal relationships and balance of powers. When it comes to Type 3, one is dealing with more radical modifications, implying the changing of rules, features of programmes, values and theories of action; a step further would involve the possibility of observing convergence in outcomes; further again, even more radical change could entail significant alterations of the overall systems such that they converge, eventually, towards a unified common 'European model'. Transformations of Type 1 concerning the discourse are particularly difficult to document (see Hassenteufel and Smith, 2002; Radaelli, 2000a). Their identification entails analysing discourses in an historical perspective. This implies dealing with the political language of small elites. The formal introduction of new terms, indicators (for instance, the employment rate), general conceptions (for instance, the ideas of activation and the notion that 'work should pay') may mean a superficial adaptation of the discourse, which might have few substantive consequences. Substantive change necessitates that a link be made to Type 3 transformations. A common discourse may be current without substantive policy changes (Barbier, 2002b; Barbier and Sylla, 2002).

For the purpose here, it is rather easy to identify Type 1 transformations (for instance, all elite actors now use the employment rate indicator; the notion of activation, not previously used in certain countries, has now been generalised in the EES discourse, including

Table 5.1: A typology of activation transformations (documented and potential) in the context of the EES

Transformations	Types
EU-level activities	Activation is introduced on the new agenda and activities
	The EES discourse features activation prominently after discussion between member states
National procedural	National agendas are altered to include activation
National substantive Type 1	The national discourse incorporates activation into its formulations, notwithstanding certain resistances
National substantive Type 2	New actors participating in the EES national process are consulted on activation strategies
	General principles of programmes formally include activation prescriptions
National substantive Type 3	Single programmes/policies are substantively altered (rules, values, theories of action) because of activation
	Programmes/policies converge in Europe due to favourable activation outcomes
	Systems are altered (rules, values, theories of action)
	Systems converge (outcomes)
	A common European Social Model of activation emerges

Source: © adapted from Barbier (2004b)

in new member states, and so forth). As for Type 2 transformations, it can be noted that the formal principle of activation is now present everywhere, although this change might originate in diverse (and previous) causes (Barbier, 2004c). It is also not hard to observe the transformations of systems of actors involved in national policy arenas (for instance, the social partner organisations are now consulted during the process of drafting the National Action Plans), although their influence in the eventual programmes and outcomes remains to be seen, especially in relation to the type of activation effectively promoted at the national level (de la Porte and Pochet 2002, 2003). However, Type 3 transformations do remain empirically undocumented: the existence of an 'activation ESM' indeed remains purely conjectural. Superficial face-value imitation cases may be very mendacious: they are bound to appear because programmes are described and discussed in English.

Further documentation of diversity is possible from a comparison of specific programmes, which, in the current EES guidelines, have been classified under the activation heading (Barbier, 2002b). Such comparison reinforces the observation according to which an existing ESM has not clearly emerged in the field under consideration. Indeed, what the analysis shows is that very different collective values and norms can coexist within a common EES value framework, within the broadly 'mobilising ESM'.

Conclusion

All in all, in the field of assistance benefits and labour market policies, the consequences of activation strategies for individuals' social rights are probably the most highly documented and discussed aspect. Nevertheless, these consequences should be considered more widely and must include the impact of the reforms upon access to *quality jobs* and to *full employment*. Although quality has been on the EU agenda for quite some time now, evaluation studies in this respect are still quite limited. The main body of literature about activation has concentrated on formal changes, very seldom exploring substantive ones. Partial evaluation data have been provided and compared (De Koning and Mosley, 2002; Martin, 1998; Pearson and Scarpetta, 2000). What is certain also is that, since the early 1990s, many empirical 'worlds of activation' have coexisted in Europe (Barbier and Ludwig-Mayerhofer, 2004) within the existing ESM. To a certain extent only, and with the notable exception of the UK, do these present clear common features when compared with the US.

What is, however, less well known and remains to be researched is the long-term impact of these reforms, including their actual influence on the substance of social citizenship across various countries. Addressing such questions certainly demands of researchers that they do not remain content with the mainstream instrumental economic studies that are supposed to evaluate policies and programmes, including the evaluation processes implemented at the EU level in the wake of the EES (Barbier, 2004b).

Notes

[1] However, this literature has paid only limited attention to the supranational EU level: this applies, for instance, to the classification of 'welfare regimes'.

[2] By contrast, Fitoussi and Saraceno (2004, p 2) define the 'neoliberal doctrine' as setting two main tasks for policy: reducing the distortionate presence of government and using the resources thus freed to increase competition by means of structural reforms.

[3] Here again the empirical data from the new member states unfortunately remain scarce: for a different instance, see Wright et al (2004), where the Slovenian case is analysed.

[4] Additionally, state income tax credits programmes should be considered.

[5] Which encompasses many different programmes, such as Medicaid, Supplemental Security Income, Food Stamps, EITC, and so forth (Morel, 2000).

[6] What is not easy to assess is the *net contribution* attributable to 'welfare reform'. Obviously the buoyant US economy has played an important role. Tentative evaluations have recently been published (Greenberg et al, 2001). One important finding of the review of previous comparable programmes is that they produced no substantial change in peoples' lives during the follow-up period. The programmes helped a substantial number of individuals to replace income from AFDC and Food Stamps with income from jobs, but had not, as of two years, lifted many families out of poverty (see Handler, this volume).

[7] Hence, TANF accounts for less than 2% of the federal budget and is of relatively marginal importance according to European social budget standards.

[8] The third TANF report to the Congress stressed, for instance, that teenage birth rates fell in all states, as did out-of-wedlock births also (Office of Family Assistance, 2000, p 4).

[9] Greenberg et al (2001, p 1) note that participation in welfare fell much more rapidly than child poverty.

[10] Note that from April 2003, a new Working Tax Credit (WTC) has combined the former WFTC and the former tax credits for disabled people. The latest official statistics available for WFTC are as of February 2003 (Inland Revenue, 2003).

[11] For a complementary distinction see Börzel and Risse (2000) who distinguish between convergence of rules and convergence of outcomes.

[12] The three categories can be also seen in the light of Hall's (1993) three different order changes.

References

Barbier, J.-C. (2002a) 'Peut-on parler d'«activation» de la protection sociale en Europe?', *Revue Française de Sociologie*, no 43-2, April-June, pp 307-32.

Barbier, J.-C. (2002b) 'Une Europe sociale normative et procédurale: le cas de la stratégie coordonnée pour l'emploi', *Sociétés Contemporaines*, no 47, pp 11-36.

Barbier, J.-C. (2004a) 'La stratégie européenne pour l'emploi: genèse, coordination communautaire et diversité nationale', avec la contribution de Ndongo S. Sylla, rapport de recherche pour la DARES (ministère du travail), CEE, Noisy le Grand, miméo.

Barbier, J.-C. (2004b) 'Research on Open Methods of Coordination and national social policies: what sociological theories and methods?', Paper presented to the Research Committee 19 international conference, Paris, 2-4 September.

Barbier, J.-C. (2004c) 'The European Employment Strategy: a channel for activating social protection?', in J. Zeitlin, P. Pochet, with L. Magnusson (eds) *The Open Method of Coordination in action: The European Employment and Social Inclusion Strategies*, Brussels: PIE-Peter Lang, pp 417-46.

Barbier, J.-C. (2004d) 'Systems of social protection in Europe: two contrasted paths to activation and maybe a third', in J. Lind, H. Knudsen, H. Jørgensen (eds) *Labour and employment regulation in Europe*, Brussels: PIE-Peter Lang, pp 233-54.

Barbier, J.-C. (2004e) 'Activation policies: a comparative perspective', in A. Serrano Pascual (ed) *Are activation policies converging in Europe? The European Employment Strategy for Young People*, Brussels: ETUI, pp 47-84.

Barbier, J.-C. and Fargion, V. (2004) 'Continental inconsistencies on the path to activation: consequences for social citizenship in Italy and France', *European Societies*, vol 6, no 4, pp 437-60.

Barbier, J.-C. and Ludwig-Mayerhofer, W. (eds) (2004) 'The many worlds of activation', *European Societies*, Special issue on activation policies, vol 6, no 4, pp 423-36.

Barbier, J.-C. and Nadel, H. (2000) *La flexibilité du travail et de l'emploi*, Paris: Domino, Flammarion [(2003) *La flessibilità del lavoro et dell'occupazione*, introduzione di L. Castelluci e E. Pugliese, Roma: Donzelli].

Barbier, J.-C. and Sylla, N. S. (2002) *Stratégie européenne de l'emploi: les représentations des acteurs en France*, Report for the Ministry of Employment, December, Noisy-le-Grand: Ministry of Employment.

Barbier, J.-C. and Théret, B. (2001) 'Welfare to work or work to welfare: the French case', in N. Gilbert and R. Van Voorhis (eds) *Activating the unemployed: A comparative appraisal of work-oriented policies*, Rutgers, NJ: Transaction Publishers, pp 135-83.

Barbier, J.-C. and Théret, B. (2003) 'The French social protection system: path dependencies and societal coherence', in N. Gilbert and R. Van Voorhis (eds) *Changing patterns of social protection*, Rutgers NJ: Transaction Publishers, pp 119-67.

Barbier, J.-C. and Théret, B. (2004) *Le nouveau système français de protection sociale*, Repères, Paris: La Découverte.

Börzel, T. and Risse, T. (2000) 'When Europe hits home: Europeanization and domestic change', European Integration online Papers (EIoP), vol 4, no 15 (http://eiop.or.at/eiop/texte/2000-015a.htm).

Bradshaw, J., Terum, L. I. and Skevik, A. (2000) 'Lone parenthood in the 1990s: new challenges, new responses?', Paper presented to the International Social Security Association research conference, Helsinki, September.

CBPP (Center on Budget and Policy Priorities) (2004) 'Census data show poverty increased, income stagnated and the number of uninsured rose to a record level in 2003', *News Release*, 27 August.

De Koning, J. and Mosley, H. (2002) 'How can active policies be made more effective?', in G. Schmid and B. Gazier (eds) *The dynamics of full employment*, Cheltenham: Edward Elgar, pp 365-92.

de la Porte, C. and Pochet, P. (eds) (2002) *Building Social Europe through the Open Method of Co-ordination*, Brussels: PLE-Peter Lang.

de la Porte C. and Pochet P. (2003) 'Participation in the Open Method of Coordination: the case of employment and social inclusion', in J. Zeitlin, P. Pochet, with L. Magnusson (eds) *The Open Method of Coordination in action: The European Employment and Social Inclusion Strategies*, Brussels: PIE-Peter Lang, pp 353-90.

Deacon, A. (1999) 'The influence of European and American ideas upon 'New Labour' thinking on welfare reform', Paper presented to the conference 'Global trajectories: ideas, transitional transfer and models of welfare reform', Florence, 25-26 March.

DWP (Department for Work and Pensions) (2002) *Client group analysis, quarterly bulletin on the population of working age on key benefits*, August, Newcastle: DWP.

DWP (2004) *Client group analysis, quarterly bulletin on the population of working age on key benefits*, May, Newcastle: DWP.

Economist, The (1999) 'Labour's crusade', 25 September, pp 49-50.

Finn D. (1998) *Welfare to work: Making it work locally*, Report for the OECD Local Economic and Employment Development Programme (LEED), October, Paris: OECD.

Fitoussi, J. P. and Passet, O. (2000) 'Réformes structurelles et politiques macro-économiques: les enseignements des modèles de pays', in *Réduction du chômage: Les réussites en Europe*, Report for the Economic Analysis Council, Paris: Documentation française, pp 11-96.

Fitoussi, J.P. and Saraceno, F. (2004) 'The Brussels–Frankfurt–Washington consensus', Working Paper No 2004-02, February, Paris: Observatoire Français des Conjonctures Economiques.

Freeman, R.B. (2000) *Single peaked versus diversified capitalism: The relation between economic institutions and outcomes*, NBER Working Paper 7556, February.

Gilbert, N. (2002) *Transformation of the welfare state, the surrender of public responsibility*, Oxford: Oxford University Press.

Goul Andersen, J., Clasen, J., van Oorschot, W. and Halvorsen, K. (2002) *Europe's new state of welfare*, Bristol: The Policy Press.

Greenberg, M., Levin-Epstein, J., Hutson, R., Ooms, T., Schumacher, R. and Turets, V. (2001) *Welfare reauthorization: An early guide to the issues*, Publication No 01-20, Washington, DC: CLASP.

Guillén, A. and Palier, B. (2004) 'EU enlargement, Europeanization and social policy', *Journal of European Social Policy*, vol 14, no 3, August, pp 203-9.

Hall, P. A. (1993) 'Policy paradigms, social learning, and the state: the case of economic policymaking in Britain', *Comparative Politics*, vol 25, no 3, April, pp 274-96.

Hall, P. A. and Soskice, D. (2001) *Varieties of capitalism: The institutional foundations of comparative advantage*, Oxford: Oxford University Press.

Handler, J. (2003) 'Social citizenship and workfare in the US and Western Europe: from status to contract', *Journal of European Social Policy*, vol 13, pp 229-43.

Hassenteufel, P. and Smith, A. (2002) 'Essouflement ou second souffle? L'analyse des politiques publiques à la française', *Revue Française de Science Politique*, vol 52, no 1, pp 53-74.

Inland Revenue (2003) 'Working Families Tax Credit statistics', London: Office for National Statistics.

Jensen, P. and Halvorsen, R. (2004) 'Activation in Scandinavian welfare policy', *European Societies*, vol 6, no 4, pp 461-84.

Jobert, B. (ed) (1994) *Le tournant néo-libéral en Europe*, Paris: L'Harmattan,

Jørgensen H. (2002) *Consensus, cooperation and conflict: The policy making process in Denmark*, Cheltenham: Edward Elgar.

King D. (1995) *Actively seeking work: The politics of unemployment and welfare policy in the United States and Great Britain*, Chicago, IL: University of Chicago Press.

Lødemel, I. and Trickey, H. (2000) '*An offer you can't refuse': Workfare in international perspective*, Bristol: The Policy Press.

Ludwig-Mayerhofer, W. and Wroblewsky, A. (2004) 'Eppur si muove?', *European Societies*, vol 6, no 4, pp 485-510.

Martin, J. P. (1998) *What works among active labour market policies: evidence from OECD countries' experiences*, Labour Market and Social Policy Occasional Papers, No 35, Paris: OECD.

Morel, S. (2000) *Les logiques de la réciprocité, les transformations de la relation d'assistance aux Etats Unis et en France*, Paris: PUF.

Office of Family Assistance (2000) *Third annual report to Congress*, DHSS, August, internet version (www.acf.hhs.gov).

Office of Family Assistance (2003) *Temporary Assistance for Needy Families (TANF): Fifth annual report to Congress* (available at www.acf.hhs.gov/programs/ofa/annualreport5/index.htm).

Pearson, M. and Scarpetta, S. (2000) 'An overview: what do we know about policies to make work pay?', *OECD Studies*, no 31, pp 11-24.

Radaelli, C. M. (2000a) *Whither Europeanization? Concept stretching and substantive change*, European integration online Papers (EioP), vol 4, no 8, (http://eiop.or.at/eiop/texte/2000-08a.htm).

Radaelli, C. M. (2000b) 'Logiques de pouvoir et récits dans les politiques publiques de l'Union européenne', *Revue Française de Science Politique*, vol 50, no 2, pp 255-76.

Rodgers, C. S. (1981) 'Work tests for welfare recipients: the gap between the goal and the reality', *Journal of Policy Analysis and Management*, vol 1, no 1, pp 5-17.

Schmid, G. and Gazier, B. (eds) (2002) *The dynamics of full employment*, Cheltenham: Edward Elgar.

Serrano Pascual, A. (2004) 'Conclusion: towards convergence of European activation policies?', in A. Serrano Pascual (ed) *Are activation policies converging in Europe? The European Employment Strategy for Young People*, Brussels: ETUI, pp 497-518.

Torfing, J. (1999) 'Workfare with welfare: recent reforms of the Danish welfare state', *Journal of European Social Policy*, vol 9, no 1, pp 5-28.

van Berkel, R. and Møller, I. H. (2002) *Active social policies in the EU: Inclusion through participation?*, Bristol: The Policy Press.

Wood, S. (2001) 'Labour market regimes under threat? Source of continuity in Germany, Britain and Sweden', in P. Pierson (ed) *The new politics of the welfare state*, Oxford: OUP, pp 368-409.

Wright, S., Kopac, A. and Slater, G. (2004) 'Continuities within paradigmatic change', *European Societies*, vol 6, no 4, pp 511-34.

SIX

The European Social Model and gender equality[1]

Lilja Mósesdóttir

At the Lisbon Council in 2000, the European Union (EU) committed itself to the 10-year strategic goal of becoming the most competitive and dynamic knowledge-based economy in the world, capable of sustainable economic growth with more and better jobs and social cohesion, including gender equality. There are, however, clear indications that the transition towards the knowledge-based economy increases the risk of social exclusion, as more people now face difficulties in attaining and remaining in secure and well-paid jobs. Moreover, progress towards gender equality has been slow, and gender gaps remain substantial across the EU. The EU has urged the member states to tackle these risks and gaps by modernising the European Social Model (ESM). The EU's main modes of intervention in the member states to tackle gender gaps are directives and, increasingly, the European Employment Strategy (EES). However, several social models exist in the member states and these have facilitated differing balances of employment, job quality and social equality. The reference to a single social model, or to the ESM, when many models are actually present within the community, signals a growing interest on the part of the EU to pressure the member states into convergence not only in the economic but also in the social sphere. However, the EU has limited power to intervene in the social sphere at the member state level, so that the outcomes of its efforts to achieve, for example, gender equality are path-dependent or influenced by national actors and different welfare state models.

This chapter will analyse how the EU has sought to create a regulation paradigm or an ESM in order to pressure the member states to tackle gender (in)equalities more effectively. This regulation paradigm involves, on the one hand, hard measures, such as legally binding directives, and, on the other hand, soft measures or guidelines and recommendations, such as the EES. The aim of this chapter is to identify the potentials and limitations of the EU's regulation mechanism or the ESM in achieving the goal of gender equality. Moreover, it will examine the extent to which this regulation paradigm in the EU15 member states is transforming gender relations.

The EU's regulation paradigm

This section will discuss the EU's regulation paradigm or legal interventions and policy interventions to achieve gender equality in the member states. The goal is to highlight the main features of the regulation paradigm and its development over time.

Legal interventions

Since the 1957 Treaty of Rome, the emphasis of the EU's directives in the field of equal opportunities has slowly shifted away from extending employment rights in order to prevent direct discrimination based on gender towards ensuring rights to reconciliation of work and family life. From the mid-1970s onwards, various directives securing equal treatment of women and men in employment and employment-related matters were implemented. These include directives on: equal pay for the same work or work of equal value (1975); equal treatment for men and women in relation to access to employment, vocational training, promotion and working conditions (1976); equal treatment for men and women in statutory social security (1978), and occupational social security schemes (1986); equal treatment for those who are self-employed (1986); and shifting the burden of proof of discrimination away from the complainant (1997). Directives that go beyond direct discrimination were increasingly implemented from the 1990s. These are directives on: the protection of pregnant workers and those who have recently given birth (1992); working time that establishes limits to hours of work (1993); a parental leave of at least three months for both men and women workers (1996); and a series of directives tackling issues of non-standard workers such as part-timers and those on fixed-term contracts (Hantrais, 1995; Verloo, 2001; Walby, 2004, pp 17-18).

The aim of the equal treatment approach is to ensure that women have the same formal rights as men and thereby enjoy opportunities equal to those of men in the labour market. It is then up to individuals (women) to use their formal rights (Verloo, 2001). A common feature of directives implemented during the 1990s is that they give rights to workers, in most cases women, who need to take temporary leave from work (parental leave) or who work non-standard hours due to family obligations. These directives are, as argued by Walby (2004, p 19), more transformative than those designed to ensure equal treatment since they ensure that women, and increasingly men, are given the opportunity to combine work and family life instead of having to choose in favour of either one or the other.

The EU's policy intervention

The main policy intervention of the ESM has become the EES, which was introduced in 1997 to stimulate activation in Europe. Serrano Pascual (2003) claims that the EES is a discursive mechanism designed to create common understandings and evaluation methods across the EU. Accordingly, the EU creates common understandings, through the EES, of the gender problems that need to be solved. These common understandings call in turn for common solutions or methods as the EU's objective is to achieve gender equality.

According to the 1997 Amsterdam Treaty, the role of the EES was not to achieve harmonisation of policies in the manner applicable to monetary policy but to facilitate convergence of employment objectives through the Open Method of Coordination (OMC) or what has been termed the Luxembourg process. The OMC involves establishing common guidelines for policy (Employment Guidelines), regular reporting by the member states on implementation (National Action Plans), peer group review and assessment, leading to specific recommendations and, finally, to the refining of the common guidelines (see Behning et al, 2001, pp 9-10; Caprile et al, 2002, p 4). The annual employment guidelines set common priorities for member states' employment policies and, until 2003, equal opportunities occupied a central position in the guidelines as one of the four pillars: (1) improving employability; (2) developing entrepreneurship and job creation; (3) encouraging adaptability of businesses and their employees; (4) strengthening equal opportunities for women and men.

When highlighting common gender problems, EU officials compare the situation prevailing in EU15 with that of the United States (US) where the employment rate of women has been, on average, higher (see, for example, recent issues of *Employment in Europe*). For the sake of unity among the member states, EU officials do not openly acknowledge that some member states actually outperform or are more competitive than the US when it comes to reducing gender gaps in employment (for example, the Nordic countries). The emphasis is, thus, on common gaps rather than on differences or different performances across the member countries (Mósesdóttir and

Thorbergsdóttir, 2004). In the annual employment guidelines (1998-2002), the member states were encouraged to implement measures to reduce gender gaps in employment, unemployment and pay, as well as gender segregation. In addition, member states were expected to implement measures to enable reconciliation of work and family life (flexible work arrangements and good-quality child care) as well as to facilitate the return to work.

The political agenda of the EES changed in 2003 from an emphasis on equal opportunities, or the context in which men and women act, to gender equality, or outcomes of efforts to change the context. This shift in the gender agenda is in line with more result-oriented employment guidelines and slow progress in closing gender gaps. Moreover, gender issues have been moved from being one of four pillars of the EES to priority six of 10 main priorities for action. This change is likely to be interpreted by the member states as a downgrading of the gender agenda in the new EES, especially as no concrete examples are given of how to approach these main objectives from a gender perspective. As argued by Rubery (2003), the new overarching objectives of full employment, improving job quality and productivity, and promoting social inclusion, address the different realities facing women across the member states well. In Sweden, young women face lack of employment opportunities[2] when entering the labour market while female employment grew in some instances in Europe because women were more likely to accept lower-quality jobs and, in particular, part-time jobs. Low-quality jobs are strongly associated with transitions out of employment into inactivity for women (Rubery et al, 2001, p 114; OECD, 2003, p 40).

Over the years, the EU has made incremental changes to the EES, which have resulted in a steady expansion in the scope of the objectives, such as, for example, the shift from equal opportunities to gender equality signals. Moreover, the EU has increasingly applied quantitative targets to pressure the member states to attain the objectives of the EES. The female employment rate in the EU is, for example, to reach 60% by the year 2010 (Lisbon Council, 2000) and, also by 2010, the member states should provide child care for at least 90% of children between three years of age and the mandatory school age and at least 33% of children under three years of age (Barcelona Council, 2002). However, the EES does not acknowledge tensions and contradictions between different policy objectives.

One of the main priorities of the EES (2003) is to eliminate gender gaps in employment, unemployment and pay. However, evidence shows that the gender pay gap is smaller in countries with a low female employment rate, such as Italy. The gender gap in employment may also become smaller due to a growth in low-paid jobs (for instance, in Spain) and gender segregation is high in countries with high female employment rates (for example, the Nordic countries). Contradictions can also be found between objectives of the EU's policy intervention and legal intervention. The employment guidelines from 2004 (Council of the European Union, 2003, para 16) state that gender gaps in employment and pay should be reduced without 'calling into question the principle of wage differentiation according to productivity and labour market situation'. As pointed out by Rubery et al (2004, p 50), this paragraph is in conflict with equality law, which unequivocally establishes the right to equal pay for work of equal value irrespective of conditions prevailing in the labour market.

The EES has not only induced the member states to close gender gaps or make gender equality a political priority. The EU has used the EES to facilitate policy-learning processes in the member states, which involves adjustment of methods and techniques in response to past experience and new information about best practices in other member countries. Moreover, the EU has provided the member states with methodological tools to achieve the goal of gender equality or to tackle gender gaps in employment, unemployment and pay, as well as gender segregation. The common methodology promoted by the EU to solve gender problems is the OMC, involving policy coordination, targets, evaluations and non-binding recommendations. Moreover, the member states have since 1998 been encouraged to adopt the two-track strategy of gender mainstreaming and specific gender policy measures as part of the EES.

Gender mainstreaming involves the integration of the gender perspective into every stage of the policy processes (design, implementation, monitoring and evaluation) to promote equality between men and women, while special measures focus on improving the position of the undervalued and/or underrepresented sex, in most cases women. The solutions provided by the EU to solve gender problems (gender mainstreaming and special measures) within the framework of the EES have, so far, resulted in greater awareness of gender issues, more ambitious and integrated equal opportunity agendas and policies, setting up of institutions (women's departments), spreading of practices (gender mainstreaming) and statistical tools (indicators). Gender mainstreaming has, however, been applied differently in the member states. Some member states have used the approach as a rhetorical concept (Spain, for instance) while others have applied it as a systematic method to integrate the gender perspective into policies (Sweden).

The potentials and limitations of the EU's regulation paradigm

The EU's regulation paradigm has, in relation to the goal of gender equality, both possibilities and shortcomings, and these will be discussed with the focus on how directives and the EES have been implemented at the national level.

Directives

The EU's legislative intervention into the regulation of European labour markets has led to a curtailing of the opportunities to discriminate against women. Hence, women have increasingly found themselves enjoying the same rights as men insofar as they behave like men on the labour market. The focus of most directives has traditionally been narrow or confined to the rights of workers. However, it has broadened out in recent years as workers are no longer treated as autonomous individuals but as persons with family obligations, which they need to reconcile with their professional requirements. This broader scope of the EU's legislative intervention has the potential to transform prevailing gender relations in the member states, especially in those countries where the male-breadwinner model has been dominant.

The EU legislation involves harmonisation of employment and social law, guaranteeing a certain minimum standard, especially in countries that have not yet achieved this standard. In Greece, Spain and Portugal, EU legislation has led to a certain degree of convergence but, before joining the EU, these countries had no previous experience of equality law or equal opportunities policies (see Booth and Bennett, 2002, p 436). However, the EU's directives are implemented differently across the member states as it depends on the political will and institutional capacity to execute them. The directive on a parental leave of at least three months for both men and women workers (1996) has, for example, been implemented with very different levels of payment in the member states. In some countries, parental leave is unpaid (Greece, Spain and the UK), while in others a fixed flat-rate allowance is payable (Austria, Belgium and Germany) and in the Nordic member states the payments are wage-related. The level of payment influences, first and foremost, men's take-up rate of parental level and the lower the payment the less likely are men to engage in the care of infants (see

Plantenga and Rembery, 2005). Hence, the transformative impact of the parental leave directive on gender relations will be curtailed by a low replacement rate of leave payments.

The EES

The EES signals a shift in the EU's regulation paradigm as it is a soft-law approach that acknowledges national diversity as opposed to harmonisation. The EES is not only an interesting experiment with governance, involving an OMC instead of ruling by directives, but also an important means to move equal opportunities to the centre of policy-making within the EU. The EU's objective to achieve gender equality through gender mainstreaming of policies at all policy levels has facilitated greater awareness of gender issues and a commitment to gender equality in some member states.

The main advantage of the gender mainstreaming strategy is that it pressures the EU and the member states to take a holistic view of gender (in)equalities involving different actors, institutional levels and measures. However, the OMC and gender mainstreaming strategies are a soft-law approach without any sanctions to punish those countries that do not comply with the European guidelines or respond to non-binding recommendations made by the EU. In addition, the encompassing concept of gender mainstreaming is vague and open to different interpretations. Hence, the methodology to solve gender problems relies on the political will of actors in power who may understand the concept differently, have insufficient resources to pursue it and be unwilling to apply it (see Behning and Serrano Pascual, 2001; Mósesdóttir, 2003; Rubery, 2003). A successful implementation of the gender mainstreaming strategy requires cooperation between the social partners, bureaucrats and experts on gender equality across various policy areas. Few member states have, so far, been able to achieve this cooperation, as it often requires cutting across traditional partnerships and ignoring strict segmentation of policy areas.

In addition, gender equality initiatives appear to be more dependent on the political parties in power than on employment regulation around which a tripartite partnership has long been established. Experts point out, for example, that a change of government in countries such as Austria, Belgium, Denmark and Italy has led to problems in relation to progress towards greater gender equality. Changes in government and lack of interest in gender issues among actors engaged in the EES have meant that some countries appear to be going round in circles instead of moving forward when it comes to the implementation of measures to promote gender equality. The Conservative government in Austria claims, for example, that its new child care allowances enabling longer care leaves encourage female participation. However, evidence shows a sharp drop in employment rates of mothers following the implementation of this measure (see discussions in the national reports of the WELLKNOW project; Rubery et al, 2004).

Mósesdóttir and Erlingsdóttir (2005) found that the social partners and the women's movements play a limited role in the design and the implementation of gender equality policies in countries such as Austria, Denmark, Finland, the Netherlands and Spain, as well as Hungary and Iceland. The adoption of the term 'gender mainstreaming' has induced these national authorities to introduce a much more technical approach to gender equality than was earlier the case. Hence, a distance has been created between gender efforts on the one hand and social and political actors on the other. Moreover, external pressures on national authorities to achieve gender equality have been weakened and many argue that gender mainstreaming has in some cases taken care of gender problems.

Path-dependent solutions

The impact of efforts at the EU level (directives and the EES) to solve gender problems across the EU is not only dependent on political will but is also path-dependent or influenced by institutional diversity across the member states. At least four welfare state models exist within the EU and these vary in their capacity to integrate and realise directives and the objectives of the EES:

* the Nordic social democratic welfare states, where access to services and social projection is based on citizenship principles;
* Continental corporatist welfare states, where the family or voluntary organisations are responsible for social reproduction and the state provides 'last resort' services and the social insurance system reproduces labour market hierarchies (insider–outsider distinctions as well as statuses);
* Mediterranean welfare states, where pensions, health care and education are highly developed while other services are catching up with the average EU levels and where the family plays a prominent role in the provision of social services; and
* the liberal regime, where the public provisions are more targeted and private initiatives encouraged (Esping-Andersen, 1990; Mósesdóttir, 2001; Taylor-Gooby, 2004).

In the Continental and the Mediterranean welfare states (examples of which are Austria, Germany, Italy and Spain) the organisation of social services is based on the assumption that women provide care within the family. The institutional structures of these welfare states are either based on the unpaid care work of women (Italy and Spain) or cash-for-care provisions (Austria and Germany), which are low in relation to wages in the formal labour market. The Continental and the Mediterranean countries have, so far, had greater difficulties in adhering to the EU's objective of closing the gender gap in employment and in providing child care facilities than the Nordic countries that had already in 1997 ensured universal access to social services and high female employment rates. The approach of the EU to gender equality is, however, more market-oriented than has traditionally been the case in the Nordic member countries as it has, so far, abstained from intervening directly in the demand side of the labour market and from encouraging measures leading to higher public spending. The child care target is an exception and signals a growing awareness within the EU that economic, employment and social objectives (including gender equality) are difficult to achieve without more universal provision of social services. However, more extensive provision of social services outside the family will be difficult to integrate into the Continental and the Mediterranean welfare states without a dramatic change in their structures, while the Nordic countries have been able to integrate new needs, such as universal access to information and communication technologies and skills, into their welfare model without a major change in its organisation (see Roivas, 2004; Taylor-Gooby, 2004).

The various welfare state models existing in Europe do not affect only the ability of the EU member states to activate women but also their ability to meet the new risks associated with the knowledge-based economy. Men and women need, for example, to have access to the new technologies and to maintain adequate levels of skills and training through their life cycle if they are to obtain and remain in stable and well-paid jobs. As demonstrated by Caprile and Potrony (2004, p 97), the development towards the knowledge-based society (KBS) and a more inclusive society is closely related to the different welfare state models existing within the EU. The Nordic social democratic welfare states (Denmark, Finland and Sweden) in 2003 scored highest on a KBS index consisting of indicators on the access of households to the internet, digital literacy, labour productivity, revealed comparative advantage of high-tech and medium high-tech industries, tertiary educational attainment, youth upper-secondary educational attainment, employment rate (full-time equivalent) and poverty rate. The Mediterranean welfare states (Greece, Italy, Portugal and Spain) were at the other end of the scale or scored lowest on this index, while the Continental welfare states (including Austria, Germany and the Netherlands) and the liberal welfare states (Ireland and the UK) occupied an intermediate position. The main difference between the Continental and liberal welfare states was that the latter had higher levels of social exclusion.

Closing the gaps?

This section will consider whether the EU's policy paradigm or the gender problems and policy solutions to them correspond to common values in the member states and the development of gender gaps across the EU15 member states. EU regulation is designed to create common understandings across the member states. Unfortunately, one is able to identify whether EU regulation harmonises with common values only from when the EES was introduced in 1997 as the latest detailed survey on equal opportunities was conducted in 1996. The development of gender gaps reveals the extent to which the EU's objective of gender equality is becoming a reality across the EU15 member states.

Common values

The common problems identified in the employment guidelines since 1997 are gender gaps in employment, unemployment and in pay, as well as segregation. The EU's objective of tackling gender gaps as a part of the EES was in line with the view of most Europeans living in the member states when the strategy was introduced. According to the latest survey on equal opportunities in the EU (1996), most Europeans were of the opinion that women's employment would have a positive effect on the wellbeing of women and that women were disadvantaged in comparison with men with regard to unemployment, salary/wage, the number and variety of occupations open to them and the chances of promotion. It was, however, not until the year 2000 when child care targets were introduced that the EU responded to fears expressed by 50% of Europeans that women's employment would have a negative effect on the wellbeing of children. In 1996, this concern was widespread in countries such as Austria and Germany but it came as a surprise that the southern countries – Greece, Italy, Portugal and Spain – had the highest percentages of people who thought that women's employment tended to be positive for the wellbeing of the child (see European Commission, 1997, chapter II).

The main focus of the employment objectives and their implementation has been on changing women's behaviour or on activating women by enhancing opportunities to reconcile work and family life. Limited attention has been given to long working hours among men in some of the member states and the low share of men caring for children and dependants inside and outside the labour market. This unbalanced approach to gender equality does not benefit all men and, to a certain extent, contradicts common views in Europe. The failure to tackle men's behaviour means that problems such as high drop-out rates of men from secondary education are not adequately addressed in the EES. The EU has responded to the needs of the KBS by integrating targets on educational attainment[3] and lifelong learning[4] into the EES. Young men in the EU are, on average, less educated than young women and adult women are over-represented among lifelong learners. This advantage of women in terms of skill attainment and lifelong learning has, so far, facilitated an increase in women's employment but not led to a narrowing of the gender pay gap. An important explanation for this lack of progress has been the growth of low-paid jobs, which have been taken up by women in countries such as Greece, Portugal and Spain (see Caprile and Potrony, 2004; and section three in this chapter).

The lifelong learning and educational targets of the EU can be criticised for being both gender-blind and better suited to deal with skill gaps (insufficient skill levels) than skill mismatches (wrong skills). Women are more likely to select general skills as they enjoy less labour market protection than men (Estevez-Abe et al, 2001; Estevez-Abe, 2002). Motherhood and career interruption increase the likelihood of dismissal and receiving lower wages than men. It therefore takes more institutional support to encourage women, in comparison with men, to make specific skill investments that in turn increase dependence on a particular employer. The EU's lifelong learning strategy and the educational targets do not provide the necessary institutional support for women to acquire skills to enter male-dominated industries and occupations, which in most cases require either firm-specific or industry-specific skills. In the member states, measures designed to respond to skill shortages focus only on the need of women to enhance their information technology skills and not on the question of their access to male-dominated technology and occupations (see Roivas, 2004).

In the survey of equal opportunities from 1996, 40% of Europeans surveyed said that both men and women had to change their behaviour to eliminate gender inequality, while 39% said that men should change first and 9% that women should change their behaviour (European Commission, 1997, p 64). According to Mósesdóttir and Erlingsdóttir (2005), member states rely more on special action/measures based on the perspectives of equal treatment and the women's perspective (difference) than on gender mainstreaming. The women's perspective is especially apparent in measures that are implemented to promote the reconciliation of work and family life, as most of them focus on enabling women to combine work and care responsibilities. This emphasis on equal treatment and the women's perspective indicates that the gender mainstreaming strategy is still at the stage of discourse. Hence, the transformative potential of the strategy still needs to be utilised when it comes to the EES.

Gender gaps

The integration of the gender mainstreaming strategy into the EES has led to a strong labour market orientation of the gender problems identified across the EU and of the measures implemented to solve them. One of the main priorities of the EES has been to achieve an overall employment rate of 70% and an employment rate of 60% for women in the EU by the year 2010. In 2003, only Denmark, the Netherlands, Sweden and the UK had met both targets. Austria, Finland and Portugal had also achieved the target of 60% employment rate for women but not that of an overall employment rate of 70%. Since the implementation of the EES, gender gaps in employment rates have fallen in all EU15 member states (see Table 6.1). This positive development may be attributed to favourable economic growth since the introduction of the EES, the growing importance of two earners to maintain acceptable living standards and women's increased skill levels and desire to enter employment. If the gender gap is compared across the member states, a sharp north–south division is seen to have prevailed during the period. Countries such as Greece, Ireland, Luxembourg and Spain had the largest gender gap at the start and the end of the period, while the Nordic member countries had the smallest gender gap. The gender gap in employment is, however, wider if the full-time equivalent (FTE) employment rates are used, which correct for different hours of work, but women work on average fewer hours than men in the labour market. In 2003, the gender gap in the FTE employment rates for the EU15 was 23.7% while in head-count employment rates it was 16.5% (European Commission, 2005, p 87).

Table 6.1: Gender gap in employment rates (head count)[a]

	1999	2001	2003
Austria	18.0	15.7	13
Belgium	17.7	17.8	15.5
Denmark	9.7	8.2	9.1
Germany	15.4	14.1	11.8
Greece	30.2	29.9	28.6
Finland	5.8	5.4	4
France	14.0	13.7	12.2
Ireland	22.5	21.5	19.2
Italy	29.0	27.4	16.9
Luxembourg	25.9	24.1	21.3
Netherlands	18.6	17.6	15.1
Portugal	16.3	15.7	13.5
Spain	30.8	29.4	27.2
Sweden	4.6	3.4	2.7
UK	13.5	13.3	12.8
EU15	19.1	18.1	16.5

Note: [a]The difference in employment rates between men and women in percentage points.
Source: European Commission (2005, p 48)

Countries such as Germany, the Netherlands and the UK perform worse if the indicator on employment rates is changed from head counts to FTE due to extensive part-time work among women in these countries.

Gender gaps in unemployment rates have also fallen over the period 1999-2003 (see Table 6.2). The greatest gender gap in unemployment has continued to be in countries with relative low female employment rates or in Greece, Ireland and Spain. In 2003, men were more prone to unemployment than women in Finland, Germany, Ireland, Sweden and the UK. According to the 2002 *Joint employment report* (Council of the European Union, 2002), the gender gap in unemployment understates the gender gap in the share of the working-age population. The inactive who wish to work in the EU account for 5.6% of the female working-age population and only 3.1% of the male working-age population (Council of the European Union, 2002).

This implies that women will continue to be the main source of labour growth across the EU in the near future.

The gender pay gap in the EU15 has remained remarkably stable (see Table 6.3). From 1997 to 2001, the gap ranged from 15 to 16 percentage points. The widest gap at both the start and the end of the period was in Austria, Germany and the UK, while Italy and Portugal had the smallest gap. The narrow pay gap in Portugal is due to the fact that women working in the public sector earn even higher average wages than their male counterparts. The small gender pay gap in Italy

Table 6.2: Gender gap in unemployment rates[a]

	1999	2001	2003
Austria	1.3	1.0	0.8
Belgium	3.0	1.6	0.8
Denmark	1.0	1.0	0.6
Germany	−1.5	−2.2	−0.8
Greece	10.0	8.6	8.3
Finland	0.9	1.1	−0.3
France	3.6	3.3	2.0
Ireland	−0.2	−0.2	−0.7
Italy	6.9	5.6	4.9
Luxembourg	1.5	1.0	1.6
Netherlands	2.1	1.1	0.4
Portugal	1.3	1.9	1.8
Spain	9.7	7.9	7.7
Sweden	0.2	−0.7	−0.8
UK	−1.4	−1.1	−1.2
EU15	2.7	2.1	1.6

Note: [a]The difference in unemployment rates between women and men in percentage points.

Source: European Commission (2005, p 49)

Table 6.3: The (unadjusted) gender pay gap[a]

	1997	1999	2001
Austria	22	21	20
Belgium	10	11	12
Denmark	13	14	15
Germany	21	19	21
Greece	13	13	18
Finland	18	19	17
France	12	12	14
Ireland	19	22	17
Italy	7	8	6
Luxembourg	–	–	–
Netherlands	22	21	19
Portugal	7	5	10
Spain	14	14	17
Sweden	17	17	18
UK	21	22	21
EU15	15	15	16

Notes: [a] Difference between men's and women's average gross hourly earnings as percentage of men's average gross hourly earnings (for paid employees at work 15+ hours).

Germany: the 'number of hours' used for calculations include paid and unpaid overtime.

Sweden: data are based on full-time equivalent monthly salaries, not hourly earnings.

France: the gender pay gap is based on net hourly earnings.

Netherlands: data are based on annual earnings including overtime pay and non-regular payments.

Sources: Eurostat (2004) (European Community Household Panel, ECHP; European Commission (2005, p 94)

is due to relatively compressed wage differences across educational groups. Moreover, the participation rate among women with less than upper-secondary education is relatively low. This favourable gender pay gap in Italy is likely to grow as more women enter the labour market to fill vacancies in the service sector, which, in most cases, offers low-paid jobs. A study carried out by the European Commission shows that women constitute the majority of the low-paid in the EU (European Commission, 2002a, pp 35-46). Working in the public sector provides a wage premium that is higher for the low-paid, suggesting that any change to the public sector may have particular significance for women. In its evaluation of the EES, the European Commission (2002b, p 28) stated that Belgium, Denmark, Ireland and the UK focused on measures to reduce the gender pay gap. These measures were followed by a slight increase in the gender pay gap in Belgium and Denmark, while it became smaller in Ireland and remained unchanged in the UK.

Gender segregation in EU15 remained almost unchanged from 1997 (see Table 6.4). This indicator highlights the extent to which men and women are segregated across occupations in the labour market. According to this indicator, the Finnish labour market was in 2003 the most gender-segregated among the EU15 member states. By contrast, the least gender-segregated labour markets were found in

Table 6.4 Gender gap in segregation[a]

	1999	2001	2003
Austria	27.6	27.2	27.8
Belgium	26.0	26.1	26.3
Denmark	29.2	28.1	27.4
Germany	26.9	27.0	26.7
Greece	20.9	21.7	21.7
Finland	28.9	29.6	29.5
France	27.0	26.6	26.5
Ireland	26.7	26.7	27.1
Italy	21.5	21.9	22.3
Luxembourg	25.3	26.8	25.1
Netherlands	24.3	25.0	24.5
Portugal	26.2	26.3	27.4
Spain	24.5	24.9	26.3
Sweden	29.3	28.0	27.7
UK	26.9	26.7	26.4
EU15	25.9	25.1	25.2

Note: [a] Gender segregation in occupations, calculated as the average national share of employment for women and men applied to each occupation; differences are added up to produce a total amount of gender imbalance presented as a proportion of total employment (ISCO classification).

Source: European Commission (2005, p 97)

Greece and Italy. In its evaluation of the EES in 2002, the European Commission considered that Denmark together with France, Spain, Sweden and the UK had concentrated on tackling gender segregation. These efforts did, however, not prevent the gender segregation from increasing in Spain since 1999, while it fell considerably in Denmark and Sweden.

Our analysis of gender gaps in employment, unemployment and segregation reveals extensive gaps across the EU member states (see also Mósesdóttir, 2003; Caprile and Potrony, 2004). However, a positive development has taken place since the implementation of the EES as (un)employment gaps have narrowed. Hence, we can argue that the ESM based on the dual-breadwinner model is slowly becoming a reality, although this was more the result of favourable economic climate than the regulatory power of the EU. The speed at which this development has and will take place varies across the member states due to different political and institutional frameworks. In the Nordic countries, a dual-breadwinner model exists with high employment rates among men and women. Moreover, the difference between men's and women's hours of work is small in the Nordic member countries and motherhood has a limited effect on women's involvement in paid work. In the liberal welfare state (the UK) and the Continental welfare states (Germany and the Netherlands), the male-breadwinner model has been modified, as women have increasingly entered the labour market as part-time workers, especially after having children. These countries have less extensive and subsidised child care than the Nordic countries, although expenditures on these services are rising (Taylor-Gooby, 2004, p 16). Moreover, the UK government has, for example, actively promoted part-time work to enable women to combine wage and household work (half-earner model), although part-time work has, so far, been concentrated in low-skilled and low-paid occupations.

A modification of the male-breadwinner model has also taken place in the Mediterranean welfare states, although this is the case more for young skilled women who have entered the labour market as full-time workers than for other groups of women. Motherhood has a great impact on women's employment in the Mediterranean countries, as many women remain outside the labour market to care for dependants. Recently, long care leave has been taken up in Spain to enable women to continue with their care responsibilities, thereby lending further support to the male-breadwinner model. This measure is likely to enhance further divisions among Spanish women or those integrated into the male-breadwinner model and those able to construct their lives around the dual-breadwinner model. Across the member states, women are still much more likely than men to make use of extended care leave rights and those who do so run the risk of losing attachment to the labour market and of being penalised in terms of career progression and pay (Eurostat, 2002; European Commission, 2004; Rubery et al, 2004, p 20).

Conclusion

The EU's regulation paradigm as it relates to gender equality is patchy and involves contradictory objectives. Its impact at the national level is constrained by national actors and variety of welfare state models. In other words, the limited scope of directives in the area of employment, the weak regulatory power of the EES and institutional diversity in the member states prevent a full convergence around an ESM based on gender equality. However, the EU has managed to use its regulation paradigm to create a common understanding of problems to be tackled, and this has in turn intensified convergence pressures across the member states. Hence the distance between the different developmental paths of the member states is narrowing and the dual-breadwinner model is slowly becoming a common feature.

The EES includes only limited efforts to tackle and achieve convergence around care-sharing among men and women, as this would require a shift from family to individual rights/responsibilities in the tax, benefit and service systems of many of the member states. The dual-breadwinner model involves, therefore, more similar employment participation of men and women across Europe and not equal division of unpaid work and equal pay. However, incremental expansion of EU regulation of gender relations through the EES in the member states will continue to take place and the effects of this expansion will eventually accumulate and lead to a radical change in countries where the welfare state model has traditionally supported the male-breadwinner model, as in Spain. The forces behind the incremental expansion of EU regulation are women's desire to work, the growing need to activate women to ensure economic growth, and to a lesser extent the soft-law approach of the EES, which will gradually legitimate EU intervention into the social sphere across the member states.

The EU recognises that the success of employment policies depends largely on the quality of their implementation and calls for strong involvement of parliamentary bodies, social partners and other relevant actors (Council of the European Union, 2003/2004, p 11). In most member states, women are poorly represented in elected bodies and among the social partners. Moreover, gender mainstreaming in the EES has not involved the active engagement of women and equality bodies in identifying gender problems and solutions. Women's opportunities to influence gender policies and measures are in most cases dependent on the political will of parties in power and are therefore often subject to short-term interests of party politics (see reports of WELLKNOW project [see www.bifrost.is/wellknow/]). Hence, women's interests are inadequately represented in the ESM and the EU treats gender problems first and foremost as a technical problem preventing the member states from achieving economic growth comparable with that of the US or in terms of economic efficiency.

The concern to achieve economic goals undermines, to a certain extent, gender equality, as women are encouraged to enter the labour market at the same time as jobs have become less rewarding (low-skilled and low-paid) and deregulation of pay systems in Europe has led to less transparency and growing inequalities. Hence, efforts to reduce gender inequalities need to move from reliance on economic growth to the active integration of women's interest into economic policies and the ESM. Moreover, the focus of hard and soft measures needs to be broadened to include men's behaviour as well as redistribution of resources among women and men and women's representation. If Europe is to move towards greater gender equality, national governments need to make gender mainstreaming a political priority with the same status as economic policies and to promote its application not only in the public but also in the private sector.

Notes

[1] This chapter is based on research results of the WELLKNOW project: 'From welfare to knowfare: a European approach to employment and gender mainstreaming in the knowledge-based society' (see www.bifrost.is/wellknow). The project received funding during the period 2003-05 from the EU's fifth framework programme as a part of the specific programme: 'Improving the human research potential and the socio-economic knowledge base'.

[2] In 2002, the youth female unemployment rate (percentage of the labour force aged 15-24) was 11.6% in Sweden while this rate was only 6.9% in the EU15 (European Commission, 2004).

[3] By 2010 at least 85% of 22-year-olds in the EU should have completed upper-secondary education and the EU average level of participation

in lifelong learning should be at least 12.5% among the adult working-age population (25-64 age group).

⁴ The indicator on lifelong learning is defined as persons (aged 25-64) in employment who answered that they had received education or training in the four weeks preceding the survey (Caprile and Potrony, 2004, pp 51 and 66).

References

Barcelona European Council (2002) *Presidency conclusions*, (www.consilium.europa.eu/ueDocs/cms_Data/docs/pressData/en/ec/71025.pdf).

Barry, U., Bettio, F., Figueiredo, H., Grimshaw, D., Maier, F. and Plasman, R. (2001) 'III. Indicators on gender gaps in pay and income', in J. Rubery, C. Fagan, D. Grimshaw, H. Figueiredo and M. Smith (eds) *Indicators on gender equality in the European Employment Strategy*, EWERC, Manchester School of Management, UMIST, available at www.mbs.ac.uk/research/centres/european-employment/projects/gender-social-inclusion/documents/Indicators2001(final).pdf

Behning, U. and Serrano Pascual, A. (eds) (2001) *Gender mainstreaming in the European Employment Strategy*, Brussels: European Trade Union Institute.

Behning, U., Foden, D. and Serrano Pascual, A. (2001) 'Introduction', in U. Behning, and A. Serrano Pascual (eds) *Gender mainstreaming within the European Union*, Brussels: European Trade Union Institute, pp 9-23.

Booth, C. and Bennett, C. (2002) 'Gender mainstreaming in the European Union', *European Journal of Women's Studies*, vol 9, no 4, pp 430-46.

Caprile, M. and Potrony, J. (2004) 'Measuring progress towards the knowledge-based society, quality of working life and gender equality', in M. Caprile (ed) *Measuring progress towards the knowledge-based society, quality of working life and gender equality*, WELLKNOWN project report no 3, pp 57-98, available at www.bifrost.is/wellknow/Files/Skra_0006771.pdf

Caprile, M., Cachon, L. and Montagut, T. (2002) *Potential of community policies for employment promotion: The role of inclusion and participation for competitiveness, growth and employment*, Copenhagen: PLS Rambøll Management A/S, available at www.europa.eu.int/comm/employment_social/news/2002/aug/annex5.pdf

Council of the European Union (2002) *Joint employment report*, Brussels: European Commission, available at http://europa.eu.int/comm/employment_social/employment_strategy/report_2002/jer2002_final_en.pdf

Council of the European Union (2003) 'Council decision of 22 July 2003 on guidelines for the employment policies of the member states', *Official Journal of the European Union*, L197/13, 5 August, p.10.

Council of the European Union (2003/04) *Joint employment report*, Brussels: European Commission, available at http://europa.eu.int/comm/employment_social/employment_strategy/report_2003/jer20034_en.pdf

Esping-Andersen, G. (1990) *The three worlds of welfare capitalism*, Cambridge: Polity Press.

Estevez-Abe, M. (2002) 'Gendering varieties of capitalism', Paper prepared for a conference on the political economy of family and work, Yale University, July.

Estevez-Abe, M., Iversen, T. and Soskice, D. (2001) 'Social protection and formation of skills: a reinterpretation of the welfare state', in P. Hall and D. Soskice (eds) *Varieties of capitalism: The institutional foundations of comparative advantage*, Oxford: Oxford University Press, pp 145-83.

European Commission (1997) *Equal opportunities for men and women in Europe?*, Eurobarometer 44.3, Luxembourg: Office for Official Publications for the European Communities, available at http://europa.eu.int/comm/public_opinion/archives/ebs/ebs_097_en.pdf

European Commission (2002a) *Employment in Europe 2002*, Luxembourg: European Commission.

European Commission (2002b) *Impact evaluation of the European Employment Strategy*, COM (2002) 416 final of 17 July.

European Commission (2004) *Employment in Europe 2004*, Luxembourg: European Commission.

European Commission (2005) *Second version: Indicators for monitoring the employment guidelines 2004-2005 compendium*, Brussels: European Commission, available at europa.eu.int/comm/employment_social/employment_strategy/indic/compendium_jer2004_en.pdf

Eurostat (2002) *The impact of children on women's employment varies between member states*, Luxembourg: Eurostat News Release 60/2002.

Eurostat (2004) European Community Household Panel (ECHP) data provided by Eurostat on 30 September 2004 to the Expert Group on Gender, Social Inclusion and Employment (EGGSIE).

Hantrais, L. (1995) *Social policy in the European Union*, London: Macmillian Press.

Lisbon European Council (2000) *Presidency conclusions*, (www.consilium.europa.eu/ueDocs/cms_Data/docs/pressData/en/ec/00100-r1.en0.htm).

Mósesdóttir, L. (2001) *The interplay between gender, markets and the state in Sweden, Germany and the United States*, London: Ashgate.

Mósesdóttir, L. (2003) 'Moving Europe towards the dual-breadwinner model', in D. Foden and L. Magnusson (eds) *Five years' experience of the Luxembourg employment strategy*, Brussels: European Trade Union Institute, pp 183-204.

Mósesdóttir, L. and Erlingsdóttir, R. G. (2005) 'Comparative analyses of policies', in L. Mósesdóttir (ed) *Policies and performances: The case of Austria, Denmark, Finland, the Netherlands, Spain, Hungary and Iceland*, WELLKNOWN project report no 4, pp 6-44, available at www.bifrost.is/wellknow/Files/Skra_0007770.pdf

Mósesdóttir, L. and Thorbergsdóttir, B. (2004) 'European policies facilitating and managing change towards the knowledge based society and gender equality', in K. Sjørup (ed) *The European Employment Strategy and national employment policies: Addressing the employment and gender challenges of the knowledge based society*, WELLKNOWN project report no 2, pp 8-25, available at www.bifrost.is/wellknow/Files/Skra_0005517.pdf

OECD (Organisation for Economic Co-operation and Development) (2003) *Employment outlook*, Paris: OECD.

Plantenga, J. and Rembery, C. (2005) *Reconciliation of work and private life: A comparative review of thirty European countries*, A report prepared by members of the coordinating team of Expert Groups on Gender, Social Inclusion and Employment (EGGSIE) for the Equal Opportunities Unit of the European Commission, available at http://europe.eu.int/comm/employment_social/gender_equality/docs/2005/reconciliation_report_en.pdf

Roivas, S. (2004) 'Towards better employment and equal opportunities – NAPs as political pedagogy?', in K. Sjørup (ed) *The European Employment Strategy and national employment policies: Addressing the employment and gender challenges of the knowledge based society*, WELLKNOWN project report no 2, pp 26-101, available at www.bifrost.is/wellknow/Files/Skra_0005517.pdf

Rubery, J. l. (2003) 'Gender mainstreaming and the Open Method of Coordination: is the Open Method too open for gender equality policy?', Paper presented at the conference 'New approaches to governance in EU social and employment policy: Open Coordination and the future of Social Europe, available at http://eucenter.wisc.edu/Conferences/OMCnetOct03/rubery.pdf

Rubery, J., Grimshaw, D., Smith, M. and Figueiredo, H. (2001) *Gender equality and the European Employment Strategy: An evaluation of the National Action Plans for Employment 2001*, EWERC, Manchester School of Management, UMIST, available at http://www.mbs.ac.uk/research/centres/european-employment/projects/gender-social-inclusion/documents/Synthesis2001.pdf

Rubery, J., Smith, M., Figueiredo, H., Fagan, C. and Grimshaw, D. (2004) *Gender equality and the European Employment Strategy and social inclusion process*, available at www.mbs.ac.uk/research/centres/european-employment/projects/gender-social-inclusion/documents/NapEmp_Inc2003.pdf

Serrano Pascual, A. (2003) 'Towards convergence of the European activation policies?', in D. Foden and L. Magnusson (eds) *Five years' experience of the Luxembourg Employment Strategy*, Brussels: European Trade Union Institute, pp 141-66.

Taylor-Gooby, P. (2004) 'New risks and social change', in P. Taylor-Gooby (ed) *New risks, new welfare: The transformation of the European welfare state*, Oxford: Oxford University Press, pp 1-28.

Verloo, M. (2001) *Another velvet revolution? Gender mainstreaming and the politics of implementation*, IWM Working Paper No 5/2001, available at www.iwm.at/p-iwmwp.htm#Verloo

Walby, S. (2004) 'The European Union and gender equality: emergent varieties of gender regime', *Social Politics*, vol 11, no 1, pp 4-29.

SEVEN

The European Social Model and enlargement

Maarten Keune

Introduction

In May 2004, after a long period of preparation, eight former state-socialist countries joined the European Union (EU). The entry of these new member states (NMS) raises a number of questions concerning the relationship between the enlargement of the EU and the European Social Model (ESM). For some, enlargement is a threat to the ESM. It is argued that, in combination with the restrictive conditions set by the European Monetary Union (EMU), enlargement may shift the balance of power on the labour market to the employers, lead to higher income inequality and result in a partial dismantling of the welfare state to the detriment of the poor (Kittel, 2002). According to others, the ESM may be undermined because of the weakness of social policy in the NMS and their inclination towards neoliberalism (Vaughan-Whitehead, 2003). If one accepts Scharpf's assertion that, in social policy terms, the EU has been incapable of effective action because of the diverging interests of the EU15 in this area (Scharpf, 1997), then enlargement is bound to diminish this effectiveness still further. For many actors in the NMS, accession to the EU has been considered the 'telos of transition' (Orenstein, 1998, p 480), the final step in breaking with the state-socialist past and in joining the modern democratic-capitalist world, a step expected to bring both economic *and* social benefits, stemming from, among other things, the ESM.

Assessment of the relationship between enlargement and the ESM depends first of all, however, on the definition of what the ESM is all about, and different definitions will lead to different perspectives. In Chapter One of this volume, Jepsen and Serrano Pascual identify two major ways of understanding the ESM: (a) an historical *acquis*, characterised by specific common institutions, values and outcomes; and (b) a European political project, aiming to solve shared problems and working towards a distinctive transnational model, including common goals, rules and standards, and a certain degree of transnational cohesion.

The historical *acquis* approach leads to two sets of questions. The first is whether the NMS are part of the ESM, whether, that is, they sufficiently resemble the EU15 in this respect, and, if so, how this has come about. Have these countries become part of the ESM through their preparation for membership of the EU? Have they been part of the ESM for a longer historical period (and is enlargement hence irrelevant)? Or can they become part of the ESM only in the future? The second set of questions concerns the effect of enlargement on the ESM: will the entry of the NMS have a significant effect on the social model of the EU15 and therefore on the ESM?

The political project approach gives rise to questions concerning Europeanisation and governance. Has the EU imposed a social model upon the NMS and has accession to the EU brought particular social rights and outcomes to the NMS? Will the ESM project change because of a different social orientation of the NMS, or will it be blocked because of decision-making difficulties?

This chapter aims to contribute to the further clarification of the relationship between enlargement and the ESM through a discussion of welfare state reform and performance in the NMS. Instead of starting out from a single conception of the ESM, the chapter will tackle this question from two different perspectives. Section two – more in keeping with the historical *acquis* approach – will consider the question of the extent to which the NMS' welfare states resemble, and to what extent they differ from, the EU15 welfare states.

Section three – more in keeping with the political project approach – will examine to what extent the EU has imposed upon the NMS, in particular in the run-up to membership, institutional and policy innovations that stem from the ESM. In particular, following the focus of most of the contributions to this volume, section three will review the role of the EU in shaping employment policy and labour legislation in the NMS. Section four, finally, will present conclusions.

The historical *acquis* perspective: NMS' welfare states and their performance

This section will discuss the relationship between enlargement and the ESM from the historical *acquis* perspective. According to this perspective, the countries belonging to the ESM share common values, institutions and outcomes. Here the focus of the analysis will be on institutions and outcomes, whereas values will not be dealt with. First, a brief account of the historical development of NMS' welfare states will be provided, as well as of the direction in which they have been changing over the last 15 years. The next step will be to examine the performance of these welfare states in recent years, considering to what extent this is divergent among the NMS themselves as well as between the group of NMS and the EU15. On the basis of this examination, the question of whether the NMS fit the ESM will be discussed.

Historical continuity and discontinuity

Welfare states in the EU15 are generally grouped into four welfare families, which, while dealing with welfare issues in quite diverse ways, each show a great deal of historical continuity (Esping-Andersen, 1990; Ferrera, 1996). The NMS' welfare states have experienced much less continuity. In the past 65 years, they have undergone two fundamental, systemic changes, from capitalism to state-socialism in the 1940s and back to capitalism after 1989 (Hemerijck et al, 2006). On both occasions, the complete array of social and economic institutions, as well as the normative and cognitive frames underpinning them, were called into question and the resulting institutional innovations were indeed radical.

In the first decades of the 20th century, the countries of Central and Eastern Europe (CEE) developed welfare states that largely followed the employment-related insurance-based Bismarckian or Continental welfare state model (see, for example, Potůček, 2004; Cerami, 2005). They differentiated strongly between occupational groups and generally favoured urban industrial workers over agricultural workers. Large welfare disparities could be observed across inter-war CEE, with the highly industrialised Czechoslovakia belonging to the more affluent European countries while Poland or Hungary were far more agricultural and more deeply affected by poverty.

With the emergence of state-socialism in the 1940s, the CEE welfare states increasingly acquired a universal character. This was not so much because welfare entitlements became based on citizenship, as in the Nordic welfare model, but rather because the emergence of full employment led to universal coverage of welfare arrangements. Indeed, although centrally regulated by the state, the system remained firmly employment-based. This is further underlined by the fact that full employment was initially not an integral part of the state-socialist ideology. Rather, it emerged over time as a by-product of the rapid industrial growth and the resulting continuous demand for labour. Once established, however, full employment and the resulting universal coverage of welfare state arrangements increasingly became part of the state-socialist discourse and became fundamental parts of the system as such (Róna-Tas, 1997; Baxandall, 2003). Furthermore, welfare entitlements were often provided through the state enterprise (Kornai, 1992), which further strengthened the link to employment.

As is true of any empirical case, the state-socialist welfare state was to some extent a mixed system. It included also certain non-employment-related, universal cash benefits such as child and family benefits, covering the population under working age. In addition, the state subsidised food, housing and transport, and maintained a formally free health system and education system, although some formally free services were not in fact entirely free (tipping of doctors, for example, was standard practice).

The state-socialist welfare state strongly reduced pre-war income inequalities, largely abolished extreme poverty and created high employment levels. This does not mean that everybody was equal: important differences prevailed between elites and non-elites, between priority sectors and non-priority sectors, and intra-enterprise differences between groups with more and less bargaining power. Also, although the state-socialist system, plagued by continuous labour shortages, facilitated female employment by providing child care, extended maternity leave and child-raising benefits, little changed in the household responsibilities for women. Women suffered from a double burden, while the division of labour also remained sexist (Deacon, 2000). What is more, the state-socialist welfare state was strongly interventionist, offering mainly low-quality services, limited choice and a generally low standard of living, while also including widespread underemployment.

Institutional reforms after 1989

In the years 1989-91, the state-socialist system was abandoned in favour of democratic capitalism. The first half of the 1990s was characterised by a deep economic crisis across the entire CEE region, although its depth varied substantially. By 1994, all NMS had seen their Gross Domestic Product (GDP) drop, with GDP losses ranging from 8% in Poland to close on 50% in Latvia, as compared to the 1989 level. Also, inflation had exploded (reaching up to 1000% in the Baltic countries in 1992) and full employment had come to an end, with employment losses ranging from some 10% in the Czech Republic to some 30% in Hungary (Keune, 2003).

The depth of the crisis of the early 1990s dampened the initial optimistic expectations of a speedy and unproblematic 'transition' to capitalism, which would rapidly replace and outperform the obsolete state-socialist economy. Indeed, the new political elites feared that the high social costs of the initial crisis would undermine the support of the population for economic and political reform. Hence, radical economic reforms were accompanied by more cautious welfare state reforms. Indeed, in these initial years the welfare state was to an important extent used as a buffer aiming to absorb the most dramatic social effects of the economic crisis, in particular the loss of income through the loss of employment.

One important way of absorbing part of the employment and income losses was the widespread use of early retirement provisions and disability pensions for redundant workers (Fultz and Ruck, 2001; Müller, 2002). As a further means of reducing the impact of employment losses, unemployment benefit schemes were set up around the region (Nesporova, 1999). In addition, all CEE countries introduced a minimum wage to put a wage floor in the labour market. Finally, social assistance schemes were introduced to prevent those without other means of existence from falling into poverty.

This succeeded only partially. By the mid-1990s, the NMS had returned to economic growth and brought inflation under control but, in spite of the welfare state, poverty had been on the rise, while welfare schemes had come under increasing financial strain because of the dramatic increase in benefit recipients, unfavourable demographic developments and falling tax and social contributions (Hemerijck et al, 2006).

Hence, welfare reform returned to the agenda but this time with a view to reducing costs and increasing efficiency, reducing welfare dependency and changing incentive structures and governance systems. However, while some dimensions of the welfare state were profoundly reformed, others have been changed only marginally. In addition, comparing the various countries, both converging and diverging elements can be observed in their reform paths.

Space does not allow for a comprehensive overview of welfare state reform in this chapter. Industrial relations and social dialogue are reviewed elsewhere in this volume. Here, a summary will be provided of reforms in the two areas that dominate social expenditure: old-age pensions and health care.

Old-age pensions

State-socialist pension systems were largely financed on a pay-as-you-earn (PAYE) basis through transfers from state firms to the state budget; direct contributions by workers were rare and retirement ages were low (Fultz and Ruck, 2001; Guardiancich, 2004). As of 1994, far-reaching reform of pension systems, taking up the largest share of social expenditure, was on the agenda. This was a result of budgetary and demographic pressures, but also because of strong reform advocacy by the World Bank, pushing for privatisation and individualisation of savings (World Bank, 1994).

While all NMS introduced adaptations to the traditional pension scheme – including the raising of the retirement age, the improvement of the collection of contributions, and the changing of benefit formulas – not all did this in the same way. Poland and Latvia made pensions more individualised, more dependent on lifetime contributions and life expectancy, more earnings-related and less redistributive (Fultz, 2003). Hungary retained the traditional system but reduced redistribution to low-income workers, while the Czech Republic and Slovenia increased redistribution toward low-wage workers (Mácha, 2002; Stanovik, 2002).

Hungary, Poland, Latvia, Estonia and Slovakia went a step further and introduced, alongside the public pillar, mandatory, commercially managed, individual savings accounts, shifting pension risks from society to the individual and reducing risk pooling and redistribution (Müller, 2002; Fultz, 2003). Finally, all NMS introduced voluntary supplementary pensions. Hence, whereas pension reform has been ongoing throughout CEE, elements of convergence – a stronger relation of pensions to employment histories, an increasing pension age and the introduction of voluntary schemes – combine with elements of divergence in the form of mandatory private savings accounts (or not) and a greater or lesser degree of redistribution. Hence, a general Bismarckian trend is mixed with some egalitarian and market elements.

Health care

Whereas, before the Second World War, most CEE countries had a Bismarckian system of health insurance, under the state-socialist system free universal health care was provided by the state. After the demise of state socialism, all NMS opted for a Bismarckian-type health insurance system under which the insured, in return for the payment of health insurance contributions, receive health care services (Cerami, 2005). However, this Bismarckian orientation, reaching back to pre-war traditions, is combined with the strong universal and egalitarian aspirations that were prevalent during the state-socialist period. Today, the state largely continues to guarantee the provision of health services to the non-insured, while it also covers the deficits of the newly established health insurance funds (Cerami, 2005). Most systems also operate on the principle of solidarity whereby the premiums paid by the insured are not risk- but income-proportionate (see, for example, Hungarian Ministry of Health, Social and Family Affairs, 2004). These Bismarckian and universalist dimensions were subsequently further combined with market influence, including market-based services (Cerami, 2005).

Health care and pension reforms indicate the more general trend of welfare reform in the NMS. Most reforms have, first of all, a Bismarckian character, increasing the importance of insurance-based benefits as well as of employment-related factors in defining benefits. This is also true of, for instance, invalidity pensions (Fultz, 2002) and unemployment benefits. However, this does not mean that NMS' welfare states are simply on a Bismarckian track, re-establishing pre-war traditions. Indeed, universalist legacies from the state-socialist era play an important role, while state and market are important governance mechanisms. Thus, as shown by Cerami (2005, pp 143-4), all NMS' welfare states present their own mix of market orientation, targeting and universality, combining their Bismarckian and state-socialist heritages with the market dogmatism projected onto the region in the past 15 years. In such institutional terms, welfare states in the NMS do not seem to fit easily into the traditional welfare-families typology developed for the EU15; nor, however, are they dramatically different from these. Rather, they seem to represent their own peculiar combination of elements to be found in the four worlds of welfare. This seems quite compatible with the idea of their incorporation into the ESM.

Welfare financing and performance

More clear-cut divergence within the NMS, as well as between the NMS and the EU15, can, however, be observed in welfare expenditure and, in particular, welfare performance. As far as finance is concerned, Table 7.1 provides the size and structure of social expenditure in the NMS as well as the average for the EU15. Two main observations can be made upon the basis of this table. First of all, among the NMS, there is a clear divide between low spenders (the Baltic countries), medium spenders (Slovakia, the Czech Republic and Hungary) and high spenders (Poland and Slovenia). These differences have been more or less stable since the mid-1990s (European Commission, 2003). Moreover, lower or higher social expenditure is not simply the result of budgetary pressures. With the exception of Slovenia, the NMS with medium or high social expenditure are also the ones with the highest fiscal deficits and the highest public debt, in other words, the ones that in theory could least afford such expenditure.

At the same time, social expenditure in all NMS remains below the average for the EU15, which stood at 27.6% of GDP in 2001. Only two NMS come anywhere near this average, with the rest remaining far behind. In fact, the Baltic countries, together with Ireland, have the lowest social expenditure of the entire EU, followed by the Czech Republic, Hungary and Slovakia. The new member state with the highest social expenditure, that is, Slovenia, falls in the same range as Italy and Finland and outperforms four of the EU15 countries. Hence, most NMS remain inside the social expenditure range defined by the highest (31.4%) and lowest (15.3%) level of expenditure in the EU15. The Baltic countries are below the lowest level, but the differences with Ireland are small. At the same time, the NMS are clearly (among) the countries with the lowest social expenditure as a percentage of GDP and so they clearly pull down the EU average. Indeed, they belong to the minimal welfare states of the EU, where social transfers are lowest.

As far as welfare state performance is concerned, Table 7.2 presents some of the main indicators for the NMS as well as the average and minimum–maximum range for the EU15. Of prime importance is the average level of income, expressed by GDP per capita. Differences within the NMS are large: GDP per capita in Latvia is only 53.2% of that of Slovenia. The Baltic countries together with Poland make up the poorer group of the NMS, while the richer group consists of Hungary, the Czech Republic and Slovenia, with Slovakia in between the two groups. In recent years, however, differences between NMS have diminished as the poorer Baltic countries as well as Slovakia have been growing much faster in 2001-04 than the richer NMS. The exception to this trend is Poland, which has seen its relative position worsen recently.

In comparison with the EU15, GDP per capita is far below the average for the EU15 in all NMS. Only Slovenia has a per capita GDP very slightly above that of the poorest old member state (Portugal). Clearly, the NMS as a group make up the poorer part of the enlarged

Table 7.1: Social expenditure in the NMS and EU15 (2001)

| | Total social expenditure (% GDP) | Old-age and survivor pensions | Structure of social expenditure (% of total) | | | | | |
			Sickness	Family benefits	Disability pension	Unemployment	Social exclusion	Housing
Estonia	14.3	42.6	31.0	14.6	7.8	1.3	2.2	0.6
Latvia	14.3	56.4	19.1	10.1	9.6	3.6	0.6	0.7
Lithuania	15.2	47.5	30.0	8.3	8.8	1.9	2.3	1.2
Slovakia	19.1	38.2	35.0	8.2	8.1	3.6	6.5	0.4
Czech Republic	19.2	42.5	34.6	8.2	8.5	3.1	2.7	0.6
Hungary	19.8	42.4	27.5	12.9	10.3	3.4	1	2.5
Poland	22.1	55.3	19.2	7.8	13.3	4.3	0.2	0.0
Slovenia	25.5	45.5	31.4	8.9	8.7	3.7	1.8	0.0
Average	18.7	46.3	28.5	9.9	9.4	3.1	2.2	0.8
EU15	27.6	46.1	28.0	8.0	8.2	6.3	1.5	2.1
EU15 min–max	15.3–31.4	–	–	–	–	–	–	–

Source: Eurostat

Table 7.2: Welfare state performance in the NMS and EU15

	GDP per capita in purchasing power standard EU25=100 (2003)	Average yearly GDP growth (2001-04)	Poverty after social transfers (2001) (%)*	Employment rate (2003) (%)	Old-age dependency ratio (2003)
Latvia	41	6.9	16	61.8	23.3
Poland	46	2.7	15	51.2	18.4
Lithuania	46	7.3	17	61.1	22.0
Estonia	49	6.0	18	62.9	23.5
Slovakia	52	4.1	21	57.7	16.5
Hungary	61	3.3	10	57.0	22.4
Czech Republic	69	2.5	8	64.7	19.7
Slovenia	77	2.9	11	62.6	21.0
EU15	109	1.3	15	64.3	25.0
EU15 min–max	74–215	0.4–4.6	9–21	56.1–75.1	16.4–26.9

Note: * Relative poverty: population with income below 60% of mean income.

Source: Eurostat

EU and half of the NMS have a GDP per capita below 50% of the EU15 average. Hence, there is much less social cohesion in the enlarged EU than was the case before May 2004. Nonetheless, the differences are getting smaller. Whereas in the EU15, average yearly GDP growth in 2001-04 was 1.3%, in all NMS growth was much higher, ranging from double the EU15 figure in the Czech Republic to 5.6 times that figure in Lithuania.

In terms of relative poverty, however, the situation is different. In the richer NMS, poverty after social transfers, as well as income inequality, is much lower than in the poorer NMS. Differences in income inequality are further confirmed when comparing the Gini coefficient for the NMS: in 2002, this ranged from 0.234 in the Czech Republic and 0.244 in Slovenia, to between 0.353 and 0.393 for Poland and the Baltic countries (UNICEF, 2004). Within the enlarged EU, the NMS can be found at the two extremes: the Baltic countries and Slovakia, together with the United Kingdom (UK), Spain, Portugal and Greece are the EU countries with the highest income inequality, while Hungary, the Czech Republic and Slovenia are, together with Denmark and Sweden, the ones with the most income equality (European Commission, 2004, p 69). Hence, where absolute poverty is much higher in the NMS than in the rest of the EU, relative poverty and income inequality in the NMS are located at the two extremes of the enlarged EU, spanning largely the same range as in the EU15.

The NMS employment rates differ again substantially, ranging from 51.2% in Poland to 64.7% in the Czech Republic. Poland has by far the lowest employment rate in the enlarged EU, five percentage points below the worst performer of the EU15 (Italy), and some six percentage points below Hungary and Slovakia. The Czech Republic is the only new member state with an employment rate above the EU15 average. In particular, Hungary, Slovakia and Poland belong to the worst performers in the enlarged EU, but the latter alone falls below all EU15 countries.

Finally, the old-age dependency ratio in the NMS varies once again quite considerably, from 16.5 in Slovakia to 23.5 in Estonia. In the Baltic countries and Hungary, in the short term, providing income for the elderly is more of a challenge, although this will change in the future. Projections suggest that by 2020 the old-age dependency ratio will be highest in Slovenia and the Czech Republic and as a longer-term challenge the ageing of the population weighs more on these countries. In comparison with the EU15, the situation is more favourable in the NMS since all these countries remain below the EU15 average.

Do the NMS fit the ESM?

The main interpretation of what the ESM is all about claims that the countries belonging to the ESM share a historical *acquis*, including common institutions, values and outcomes. The adherents to this interpretation have long assumed that the ESM was made up of the EU15, although some exclude the Anglo-Saxon countries with their liberal welfare states and emphasis on market coordination (Jepsen and Serrano Pascual, this volume). But do the NMS belong to the ESM as well? Following the historical *acquis* approach, this would be the case if they share these same institutions, values and outcomes. Assessing whether this is indeed the case gives rise, however, to serious problems. As argued by Jepsen and Serrano Pascual, these common factors are generally defined only in fairly abstract and vague terms. For example, the ESM is often regarded as encompassing generous welfare state transfers, but it is not specified what level of transfers this entails or what degree of income inequality is or is not acceptable. The closest one comes to specification is often in terms of a comparison with the United States (US), the claim being that the ESM provides greater equality and more generous social benefits. What is more, across the EU there is wide diversity of both welfare institutions and outcomes, which further complicates a more precise identification of the factors common to the countries belonging to the ESM.

Here no attempt will be made to define the common denominators of the ESM. Rather, it is assumed that the institutions, values and outcomes that can be observed in EU15 countries are in correspondence with the ESM. As to the relationship between enlargement and the ESM, the question then becomes whether the institutions, values and outcomes prevalent in the NMS can plausibly be considered sufficiently similar to any of those found in the EU15.

What does the above analysis of welfare state institutions and outcomes tell us about this question? Are NMS' welfare state institutions and outcomes like any of those found in the EU15? In an historical perspective this does not seem to be the case. During the state-socialist era the welfare state was indeed substantially different from any of the EU15, both in institutional terms and in outcomes. Institutionally, the extreme dominance of the state, the key role of the state enterprise, extended maternity leave entitlements, the obligation to work, and many other elements combined to form a system that would be hard to fit into the ESM. In terms of outcomes, income equality was much higher than in any of the EU15, there was full employment (combined with widespread underemployment), and the standard of living in most CEE countries was much lower than in any of the EU15.

After 1989 this picture changed. As it was argued above, in recent years, after a period of deep reform, although in institutional terms welfare states in the NMS do not correspond to any one of the four traditional EU15 welfare families, neither do they dramatically differ. They seem to represent peculiar combinations of elements that are also to be found in the four worlds of welfare and which do not seem to contradict the shared *acquis* view of the ESM. This is not to say that NMS' welfare states resemble EU15 welfare states. Rather, the range of welfare state arrangements in the EU15 is so broad that those found in the NMS largely fit within the range. Indeed, they are not sufficiently different to claim they would not fit the ESM. The only slight exception to this general claim might seem to be the very low social expenditure in Estonia and Latvia, which, in terms of the percentage of GDP, falls below the lowest level in the EU15. And yet the difference is only one percentage point, which hardly seems decisive. Equally, if Ireland with social expenditure of 15.3% of GDP belongs to the ESM, it seems exaggerated to claim that Estonia and Latvia with 14.3% of GDP do not! Rather, the conclusion would be that most NMS belong to the EU countries that spend a minimal amount on social expenditure.

Where welfare state outcomes are concerned, it was shown that most of these fall into the range defined by the minimum and maximum prevalent in the EU15. There is one major exception, however, which is the level of income as expressed in GDP per capita. Only one new member state has a slightly higher GDP per capita than the poorest EU15 country. Indeed, NMS' welfare states are not only minimal welfare states in terms of social expenditure, they are also low–income welfare states. How does one interpret this? Can the ESM apply to countries that are simply much poorer than the EU15? It is left to the reader to answer this question. However, if there is one welfare-related factor that sets the NMS apart from the EU15, it is clearly the huge differences in income. Hence, if the NMS have become part of the ESM, this means that both the empirical diversity as well as the social disparities covered by the ESM concept have increased since May 2004.

The political project perspective: the social *acquis* and its impact on the NMS

The weight of Social Europe

The second perspective towards enlargement and the ESM taken in this chapter is that of the ESM as a political project. The main question here is to what extent enlargement has been a process of 'coercive isomorphism' (DiMaggio and Powell, 1983), in other words, to what extent has the EU put pressure on the NMS with the aim of imposing a 'social model', in particular in the run-up to membership? Or: how important has the social dimension of the accession process been? Indeed, if one starts out from the assumption that the ESM is a political project working towards a distinctive transnational model, including common goals, rules and standards, one could expect the elements of this model to be part and parcel of the conditions imposed in exchange for EU membership.

This section will briefly examine to what extent this has been the case in the area of employment policy and labour legislation. Prior to this, however, two broader questions need to be considered: (a) is there a coherent ESM in place at the European level; and (b) to what extent were social policy issues priority issues for the EU in the run up to the enlargement of May 2004?

The first question is answered by Goetschy in this volume. She shows that no coherent ESM is enshrined in the European Community social provisions. Employment, social protection and industrial relations policies remain largely matters of national responsibility and European-level regulations are largely complementary in nature. This is not to say that European regulations are insignificant. As argued by Goetschy (this volume), Social Europe today comprises several elements of an ESM: social values and principles enshrined in the Charter of Fundamental Rights; Community social law consisting of a fragmentary set of directives; and a variety of modes of regulation on which Europe's political and social players can draw (legislation, European-level social dialogue, the Open Method of Coordination [OMC] in a series of policy areas, and redistributive Structural Funds).

As to the importance given by the EU to social policy issues in the run up to the entry of the NMS, Lendvai (2004) shows that there is a widespread consensus in the literature that the social dimension of accession and enlargement has been weak, that the EU has been a weak transnational actor where social policy is concerned and that economic issues have had clear primacy over social issues. Indeed, of the 29 thematic chapters that made up the Regular Reports that yearly reviewed the 'progress' made by the-then candidate countries in their preparation for accession, only one chapter dealt with employment and social policy, while there were individual chapters on taxation policy, monetary policy, competition policy, company law, transport policy, the free movement of goods, and so on, giving the assessment a strongly economistic character. Indeed, many authors argue that the international financial institutions, notably the World Bank, have exercised much greater influence on the reform of social policy in the NMS than the EU (for example, Müller, 2003; Ferge and Juhász, 2004).

The social acquis *and the labour market*

At the EU level there is no coherent ESM in place, and in the enlargement process social issues had a secondary status in comparison with economic issues. This does not mean, however, that no coercive isomorphism occurred between the EU and the-then candidate countries in the social field. A social *acquis* does exist as part of the larger *acquis communautaire* and the candidate countries were indeed required to adopt this social *acquis*. The social *acquis* is justified on normative grounds, that is, as incorporating social values. At the same time, increasingly, and reflecting the primacy of the economic dimension of the EU project, the social *acquis* is justified using cognitive, economic arguments: 'good social policy is good economic policy' (Diamantopoulou, 2001). The social *acquis* consists, first of all, of the EU social directives covering health and safety issues, labour legislation, gender equality, and the free movement of labour (Goetschy, this volume). These directives could be considered the 'hard' *acquis*, in other words, their incorporation into national regulations is compulsory. There is also a 'soft' *acquis*, referring to the adoption of practices common in the EU as well as the (preparation for) participation in EU processes. This relates, first of all, to social dialogue: the EU expects applicant countries to practise meaningful social dialogue and to prepare the social partners for participation in European-level social dialogue (Vaughan-Whitehead, 2000). Another example is the capacity to participate in the OMC governing a number of social policy areas, including pensions, employment, social inclusion, social protection, and others. During the years previous to accession, the NMS were gradually incorporated into these OMCs, but these processes are essentially voluntaristic in character and do not impose specific regulations. They do have importance in terms of agenda setting and the spreading of certain discourses, as will be demonstrated below.

In the field of employment policy and labour legislation, the hard *acquis* consists of a set of directives regulating, among other things, the freedom of movement for workers and the portability of social security rights across borders; equal treatment of men and women; some elements of working-time regulations; some elements of workers' participation rights; posted workers; workers' rights in case of collective redundancy or transfer of undertakings; and aspects of part-time employment. The EU regulations on these issues had to be transposed by the NMS into their domestic legislation as part of the accession process. This is a clear example of coercive isomorphism and of a direct impact of EU requirements on domestic regulations. At the same time, the body of labour regulations is indeed not comprehensive and does not have a decisive impact upon most aspects of individual and collective labour relations or employment policy. For example, it has little or no impact on employment protection regulations, industrial relations and collective bargaining, wage regulations, labour market policies, and so on. Hence, no clear model is imposed on the NMS.

Also, contradicting a simplistic convergence thesis, the impact of EU regulations on national institutions varies because it is mediated by the varying degrees of compatibility between EU and national institutions as well as varying domestic responses to adaptive pressures (Martinsen, 2005). Moreover, the transposition of the *acquis communautaire* into domestic regulations may be symbolic rather than really affecting national practices (Jacoby, 2002). For example, the Czech Republic amended its Labour Code in 2000 to transpose a number of EU regulations, including providing the possibility to establish works councils, previously non-existent in the Czech Republic. However, the social democratic government was also keen not to see the rights and position of trades unions negatively affected in any way. Hence, the amendment was made in such a way that it would satisfy the EU accession criteria but would not have a strong effect on industrial relations in general or on the role of unions at the enterprise level. Following the amendment, works councils can be established only in undertakings where no trades unions are present; they have no collective bargaining powers and cannot call strikes; and they can exercise information and consultation rights only within the meaning of the EU directive. The works councils thus cannot replace trades unions or exercise their core functions. Clearly, the Czech version of works councils is aimed at satisfying the EU without changing national practice in any meaningful way.

To summarise, the hard *acquis* has had a limited impact on labour regulations because it covers only a limited number of labour aspects instead of imposing a model of some kind. Also, in the areas it does cover it does not necessarily lead to convergence in domestic practices.

As to the soft *acquis*, the key issue is the role of the European Employment Strategy (EES). The soft *acquis* is soft in that it does not aim to impose specific regulations; it is not soft in that it does require participation of the prospective member states in EES processes. The EES is based on the OMC procedure and comprises 'a voluntary adaptation of national policies by involvement in a multi-level process of benchmarking multilateral surveillance, peer review, exchanges of information, cooperation and consultation' (Schüttpelz, 2004, p 2). It leaves detailed policy decisions to national authorities and rather promotes a cognitive model, which aims to alter beliefs and expectations of national actors (Schüttpelz, 2004). The EES is not a comprehensive full-employment strategy; rather it emphasises supply-side problems in the labour market, aiming at increasing flexibility, employability and activation of the labour force, and argues that labour market problems originate largely in the individual characteristics of the unemployed or inactive (Watt, 2004).

For the NMS, the preparation for EU accession included the incorporation into the EES processes. The-then candidate countries started to 'shadow' the EES largely as of 1999. Most importantly, together with the European Commission, they started to elaborate their first joint assessment papers (JAPs) of employment policy priorities, signed for most NMS in 2000-01, and to evaluate implementation. As mentioned in the JAPs, they contain an 'agreed set of employment and labour market objectives necessary to advance the country's labour market transformation, to make progress in adapting the employment system so as to be able to implement the European Employment Strategy and to prepare for accession to the European Union'. The JAPs present an analysis of labour market problems as well as a long list of (often vaguely formulated) commitments and tasks for the future. The EES is also clearly reflected in the NMS employment policy. For example, the Polish National Strategy of Employment Growth and Human Resource Developments 2000-06 was modelled on the four pillars of the EES and owed much to the ideology of the strategy (Mailand, 2005), while Czech employment policy also was developed on the basis of EES principles (Schüttpelz, 2004). Indeed, the EES discourse, structure and objectives were adopted to a large extent in most NMS (Ferge and Juhász, 2004; Schüttpelz, 2004; Mailand, 2005). The EES was also used in the NMS to justify certain types of reform to labour legislation, in particular those aiming to increase labour market flexibility (for example, Keune, 2003). Moreover, the NMS had a clear interest in adopting the EES discourse since this was a requirement for membership and because funding criteria for the European Social Funds were aligned upon the EES priorities.

It is less clear, however, to what extent the EES has really influenced the content of employment policy. Because of the relatively recent incorporation of the NMS in the EES process, its real impact on policy is not yet easy to assess. Mailand (2005) suggests that in Poland the influence of the EES on policy content is much more limited than that on the way policy is framed and structured. Schüttpelz (2004), meanwhile, argues that, as in the EU15, there is a gap between strategic orientations and implementation. Finally, Ferge and Juhász (2004, p 242) show that although the successive Hungarian governments follow the EES discourse on the importance of giving precedence to active instead of passive labour market policies, the funds spent on active measures are quite limited.

This latter point is underscored by the data provided in Table 7.3. Although all NMS acknowledge the crucial importance of labour market policies, expenditure on such policies as a percentage of GDP remains very low and far below the average for the EU15. In Slovenia alone, such expenditure exceeds 1% of GDP, while in Estonia, Latvia and the Czech Republic it remains below the lowest level to be found in the EU15. More in line with the EU15 is that most NMS spend more on passive than on active labour market policies. Hence, in the short term, the participation of the NMS in the EES has had more impact on discourse than on policy. This may well change as time goes on, however.

Table 7.3: Expenditure on labour market policies in the NMS (2001)

	Expenditure on labour market policies (% GDP)	Passive (% total)	Active (% total)
Czech Republic	0.44	56.8	43.2
Estonia	0.18[a]	61.5	38.5
Hungary	0.85[b]	43.0	57.0
Latvia	0.36	78.1	21.9
Lithuania	0.64	41.0	59.0
Poland	0.96[c]	87.9[d]	12.1[d]
Slovakia	0.73	68.5	31.5
Slovenia	1.30	68.5	31.5
EU15	1.93	65.8	34.2
EU15 min–max	0.48–3.91	0.40–2.29	0.08–1.62

Notes: [a] = 2002; [b] = 2003; [c] = 2000; [d] = 2004.

Sources: Eurostat; Ministries of Labour; Eamets et al (2003)

Conclusions

This chapter set out to contribute to the clarification of the relationship between enlargement and the ESM through a discussion of welfare state reform and performance in the NMS. It has discussed this relationship from two different perspectives, corresponding to the two major ways of understanding the ESM: the historical *acquis* perspective and the political project perspective. From the first perspective it was concluded that the NMS are not sufficiently different from the EU15 to conclude that they do not fit the ESM, the main exception being the level of income. Also, their inclusion in the ESM would mean that both the empirical diversity as well as the social disparities covered by the ESM concept would increase.

From the second perspective, it was shown that, at the European level, no coherent ESM is in place and also that no comprehensive social model was imposed on the NMS during the accession process. Clearly, from the side of the EU, enlargement was more about economic than about social integration and convergence. This does not mean that no coercive isomorphism has taken place, but that it has been limited in scope, has been mediated by domestic factors and EU influence has for the moment been stronger on domestic discourses than on policy content.

From neither perspective does the ESM emerge as a particularly well-defined concept or model. From the historical *acquis* perspective, it can quite easily incorporate a group of eight countries with a rather different history because the diversity covered by the ESM is already very wide. From the political project perspective, it does not place any particularly great demands on new members. In other words, the ESM, viewed from either of the two perspectives examined, can incorporate a very wide spectrum of national-level diversity.

References

Baxandall, P. (2003) 'Postcommunist unemployment politics: historical legacies and the curious acceptance of job loss', in G. Ekiert and S. Hanson (eds) *Capitalism and democracy in Central and Eastern Europe: Assessing the legacy of communist rule*, Cambridge: Cambridge University Press, pp 248–88.

Cerami, A. (2005) 'Social policy in Central and Eastern Europe: The emergence of a new European model of solidarity?', PhD thesis, University of Erfurt, Germany.

Deacon, B. (2000) 'Eastern European welfare states: the impact of the politics of globalisation', *Journal of European Social Policy*, vol 10, no 2, pp 146-61.

Diamantopoulou, A. (2001) 'The European Employment Strategy and Social Model', speech delivered in Warsaw, 29 January, available at http://europa.eu.int/comm/employment_social/speeches/2001/010129ad.pdf

DiMaggio, P. and Powell, W. (1983) 'The iron cage revisited: institutional isomorphism and collective rationality in organizational fields', *American Sociological Review*, vol 48, no 2, pp 147-60.

Esping-Andersen, G. (1990) *The three worlds of welfare capitalism*, Princeton, NJ: Princeton University Press.

European Commission (2003) *Social protection in the 13 candidate countries: A comparative analysis*, Luxembourg: Office for Official Publications of the European Communities.

European Commission (2004) *The social situation in the European Union 2004*, Luxembourg: Office for Official Publications of the European Communities.

Ferge, Z. and Juhász, G. (2004) 'Accession and social policy: the case of Hungary', *Journal of European Social Policy*, vol 14, no 3, pp 233-51.

Ferrera, M. (1996) 'The southern model of welfare in Social Europe', *Journal of European Social Policy*, vol 6, no 1, pp 17-37.

Fultz, E. (2002) 'A comparative overview of disability pension reform in the Czech Republic, Estonia and Poland', in E. Fultz and M. Ruck (eds) *Reforming worker protections: Disability pensions in transformation*, Budapest: International Labour Office.

Fultz, E. (2003) 'Recent trends in pension reform and implementation in the EU accession countries', Paper presented at the International Labour Conference, Geneva, 10 June.

Fultz, E. and Ruck, M. (2001) 'Pension reform in Central and Eastern Europe: emerging issues and patterns', *International Labour Review*, vol 140, no 1, pp 19-43.

Guardiancich, I. (2004) 'Welfare state retrenchment in Central and Eastern Europe: the case of pension reforms in Poland and Slovenia', *Managing Global Transitions*, vol 2, no 1, pp 41-64.

Hemerijck, A., Keune, M. and Rhodes, M. (2006: forthcoming) 'European welfare states: diversity, challenges and reforms', in P. Heywood, E. Jones, M. Rhodes and U. Sedelmeier (eds) *Developments in European politics*, Basingstoke, Hampshire: Macmillan/Palgrave.

Hungarian Ministry of Health, Social and Family Affairs (2004) *Health and social services in Hungary: 2004 – year of changes*, Budapest, available at www.eszcsm.hu

Jacoby, W. (2002) 'Talking the talk and walking the walk: the cultural and institutional effects of western models', in F. Bönker, K. Müller and A. Pickel (eds) *Postcommunist transformation and the social sciences: Cross-disciplinary approaches*, Lanham: Rowan and Littlefield Publishers, pp 129-52.

Keune, M. (2003) 'Capitalist divergence and labour market flexibility in the Czech Republic and Hungary: a comparative analysis of standard and non-standard employment', *Czech Sociological Review*, vol 39, no 6, pp 607-24.

Kittel, B. (2002) *EMU, EU Enlargement, and the European Social Model: trends, challenges and questions*, MPIfG Working Paper 02/1, February, Cologne: Max-Planck Institut für Gessellschaftforschung.

Kornai, J. (1992) *The socialist system: The political economy of communism*, Oxford: Oxford University Press.

Lendvai, N. (2004) 'The weakest link? EU accession and enlargement: dialoguing EU and post-communist social policy', *Journal of European Social Policy*, vol 14, no 3, pp 319-33.

Mácha, M. (2002) 'The political economy of pension reform in the Czech Republic', in E. Fultz (ed) *Pension reform in Central and Eastern Europe vol 2: Restructuring of public pension schemes: Case studies of the Czech Republic and Slovenia*, Budapest: International Labour Office, pp 75-112.

Mailand, M. (2005) *Implementing the revised European Employment Strategy – North, South, East and West*, Working Paper, Copenhagen: FAOS.

Martinsen, D. (2005) 'The Europeanisation of welfare – the domestic impact of intra-European social security', *Journal of Common Market Studies*, vol 43, no 5, pp 1003-30.

Müller, K. (2002) 'Pension reform paths in Central-Eastern Europe and the former Soviet Union', *Social Policy and Administration*, vol 36, no 2, pp 725-48.

Müller, K. (2003) 'The making of pension privatization in Latin America and Eastern Europe', in R. Holzman, M. Orenstein and M. Rutowski (eds) *Pension reform in Europe: Process and progress*, Washington, DC: World Bank, pp 47-78.

Nesporova, A. (1999) *Employment and labour market policies in transition economies*, Geneva: International Labour Office.

Orenstein, M. (1998) 'A genealogy of Communist successor parties in East-Central Europe and the determinants of their success', *East European Politics and Society*, vol 12, pp 472-99.

Potůček, M. (2004) 'Accession and social policy: the case of the Czech Republic', *Journal of European Social Policy*, vol 14, no 3, pp 253-66.

Róna-Tas, Á. (1997) *The great surprise of the small transformation: The demise of communism and the rise of the private sector in Hungary*, Ann Arbor, MI: University of Michigan Press.

Scharpf, F. (1997) 'Economic integration, democracy and the welfare state', *Journal of European Public Policy*, vol 4, no 1, pp 18-36.

Schüttpelz, A. (2004) *Policy transfer and pre-accession Europeanization of the Czech employment policy*, Discussion Paper SP III 2004-2001, Berlin: WZB.

Stanovnik, T. (2002) 'The political economy of pension reform in Slovenia', in E. Fultz (ed) *Pension reform in Central and Eastern Europe, vol 2: Restructuring of public pension schemes: Case studies of the Czech Republic and Slovenia*, Budapest: International Labour Office.

UNICEF (United Nations Children's Fund) (2004) *UNICEF innocenti social monitor 2004*, Florence: UNICEF.

Vaughan-Whitehead, D. (2000) 'Social dialogue in EU enlargement: acquis and responsibilities', *Transfer: European Review of Labour and Research*, vol 6, no 3, pp 387-98.

Vaughan-Whitehead, D. (2003) *EU enlargement versus Social Europe? The uncertain future of the European social mode*, Cheltenham: Edward Elgar.

Watt, A. (2004) 'Reform of the European Employment Strategy after five years: a change of course or merely of presentation?', *European Journal of Industrial Relations*, vol 10, no 2, pp 117-37.

World Bank (1994) *Averting the old age crisis*, Washington, DC: World Bank.

EIGHT

Reforming the European Social Model and the politics of indicators: from the unemployment rate to the employment rate in the European Employment Strategy[1]

Robert Salais

Introduction

The Open Method of Coordination (OMC) was introduced for the purpose of monitoring the 'modernisation' of the European Social Model (ESM) from a hypothetical 'centre' towards greater flexibility, better economic efficiency and lower costs. What verdict can be issued concerning the OMC, in the context of reform of the ESM? This chapter will focus on the European Employment Strategy (EES) as an exemplar of what could be called 'a politics of indicators', by which is meant the specific type of political action and monitoring introduced by the OMC.

Under the EES the benchmarking of national employment policies, by means of a set of indicators, plays a key role. In benchmarking management techniques, identifying good practices is the precondition for finding ways of applying them (Tronti, 2001). The performance gaps between firms have to be measured in a consistent and reliable manner and properly correlated with the objectives of the firm. They must be clearly attributable to the causes, that is, the good practices. It is at this decisive point that the indicators appear on the scene. While, in the case of a firm, it is fairly easy to agree on objectives (profit, growth, cost reduction, share value, productivity, and so on), on how they are to be quantified, and on some of their interrelationships, this is much more difficult for public policies, the purposes of which are extremely varied and, in some cases, mutually contradictory. It is often quite impossible to disentangle the complex web of interactions existing between quantitative performance and the identification of good practices. In any case, political deliberation is needed for agreement – or minimum compromise – to be reached on the values and standards on the basis of which public decisions are to be taken. It is precisely from such political deliberation that the OMC is seeking to take its distance.

The general line of argument that will be followed here is that there exist, empirically and politically, so many obstacles to the effective and efficient use of this method within the EES that benchmarking ultimately boils down to little more than scoring. Member states are simply ranked by performance on a series of quantitative indicators, with the worst performers then being urged to do better. The way thus lies open for the degeneration of the method into a game in which member states and the European Commission implicitly collude with one another. The purpose of the game relates to the statistical yield (or return) of the national employment policies, assessed from the standpoint of the selected indicators. However, such degeneration is likely to have very real consequences for the ways of conceiving the functioning of labour markets and the reform of social policies in Europe. Far from any effort to eradicate unemployment (as might seem to be implied by the policy orientation in favour of higher employment rates), there is encouragement for public policies in Europe to make optimal use of it for economic purposes (namely price and wage stability).

In section two, the author examines the selection bias of action variables made by the table of European indicators, with regard to their most important issues: employment and employability. Section three offers a reminder that the origins of the EES and the OMC are to be found in the national labour markets' need for flexibility, as required by the European economic and monetary authorities. Section four stresses the risk that the EES could well degenerate into a rational game in which statistical improvement of indicators would no longer be linked with any real improvement in employability or in the operation of labour markets. Section five concludes on the possible emergence on a European scenario by which unemployment would be subject to a process of pure 'fabrication'. The worries are that such a process can achieve neither flexibility nor employment growth.

The 'anomalies' in the benchmarking of employment policies

Under the EES, benchmarking by means of indicators is carried out in two ways, respectively labelled as performance indicators and key indicators[2] (see Table 8.1 in the Appendix to this chapter). There are several anomalies that need to be pointed out.

Characteristics of the table of indicators

The main performance indicators (which appear at the top of the EES list) are the employment rates. These are gross targets, covering all types of job and, in particular, they are *not* calculated in full-time equivalents. Any kind of task counts, regardless of length, number of hours worked per week, status, or any other aspect – in a word, quality! – on the sole condition that it is regarded as a 'job' by the national or European statistical source in question. Although a part-time equivalent rate is now used for the working-age population aged 15 to 64[3], the annual reports on the EES continue to pay political attention to the gross employment rate alone.

The data used for the performance indicators come, for the most part, from Eurostat. They are known as 'harmonised' data. The national sources have been designed, either upstream in devising the questionnaire, or downstream in the statistical processing procedures, to supply figures that fit the categories and accounting frameworks defined at the European level. Beyond harmonisation, notwithstanding the naive positivism displayed by so many users of figures, institutional and instrumental formatting of this data at the national level remains considerable and distorts comparability at the European level. In relation to employment contracts, for example, national legislations differ and countries where labour law is rather loose and minimalist are at an advantage in employment rate scoring insofar as any task at all can be counted as a job. Similarly, inequalities in education and vocational training and the various forms taken by it – whether, for example, training takes place outside or within the company – call into question the pertinence of the category 'young persons aged 15 to 24'. The employment rate of 'young persons aged 15 to 24' is statistically low for those countries which have longstanding investment in training of their workforces (whose access to the labour market is accordingly delayed).[4] Are these countries going to be required to reduce their commitment to education, when the priority objective of the Lisbon Strategy is precisely to develop a knowledge economy? These examples, while to some extent caricatures, are nonetheless symptomatic of the internal contradictions and the way distortions are generated under the OMC as it is currently applied, which will be examined in section four.

For the key indicators, the results are supplied by the member states in their National Action Plan on Employment (NAPE). From three standpoints – prevention, activation and return to employment – indicators are designed to evaluate the effectiveness of the NAPE in terms of what offers (and how soon after the beginning of the unemployment period) are made to unemployed persons to improve their employability; what degree of participation in employment policy schemes takes place; what returns to employment have been made. No serious control is undertaken by the Commission to ensure reliability of national data.

All these data remain beset by a range of problems, both statistical and theoretical.

No definition of 'job' or 'unemployed person'

On the definitions and computations for either a 'job' or an 'unemployed person' depend the estimate of employment and unemployment rates and the extent to which the national figures may be legitimately interpreted and compared. Two problems remain unaddressed:

• Administrative categories concerning what constitutes a job search or an unemployed person in receipt of benefit differ from one country to another. The data on job search are closely dependent on the particular rules of registration, administration and deletion from the records applied by the employment agencies; moreover, the data relate to an individual period of search and not to the jobseeker. Data on unemployed persons in receipt of benefit depend on the rules applicable under the unemployment benefit systems (eligibility, duration and level of benefit, reasons for its withdrawal). All these rules are at the discretion of the governments (in some cases the social partners). Changes made to them do not only affect the terms of assistance but also have a direct impact on the statistics concerning jobseekers and beneficiaries, as well as their composition. Not only is comparability not guaranteed but there may be inbuilt bias. For example, if the counter for the period of unemployment registration is switched back to zero when a jobseeker returns to the agency after a short-term placement or contract, the period of unemployment and hence the long-term unemployment statistics are artificially reduced, the effect of which is far from marginal. Who, in Europe, is aware that in France the monthly statistics on jobseekers (a figure that has a major political impact) include 'reduced-activity' jobseekers? These are jobseekers working less than 78 hours a month and their inclusion raises the average duration of unemployment.

• Depending on the definition of a job and, especially, of its *quality*, the employment rate, and hence the evaluation of performance, may vary significantly. Depending, for example, on whether or not the rate is corrected for the varying incidence of part-time work, levels and scoring will change. For example, correcting for part-time work reduces the female employment rate in the UK from 65.1% to 50.2% in 2001; the corresponding fall in France is from 56.1% to 50%. On the basis of these corrected figures, the performance of the two countries becomes comparable and France moves up from 10th to 7th position. A further conclusion may be that women's employment is on average of rather better quality in France than in Britain. Similarly, assessment of the effectiveness of activation could drop sharply if criteria concerning the quality of return to employment were introduced (for example, length and type of contract, or wage compared to previous wage).

No evaluation of the effectiveness of the national employment policies

Measurement of effort takes place by counting the number of unemployed persons who began (and thus who were offered) an 'individual action plan' before they had been unemployed for six months (young persons) or for 12 months (adults). The activation rate is measured by counting the number of participants in 'training measures or similar' previously registered as unemployed. But there is no examination of the effectiveness of the measures with regard to the future of the beneficiaries in the labour market. Nor is any definition of an action plan, or of what constitutes 'training measures or similar', recommended by the European Commission. Yet the content of the plans and the nature of these measures – especially the extent to which they are appropriate to the jobseekers' situation and capabilities – significantly influence their return to work and the quality and duration of employment.

The overall problem is the strategic bias in the decisions of the Commission. This bias is exacerbated by the weakness of the

Commission's position in seeking to build a presence (*dixit* Teague, 2001) in a field where its competences are barely enshrined in law and hence open to question. The strategic advantage of the procedure takes precedence over a debate on norms and values that, under different circumstances, would be considered indispensable. It eliminates in advance from the EES what constitutes the essence of a public policy, namely the obligation to justify its means (instrumental) in the light of its ends (normative). Any technical decision (especially that relative to indicators) is full of normative consequences that ought to be debated and explicitly taken on board. Yet it obeys considerations of what appears strategically opportune, for example the need to obtain the agreement of a certain country under specific current circumstances. Outcomes are not neutral from this standpoint. What, for example, can be the meaning of an employment rate that is measured without regard for the quality of the jobs that it covers? Differing standard models are in this way implicitly placed in (unequal) competition, according to indicators that in fact favour specific models and, above all, the liberal market model. At the same time, member states are given a free hand to draw up national replies according to their own views and preferences, provided the outcome is that best suited to the accounting expectations of the Commission.

A selective and biased presentation of the labour market and employment: towards a market model approach

As shown in Figure 8.1, there are two aspects in labour market dynamics: employability (returning to employment) and vulnerability (losing a job and falling into unemployment). According to the conception of the labour market validated by the European indicators, the return-to-employment rate is acquiring target status in connection with policies specifically designed to enhance individual employability. The vulnerability to unemployment experienced by those currently in work is the subject of none of the indicators. Yet analysis of probability differentials in falling into unemployment has been a pillar of labour economics since 1970. This is an essential complement for understanding labour market dynamics. The 'employability' part ('half' of the labour market) alone is covered by the list of indicators. The 'vulnerability' aspect is missing from the EES.

Insofar as employment is of relevance to economic and monetary policy, the EES is geared to the optimum operation of the labour market, leading to a special conception of 'prevention'. It is supposed that the prevention of unemployment becomes an issue only once the

Figure 8.1: A dynamic modelling of the labour market

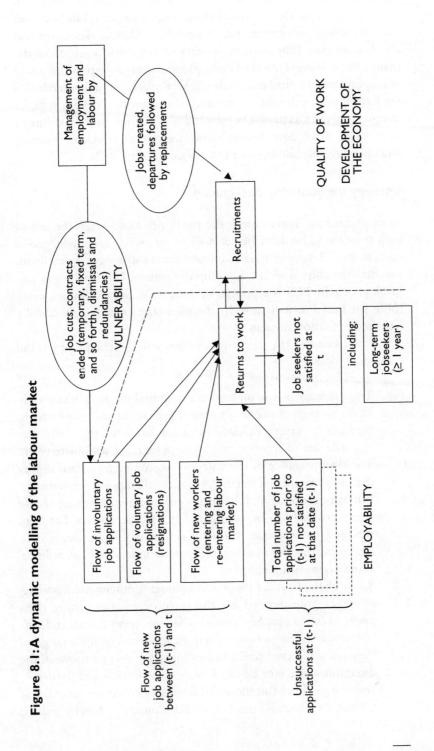

individuals have arrived on the labour market. The dynamics of employment and its determinants (number of jobs, job and staff management by firms: recruitment, mobility, redundancies, dismissals) are thus missing. Employment policies so conceived exclude all the many efforts at prevention of unemployment made within the world of employment. Be they undertaken at workplace, sectoral or territorial level, these efforts should be encouraged by Europe. They include, for instance: changes to products, jobs and organisation in the workplace in order to reach new demands and markets; in-company training; and collective bargaining on modernisation of workplaces.

Unveiling the normative background

In short, far from representing the pursuit of knowledge, the use of indicators has to be described as politics, albeit not acknowledged as such. Indeed, it is presented in a technical and ostensibly neutral form. But this neutrality does not stand up to scrutiny. This is why one can speak about the EES as a 'politics of indicators'. Such a politics leaves room for instrumentalisation by member states through specifically designed activation measures.

The argument in the next two sections will be structured around two conclusions:

(1) The category of 'unemployment' acquired meaning historically in the shaping of full-employment policies by means of which, through a variety of devices, states took on the collective responsibility of ensuring employment for those wishing to work. The disappearance of this category would by no means signify the disappearance of unemployment and employment statistics. But, via economic and monetary policy, unemployment would come gradually to be considered as a matter of fact. Far from working to eradicate it, public action would be devoted to exploiting this fact in a threefold – economic, social and political – and coordinated effort.

(2) Through the OMC, Europe is encouraging employment policies to be ex ante devised for the purpose of maximising their performance scores. Such policies become instrumental and self-referential in the pursuit of statistical returns along a range of indicators. Do they really, in this form, represent a move in the direction wished for by the European economic and monetary authorities, that of an increased flexibility of the labour market? Or do they merely 'smash the thermometer', thereby risking

causing bias in the informational basis on which these authorities seek to found their policy?

The employment rate or the search for labour market flexibility

Since the Lisbon Summit (22-24 March 2000), maximising the employment rate has become a key European policy target.

Is the employment rate a good economic policy choice?

Other things being equal, a high employment rate seems good for society because it enables integration into employment of a larger proportion of the working-age population and represents a move in the direction of reducing unemployment. The argument becomes even more acceptable if accompanied by a rhetoric of 'better employment'. By widening the tax and social security contribution base, a high level of employment offers a virtuous route to the reduction of public and social deficits. But there exist simple economic counter-arguments to this apparent common sense. First, if the increase in participation in employment is accompanied by a correlative increase in contract terminations leading to unemployment (for instance, increasing short-term contracts, hence precariousness), then, under given conditions of registration and declaration, the unemployment rate will not diminish in spite of the rise in the employment rate. Second, jobs must be financially profitable, that is to say, they must bring in more in terms of taxes and social security contributions than they cost in terms of subsidies and reduced contributions. They must therefore produce enough added value and hence be of a certain minimum quality in productivity terms. Otherwise, assuming constant conditions of contribution, eligibility and benefit, the increase in the employment rate will be accompanied by continuing deficits. A cost-benefit analysis of the employment policy measures would presumably not be in favour of creating low-quality jobs, with low added value.

Furthermore, using a dynamic modelling of the labour market,[5] Figure 8.1 shows that employability is more a consequence of macroeconomic imbalance on the labour market than a policy action variable. The employment sphere constantly feeds the market with flows of new jobseekers, especially those who, because of their condition or their situation, have turned out to be the most vulnerable to employment fluctuations. It also controls the extent of returns to employment by means of the volume and the quality of recruitments, which are, in turn, the result of new job creation and vacancies arising in existing posts. The stock of jobseekers is thus constantly increased by the flows of new arrivals and reduced by the exit of unemployed workers who have found employment (or fallen prey to discouragement). Over time there will be an effect of accumulation (or absorption). If the employment level stagnates or falls (due to job cuts, for example, as a result of restructuring; or little job creation), the number of arrivals on the labour market will be, each month, higher than the number of exits. The stock increases and the average duration of unemployment rises. This affects employability, which will tend to deteriorate. Whatever their competences, each unemployed person will take longer to find a new job, which will frequently be a worse-quality job than the previous one. There are, quite simply, more candidates for fewer jobs so that selection inevitably becomes more stringent. By improving information and job-search facilities, it may be possible somewhat to reduce the average time spent on the job market, but creating good jobs would have even greater impact.

Thus, it would be economically efficient to supplement the employment rate with indicators relative to the employment sphere (job quality and security, for example). However, the European authorities are promoting only the employment rate and employability. They interpret these variables within the – very different – theoretical and practical framework put in place in monetary and macroeconomic policies. Here lies the real change of structural standpoint, which accompanies the transition from unemployment rate to employment rate as the key economic policy indicator.

The European macroeconomic action framework and the NAIRU

Current European economic policy has been much criticised, because of the excessive limits it sets on the member states' budgetary policies. It is considered that it prohibits any economic recovery, imposes a state of chronic unemployment and, overall, excessively weak growth. While not without relevance, such criticisms omit to consider that, for the European Central Bank (ECB) and the Council of Ministers for Economic and Financial Affairs (EcoFin), unemployment remains an important target. These authorities are simply devising and putting in place a decision-taking model in broad agreement with the ideas of Milton Friedman, the famous monetarist economist.

In this model, below a certain rate of unemployment (the so-called 'natural unemployment rate' or its abbreviated variant, the NAIRU), any increase in the money supply translates exclusively into inflation.

The NAIRU is thus the unemployment rate that is compatible with an absence of inflationary pressure in the short term. A gap is, however, to be observed between the real Gross Domestic Product (GDP) and the potential GDP that *could be achieved in the absence of inflationary pressure*. Maximising the employment rate means reducing the output gap, that is, succeeding in creating jobs to make up the difference between the actual unemployment rate and the NAIRU, while respecting price stability. This should be achieved, first, by adequate monetary policy, and second, by making the labour market more flexible (in European language, developing 'employment-friendly' regulations).

In effect, maximising employment under the constraint of price stability will be achieved all the more rapidly if employment and unemployment react promptly (through job cuts or recruitments) to cyclical fluctuations in the economy. For example, if, in the event of an economic upturn, employment and unemployment make a rapid adjustment, the increase in growth will be greater. The reasoning is short term but the intended result is medium term. Let us consider a 100 metre race. The athlete who 'steals' the start has good chances of retaining an advantage at the end of the race, and even of gradually increasing it. But perhaps the economy is a long-distance race in which long-term concerns should be uppermost?

The need for flexibility and the OMC

In any case, the need for flexibility is, as a result, the *true foundation of the OMC*. The single currency and the convergence process have deprived the member states of two of the three levers that formerly enabled adjustment to external shocks: the exchange rate and, by and large, budgetary policy. This leaves adjustment by means of market mechanisms. However, for the ECB, labour markets being mostly national, adjustment to shocks cannot be directly effected on the European scale but must be achieved via a coordination of national-level adjustments. For this task, the main remaining instrument is the flexibility of national labour markets. National political initiatives to make these markets flexible are of the utmost importance (Hodson and Maher, 2001), for only the member states have sufficient knowledge and understanding of their labour markets; only they, accordingly, are in a position to devise the most appropriate policy to be followed.

In this economic framework, the EES is expected to encourage national adjustments, in other words to constitute above all a coordinated approach to making national labour markets more flexible.

It has to take charge of what the monetary policies cannot handle, namely, *the structural reduction of the NAIRU*. The stakes are far from negligible, for the estimated NAIRU is much higher in Europe than in the United States (US). Refocusing the operation of labour markets on improving individual employability is seen as facilitating adjustments of labour supply to job offers. The limitations of this model will be developed in section four.

In such a politics, the category 'unemployment' is losing its status as the goal of full-employment policies. Activation deprives the 'unemployment' category of support. Insofar as every supposedly employable person, although they may frequently pass through the labour market, spends very little time there, no serious foundation remains for the payment of passive benefits. The job search becomes a private matter to be handled as a question of individual freedom and responsibility. Meanwhile, unemployment becomes functional for the purpose of promoting growth (price and wage stability). Far from striving to eradicate it, public action should be devoted to deriving optimum benefit from it. It is therefore perfectly honest to speak, as the European Constitution[6] almost invariably does, not of 'full employment' but of 'a high level of employment'.

The instrumental drift of the EES

In general, political science takes the EES as if it were a purely political procedure, with virtual disregard for other factors. Most of the studies have focused on the wide range of actors for whose involvement the European texts contain provision and on the procedures laid down to organise their complex interactions; this is the famous 'multi-level governance'[7], the rules and foundations of which are described in the closest detail. As actors are assumed to be rational and involved in a strategic interplay of transactions, public policy is mostly conceived of, in such approaches, as no more than regulation designed to prevent opportunist behaviour. The actual content of the actions and their (in a broad sense) material outcomes become of little concern to public authorities and, thus, research. As opposed to such biases, discourses and arguments are to be benchmarked against practices and their outcomes. Empirical observation of what actually goes on within the processes, committees and various bodies has to be undertaken.

A set of unmet conditions

A further danger is to assume that the hypotheses underlying the principle of the OMC are necessarily sound. Yet these hypotheses, on which its effectiveness – and, in turn, that of the EES – depend, are far from self-evident. They consist of mutual learning, the creation of knowledge through exchange of experience ('good practice') and the possibility of substantially correcting, in accordance with the results of the benchmarking, the national and European policies conducted.

What emerges from a number of studies is a tremendous paradox: to be effective the OMC would require a set of conditions by which this method *in fact declines to be bound*:

- The Commission would need to be strong in political and operational terms in order to further its objectives. Yet it is in fact weak in both respects. Since the competences of the member states must be respected, the process rests on their goodwill and would require a greater degree of commitment than the ordinary process of national implementation of directives and regulations (according to Jacobsson, 2001, quoted in de la Porte and Pochet, 2002). The European Union has at its disposal no dissuasive instrument of the type necessary, such as the granting of subsidies or issuing of credible threats (Teague, 2001). The Commission is in possession of far less information than the member states (Teague, 2001), an asymmetry all the more prejudicial in that the Commission does little to remedy it.
- In order to promote collective learning, the process should be transparent and reflective (Zeitlin, 2002, 2005). Yet it is for the most part opaque and confined to a limited sphere of experts lacking any real democratic mandate. Committees interact with one another and demarcation and exercise of responsibilities are imprecise. The agendas of the Cambridge Process meetings (peer review) of the EES are too overcrowded to allow in-depth discussion. 'The problem is that the Council merely endorses the committees' conclusions, so it is at this level that the essential work takes place. During the Council ministers confine themselves to formal and high-flown speeches on the importance of employment and the need to combat difficulties attributable to economic cycles. It is a recording studio'.[8]

The reversal of the order of priorities – strategic, technical, political – from what should be the case (the political should influence the technical decision and this should be implemented by an appropriate strategy) systematically encourages actors to select options in a purely instrumental manner.[9]

The EES builds on national instrumental employment policies

The EES was launched in the context of a political opportunity that arose in 1997 to kill two birds with one stone: on the one hand, to show public opinion that, in the face of a high level of unemployment, the member states were not contemplating the situation idly; on the other hand, to move in the direction of a strategy of labour market flexibility. The former objective aided digestion of the latter, which, at bottom, was the more important. But there had been some underestimation of the impact that would be exerted on its development by the fact that the member states had not waited for Europe in order to exploit employment policies for their own purposes. They had themselves embarked on this path long before – with the beginnings of mass unemployment in the 1970s. The member states adjusted to the EES in such a way that they could continue with these policies by fine-tuning them (and, if possible, so as to have at their disposal new arguments and means).

These policies have been guided by two objectives, namely, to alleviate the plight of persons affected by unemployment and to influence the political indicator constituted by the unemployment statistics. Halfway houses (the so-called transitions) have been created between traditional standardised positions shown in Figure 7.1. Between 'return to employment' and 'recruitment', various schemes have been inserted, such as different kinds of traineeship or assisted contract or forms of recruitment requiring derogation from labour law. Between 'return to employment' and 'chronic long-term unemployment' a range of schemes have been intercalated to provide help such as access to the labour market or specific social welfare. Efforts have also been made to slow down, by means of early retirement systems, the inflows into unemployment resulting from mass redundancies. Social funds and public money not originally intended for this purpose have been diverted and channelled in this direction. All these schemes (assisted contracts, traineeships, dispensation from contributions in the case of recruitment of unemployed or young workers), as well as a series of reforms of employment agencies (tighter controls and shorter periods of eligibility), or the tightening of conditions of eligibility, systems of early retirement, changes in definition of the barometer (in France there are now eight different categories of jobseeker), and so on, have been used in most European countries not for this purpose alone, but always with the motive to optimise the statistical yield of the employment policies. Though some of the beneficiaries of such schemes are able to return to (mostly short-term) employment, the main objective was to reduce the number of people registered as unemployed.

In the case of France (but the same could said of other countries[10]), Benarrosh (2000) and Martinon (2002) reveal to what extent the merging of these two objectives – assistance for jobseekers and statistical return – is apparent in the daily operation of the local employment agencies. Applicants attending a local agency are assessed with regard to their likely employability. At the lowest level (lack of autonomy, no improvement possible), applicants are not registered as jobseekers. At upper levels, every applicant still on the books after six months is offered an employment policy scheme. Within a national quota set by budgetary constraints, the number and distribution of benefits and schemes offered are linked to objectives fixed for each individual agency. As a consequence, the range and quality of schemes offered to applicants are targeted according to an employability scale. The most employable people benefit from schemes that individually cost little and can lead to cumulative results; less employable ones from schemes that are much more costly (because of the distance to be covered before employment becomes likely) and, thus, offered to a much smaller number of persons. So the outcome will be mostly to reproduce the hierarchy of individuals in accordance with their employability, without any substantial improvement (Aucouturier, 1993, 1998). Whatever the – frequently considerable – competence and involvement of the staff who counsel the applicants, the organisation exerts material pressure on them to observe the recruitment selection criteria and to sort the applicants according to an employability standard.

If employability is taken as a selection criterion ex ante, it is pointless to expect an average increase in employability at the end of the schemes, other than by exclusion of the least employable. It is accordingly not surprising that evaluation of the effect of the employment policy measures is generally rather inconclusive. The longitudinal studies that are available on what becomes of the unemployed[11] describe their difficulty in finding new jobs equivalent, in terms of stability, security and pay, to the ones lost. The arrival in the queue of new applicants exacerbates competition and drags down the recruitment conditions of those who have been in the queue for some time. Accordingly, the emphasis placed by the EES on assisting applicants immediately they arrive in the queue is actually likely, at best, for any given number of available jobs, to improve the stakes in favour of those newly arrived in the agencies and to create increased inequality to the detriment of those who have been unemployed for longer.[12] In its five-year evaluation (1997-2002) the Commission has not succeeded in determining the impact of the EES taken alone on the major economic variables, like the number of jobs created or the reduction in unemployment.[13]

Improving the score is different from improving the true situation

Improving the score should not be confused with true improvement in the corresponding employment situation. Traineeships or temporary jobs in the public sector take the beneficiaries out of the jobseeker statistics (better score on the corresponding indicators) but does not necessarily improve their future employability on the scheme's termination (the actual substantive goal). The obligation – as in the British New Deal – to accept one of the offers made removes those who refuse from statistics (sometimes they prefer to remove themselves by no longer turning up to sign on at the local agency). But will these individuals become any more employable as a result? If, as rather often happens, the active measure selected fails as a step towards a proper job, the beneficiary returning to register is regarded as a new jobseeker. The 'percentage of long-term unemployment' indicator undergoes 'mechanical' improvement without any actual change in the reality of long-term unemployment. As a first step, the Indicator Group (EMCO, 2004) has recommended that short breaks (less than one month) between two unemployment spells have to be cancelled for computing the number of long-term unemployed people. But several member states lack technical tools for implementing this recommendation. For the Commission, it would be better to have free and full access to the internal rules through which the member states manage their employment (and other) agencies or design their measures, which is far from being the case.

The type of behaviour described above would be encountered, were one to embark on a systematic search for it.[14] It is not a question of deliberate cynicism or cheating. The concern is much more serious, for it relates to models for action that have been incorporated into rules and organisations. That decision-makers and government departments do seek genuine remedies is not in question or diminished. They are simply in the position of having to try their best to reconcile incompatible demands: to achieve real improvements in the situation; to remain within a set budget; to demonstrate quantitatively favourable results, which affect the benchmarking and granting of future funding.

The EES as a proxy of a rational cooperative game

How are these limits, constraints and specific features of the EES to be explained? Quite simply by considering that it operates as if it was a cooperative game among rational actors. The point is that benchmarking by means of these indicators serves to *politically monitor* the EES and not to *economically evaluate* its outcomes.

Such a game would sound like this. Its mechanism is familiar to economic theory. Take the Commission and the member states as the players. The aim of the game is to maximise the key indicators, those intended to evaluate the policies being followed. Actors know in advance the formatting of future evaluation of their actions. Insofar as any learning outcome takes place, it is of a rational order and likely to affect the procedure. Cooperation consists, for each member state, of manipulating the rules of its own measures and their implementation to meet the requirements of European indicators. It is not a collective action aimed at genuinely improving employment in Europe. Due to the limited competences given to the European level, member states are not held responsible for a substantial improvement in European employment, nor do they feel themselves accountable to such improvement when they define their employment policy actions and coordinate with the others in the EES framework. The only constraint is that they have agreed – and this commitment derives from the management by objectives of the OMC – to be accountable vis-à-vis the Commission with regard to their scores over the whole set of indicators.

All the EES actors (the Commission included) have – albeit for differing reasons – a political interest in arguing and publicly declaring that the EES is a valuable European achievement. Each party behaves in a manner designed to exhibit measurable progress. The behaviour in question has to be described to others ('exchange of good practice') and made public (this being the purpose of the annual Joint Employment Report).

Some conditions are required for the game to be played at all and this largely accords with what can be observed. The member states display their willingness to play this game, albeit in measured doses in order to avoid any irreversible commitment. But, should disagreement arise, this willingness stops at the point where the Commission pressures would imply moving beyond procedural cooperation. The number of genuinely active players remains limited, for to publicise the rules is to place the smooth functioning of the game in jeopardy. The Commission, for its part, neither interferes in the choice of policies nor checks up on the scores reported for the key indicators, except in cases of excessive abuse. At first glance, it seems that the recommendations issued by the Commission to badly rated countries could have a binding aspect. However, as it is natural that some countries will be better at the game than others, these recommendations can act as no more than a reminder to potentially recalcitrant member states – as well as any that may be experiencing difficulties – of the rules of the game.

Playing that game is far from pointless. A community of thought is formed within the realms of senior civil servants meetings in Brussels. The member states thereby gain new arguments or European backing to strengthen their own arguments and this facilitates the taking of unpopular decisions that they believe or know to be inevitable. The results are not necessarily negative, for in some cases the national agencies concerned do provide a better service to their users. For instance, in France, the EES has constituted a turning point, according to its management, in the life of the *Agence Nationale pour l'Emploi* (ANPE – national employment agency)[15] whose services have been improved. It has obtained additional resources in terms of both funding and manpower, in part from the European Social Fund (ESF) and in part from the state budget. Counsellors spend an average of half an hour rather than 20 minutes with each jobseeker. But this improvement merely emphasises the tension between two conceptions of individualised monitoring. Does it mean compelling the individual to acknowledge his/her responsibility to accept a job adapted to his/her 'employability' (instrumental logic). Or are the jobseekers to be enabled to use the facilities and resources in order to really increase their employability (genuinely personal logic)?

To adopt a different approach would also be to enter a risk zone for the survival of the EES. For it would be a question of evaluating to what extent the employability of beneficiaries has *genuinely* improved as a result of the EES. Such evaluation would not be politically beneficial, for the initial results could be rather discouraging. It would be necessary, in particular, to look at what becomes of the beneficiaries of active measures in terms of their incorporation into employment, the types of job found and their quality, and the progress of their competences by means of representative panels. It would require also that the member states agree to supply detailed accounts of all stages in the process of production of statistics on the labour market, jobseekers and the management of agencies and employment measures. This is a complex chain, which, starting with the registration of claimants, includes the monitoring of progress, signing off, and possible re-

registration at a later date. It includes also the ways in which individual registrations are aggregated to form national statistics (coding, nomenclatures, and so on). It concludes with the translation of national data into operational European indicators. The devil is in the details.

If progress is to be observed in the evolution of the indicators, is this anything other than an artefact produced by a satisfactory performance in the game being played between the member states and the Commission? The problem is that such artificial effects require, to be significant and above all lasting, a costly and inefficient increase in public expenditure, given the need to provide ever increasing numbers of places in which the unemployed can be temporarily accommodated.

The European political process and the future of the ESM

The most likely medium–term scenario is of an uncontrolled drift towards implementing, for politically instrumental purposes, market rules in a social universe to which they are quite alien. One would have the fiction of the market, without the actual conditions of it, a scenario hardly favourable to growth and employment. As information had been framed to serve political ends, it would be of no help, insofar as it would forfeit its economic and social relevance.[16]

The irony of this prospect is that it is precisely the preference given to the employment rate as key policy variable that would foster it. The policies of the ECB, EcoFin and the EES are built on theoretical models, which might not be the most appropriate models for durably increasing the employment rate. In particular, these models, if spelt out, entail aspects quite unacceptable in a social dialogue. This is their political weakness and it cannot be regarded as negligible since political commitment to Europe is thereby placed in jeopardy. Let it be considered that, according to these models, it is necessary to accept a certain level (admittedly as low as possible) of unemployment in order to maintain wage moderation and price stability. Relaxing the employment protection regulations enables a weakening of the position of the insiders and places them in competition with outsiders, with the result that jobs become more insecure. Employability has to be as great as possible for each individual but must not be too high on average over the market as a whole, for otherwise jobseekers would not lower their reservation wage sufficiently.

An employability policy makes sense only if it goes hand in hand with a policy to counter vulnerability to unemployment (as indicated in Figure 7.1). But it is then no longer an employability policy but the first step towards a politics of capabilities as described by Amartya Sen (Salais and Villeneuve, 2004). In such a politics, the market is a last-resort solution and not a universal panacea. By giving priority to prevention *upstream from the market*, the approach would continue to require a 'high standard of employment' option (an aspect referred to as quality of employment) and to give a clear status to gender equality, local-embedded policies, a role for social dialogue and personalised follow-up. Hence, it is not a question of despairing of the OMC once and for all, but of substantially redesigning it. The OMC has to be included in a true configuration of deliberative democracy, to choose a new set of indicators, suited to the development of capabilities, and to be carefully coordinated with the development of European legislation and social dialogue. Recent political trends (de la Porte and Pochet, 2005) leave room for scepticism in that respect. Generally speaking, involvement of all types of non-state actors (social, local or civil actors) are still impeded or, at least, geared by democratic 'ambiguities'. However, such genuine involvement is needed more than ever if the building of Europe is to escape from the game played by the Commission and the member states.

Notes

[1] For a fuller and more detailed version of this chapter see my contribution, in French, to B. Zimmermann (ed) (2004) *Les sciences sociales à l'épreuve de l'action: Le savant, le politique et l'Europe*, Paris: Editions de la Maison des Sciences de l'Homme, pp 287-331.

[2] Source: 'Annex 1: The indicators – sources and definitions', in European Commission (2002a) *Joint employment report 2002,* Brussels: European Commission.

[3] See definition in the Appendix to this chapter.

[4] France appealed in vain for selection of the 20-64 age group rather than the 15-64 age group in order to avoid the statistical bias caused by casual jobs for youngsters. Source: interviews in Salais et al (2002).

[5] Adapted from Salais (1980). The reference is not recent but, with all due respect, the Phillips wage–unemployment relationship and the Okun Law, the monetary policy references, are no more so.

[6] The expression 'full employment' appears only once in the European Constitution (Article I.3). When monetary and economic policies are

developed in Part III, full employment is replaced, repeatedly, by an objective of a different nature, namely, 'a high level of employment'.

[7] Trubek and Mosher (2003).

[8] Point made by a member of the French permanent representation in Brussels. Source: Salais et al (2002, p 11).

[9] This dimension was flagrant, for the statisticians questioned, in the debates on the choice of the employment policy objectives in advance of the Lisbon Strategy. Concerning the employment rate of 55- to 64-year-olds: 'There is hypocrisy: the Dutch have their invalids; the French and Germans their early retired. If in France public funding of early retirement has diminished, it has been offset by the development of collective agreements (ARPE). The British make full use of 'spontaneous' labour market withdrawal…. In short, everyone is instrumentally using European indicators, every country pushing the definition which is most favourable for it' (Salais et al, 2002, p 38).

[10] See, in the case of Germany, Rudischhauser and Zimmermann (2004).

[11] For example, Canceill and Huyghues-Despointes (1999).

[12] The drop in employability as the period of unemployment lengthens is massively documented by econometric studies, whether on account of a selection effect (the most employable are the first to be taken on, without requiring any special assistance to this end), or on account of discouragement and stigmatisation, which leads people to become gradually resigned to their condition.

[13] Source: European Commission (2002b).

[14] As pointed out, for example, the creation of 'invalids' on the Dutch labour market. Under the British New Deal, a young person who returns after a failed work experience is regarded as a new jobseeker, and so on. Undertaking such studies should be a Eurostat priority.

[15] 'When we devised the 3rd *Contrat de progrès* we were obliged at that time to take into account the discussions and guidelines that were being finalised at European level', interview with the deputy Director-General of the ANPE (source: Salais et al, 2002).

[16] It must also be noticed that, when facing this process, social sciences have to choose between mirroring the process, denunciation or critical participation (see the French version of this chapter for details – see reference in note 1).

References

Aucouturier, A.-L. (1993) 'Contribution à la mesure de l'efficacité de la politique de l'emploi', *Travail et Emploi*, 55, January, pp 20-9.

Aucouturier, A.-L. (1998) 'Evaluation des politiques d'emploi et action publique : l'exemple de l'aide aux chômeurs créateurs d'entreprise', Thesis, University of Paris X Nanterre.

Benarrosh, Y. (2000) 'Tri des chômeurs: le nécessaire consensus des acteurs de l'emploi', *Travail et Emploi*, 81, January, pp 9-25.

Canceill, G. and Huyghues-Despointes, H. (1999) 'L'inscription à l'ANPE et après: itinéraires de chômeurs', *Premières Synthèses, DARES*, vol 37, no 1.

de la Porte, C. and Pochet, P. (2002) 'Supple coordination at EU level and the key actors' involvement', in C. de la Porte and P. Pochet (eds) *Building Social Europe through the Open Method of Coordination*, Bruxelles: PIE-Peter Lang, pp 27-68.

de la Porte, C. and Pochet, P. (2005) 'Participation in the Open Method of Coordination: the cases of employment and social exclusion', in J. Zeitlin and P. Pochet (eds) *The Open Method of Coordination in action The European Employment and Social Inclusion Strategies*, Brussels: PIE-Peter Lang, pp 210-40.

EMCO (Employment Committee) (2004) 'Indicators Group report to EMCO on progress made in the field of indicators to monitor the employment guidelines', 22, 13 July, Brussels: EMCO.

European Commission (2002a) *Joint Employment Report 2002*, http://europe.eu.int/comm/employment_social/employment_strategy

European Commission (2002b) 'Taking stock of five years of the European Employment Strategy', COM(2002)416 final, *Communication*, Brussels: European Commission.

Hodson, D. and Maher, I. (2001) 'The Open Method as a new mode of governance: the case of soft economic policy coordination, *Journal of Common Market Studies*, vol 39, no 4, pp 719-45.

Martinon, S. (2002) 'Les enjeux du suivi individualisé des chômeurs et la mise en place du PAP: le cas d'une agence locale pour l'emploi', DEA Dissertation, University of Paris X Nanterre.

Rudischhauser, S. and Zimmermann, B. (2004) 'De la critique à l'expertise: la 'modernisation' de l'action publique: le cas du chômage en France et en Allemagne', in B. Zimmermann (ed) *Les sciences sociales à l'épreuve de l'action: Le savant, le politique et l'Europe*, Paris: Editions de la Maison des Sciences de l'Homme, pp 247-85.

Salais, R. (1980) 'Le chômage, un phénomène de file d'attente', *Economie et Statistique*, no 123, July, pp 67-78.

Salais, R. and Villeneuve, R. (eds) (2004) *Europe and the politics of capabilities*, Cambridge: Cambridge University Press.

Salais, R., Raveaud, G. and Grégoire, M. (2002) 'L'évaluation de l'impact de la Stratégie Européenne pour l'Emploi – thème 10: Elaboration des politiques', Unpublished report for the DARES, IDHE, Paris.

Teague, P. (2001) 'Deliberative governance and EU social policy', *European Journal of Industrial Relations*, vol 7, no 1, pp 7-26.

Tronti, L. (2001) 'Fruitful or fashionable? Can benchmarking improve the employment performance of national labour markets?', in E. Best and D. Bossaert (eds) *From Luxemburg to Lisbon and beyond: Making the Employment Strategy work*, Maastricht: European Institute of Public Administration, pp 67-83.

Trubek, D. and Mosher, J. (2003) 'New governance, EU employment policy and the European Social Model', in D. Trubek and J. Zeitlin (eds) *Governing work and welfare in a new economy: European and American experiments*, Oxford: Oxford University Press, pp 33-58.

Zeitlin, J. (2002) 'The Open Method of Coordination and the future of the European Employment Strategy', Presentation, Audition at the Employment and Social Affairs Committee of the European Parliament, Strasbourg, 8 July.

Zeitlin, J. (2005) 'The Open Method of Coordination in action: theoretical promises, empirical realities, reform strategy', in D. Zeitlin and P. Pochet, with L. Magnusson (eds) *The Open Method of Coordination in action: The European Employment and Social Inclusion Strategies*, Brussels, PIE-Peter Lang, pp 447-503.

Appendix Table 8.1: Main key economic indicators within the EES monitoring

Source: European Commission (2002, Annex 1)

Unemployment rate
Definition:
Total unemployed persons as a share of total active population (by gender).
Source: Eurostat unemployment harmonised series.

Employment rate
Definition:
Total employment rate (age group 15-64), broken down by gender and broken down for older workers (age 55-64). Persons in employment as a proportion of total population in the same age group.
Source: Quarterly Labour Force Data (QLFD), Eurostat.

Growth in labour productivity
Definition:
Growth in GDP per capita of employed population and per hour worked.
Source: ESA95, DG ECFIN.

Long-term unemployment rate
Definition:
Total long-term unemployed persons (12 months or more) as a proportion of total active population (by gender).
New start (a)
Definition: Share of young/adult unemployed persons becoming unemployed in month X, still unemployed in month X+6/12, and not having been offered a new start in the form of training, retraining, work experience, a job or other employability measure (LMP categories 2-7) (by gender).
Source: National data.
New start (b)
Definition: Share of young/adult unemployed persons becoming unemployed in month X, still unemployed in month X+6/12, and not having been offered a new start in the form of training, retraining, work experience, a job or other employability measure (LMP categories 1-7) (by gender).
Source: National data.

Activation of long-term unemployed
Definition:
Number of long-term registered unemployed participants in an active measure (training, retraining, work experience, or other employability measure) in relation to the sum of the long-term unemployed participants plus registered long-term unemployed (yearly averages). Broken down by types of measures and gender (LMP categories 2-7).
Source: National data (in the medium term the LMP database).

Follow-up of participants in active measures
Definition:
1. Rate of inflow of LMP participants into employment (three or six months after participation in a measure).
2. Rate of return of LMP participants into unemployment (three or six months after participation in a measure).
Source: National data.

Employment growth
Definition:
Annual change in total number of employed persons, overall and by main sector (by gender).
Source: Quarterly Labour Force Data (QLFD), Eurostat.

NINE

Assessing the European Social Model against the capability approach

Jean-Michel Bonvin

Introduction

The contemporary welfare state is undergoing a threefold transformation towards *activation* of recipients, *individualisation* or contractualisation of benefits, and *territorialisation* of modes of governance. Briefly stated, the very aim of the welfare state is tending to evolve from paying cash compensation to restoring acting capacity, mainly working and productive capacity; this in turn requires taking into account individual characteristics within the field of the intervention of the welfare state, by contrast with the conventional social programmes based on categories of risk; it also implies a decentralisation of the modes of operation in order to equip local welfare agents with the abilities to design tailor-made measures. These changes coincide with a redefinition of the assessment criteria used to determine what intervention of the welfare state is right and fair (substantial level) and what procedures ought to be mobilised (processual level). The new framework produces highly contrasted reactions, ranging from resistance to full endorsement, and it is implemented in quite diverse ways and at different paces according to the countries and categories of population concerned. The discussion surrounding the European Social Model (ESM) takes place against this background, and the purpose of this chapter is to assess the distinctive position taken and role played by the ESM in this evolution of the welfare state.

In order to grasp and assess the scope of these transformations, the conventional analyses of the welfare state, centred on statistical indicators and power–resource theories, are not, in our view, adequate. The procedural and reflexive turn of social policies cannot be captured by these tools: indicators are too static, and power–resource theories tend to rely on national-level data about political representation in Parliaments, which are unable to grasp the growing impact of local implementing agents within the course of the policy process. As a valid alternative, we suggest using the capability approach developed by Amartya Sen (for instance, 1992, 1999), which relies on distinguishing three dimensions: (a) the resources in possession of a person (goods or services); (b) their capability set or the extent to which they are really free to lead the life they have reason to value[1]; (c) their functionings or the life they actually lead. The choice of a specific rationale or mission for the welfare state makes a very significant difference. Is the purpose of social protection to redistribute cash or other in-kind resources? Is it to impose on the beneficiaries certain behaviours or functionings? Or is it to promote, that is, to guarantee the conditions for, their real freedom of action in all spheres of life? This chapter will strive to answer this topical set of questions in two main respects:

- To what extent do welfare programmes increase recipients' real freedom to choose the work they have reason to value (that is *capability for work*)? The postulate here is that valuable work is an essential part of human identity and flourishing.
- To what extent are benefit recipients allowed to take part actively in the welfare intervention? Drawing on Amartya Sen's perspective, we suggest calling this *capability for voice*, that is, the ability to express one's true opinions and thoughts (versus adaptive preferences) and to make them count in the course of public discussion. In our view, this notion of capability for voice adequately captures the promises conveyed by localism in welfare policies.

These two dimensions – capability for work and capability for voice – constitute the yardsticks against which the ESM will be assessed. The chapter runs as follows. The first section recalls the main substantial transformations induced by the activation of the welfare state and the individualisation of social benefits. The position of the ESM in this debate is evaluated against the *capability for work* approach. The second section focuses on processes and regulatory modes mobilised to implement the new pattern of social policies. The distinctiveness, if any, of the ESM is assessed against the *capability for voice* framework. The third section draws some tentative conclusions concerning the position of the ESM in the general capability framework: to what degree does it focus on resources, capabilities, or functionings?

The ESM and capability for work

The trend towards activation coincides with significant modifications of social protection in the three following respects: (a) the 'wealth' to be redistributed or equalised, where one can observe a move from resources to opportunities or capacity to act; (b) the emergence of a new approach based on the development of human capital; and (c) the target groups who are increasingly defined in individual terms by contrast with the previous approach centred on categories. The following paragraphs successively tackle these three issues, pointing out national diversity as well as the specific position of the ESM in these debates.

What is to be redistributed? From resources to opportunities

During the so-called golden era of the welfare state, the main aim of the welfare interventions is to compensate for the loss of income. Social security and protection are everywhere envisaged in relation to the issue of material resources, although the extent of cash redistribution provided by the welfare state varies considerably along national lines (for the worst-off alone in the liberal regimes; for everybody, but with a view to maintaining the inequalities prevailing on the labour market, in the conservative regimes; for everybody with a genuinely egalitarian ambition in the social democratic regimes – see Esping-Andersen, 1990). In this perspective, the creation of employment opportunities is not the business of the welfare state: macroeconomic opportunities are provided mainly via Keynesian demand-side policies, and it is then up to the individuals to seize these opportunities or not. Individual behaviours and their ethical appropriateness are out of the reach of the welfare state, except for social assistance recipients where such intrusion in the private sphere is envisaged as a social control device aiming to enforce compliance with prevailing social norms (in this case, work ethic). Thus, two broad categories of population can be identified in this framework: those belonging to the communities of recognised social risks (illness, maternity, disability, unemployment, and so forth) for whom equalisation of resources is guaranteed mainly via social insurance mechanisms; and those who do not pertain to these groups and are considered to be deviant, for whom cash provision is conditional upon compliance with social norms. In other words, resources for social insurance recipients on the one hand; constraints for social assistance beneficiaries on the other. The language of opportunities and capabilities is altogether absent from the rhetoric of the conventional welfare state, which is confined to providing cash resources, and is not concerned with the issues connected with acting or working capacity.

From the 1980s onwards, the main pitfall of this system is found to be the moral hazard entailed in unconditional cash benefits (inducing the so-called dependency trap). Neoliberal policies suggest eliminating this trap by reducing or suppressing cash benefits, or by introducing much stricter eligibility conditions. The underlying postulate is that if people are not provided with resources, they will make more effort to earn a livelihood. Less guaranteed resources will in the end result in more initiatives from individuals, which will bring about more opportunities. The retreat of the welfare state is thus envisaged as the very precondition for promoting individual responsibility.

Third Way social policies emerging in the mid-1990s propose yet another policy orientation: in Giddens' words, the main objective is 'investment in human capital wherever possible, rather than direct provision of economic maintenance. In place of the welfare state we should put the social investment state' (1998, p 117). In this perspective, the intervention of the state is granted legitimacy only if it is a productive investment, in other words, equalisation of resources is legitimate only if it contributes to creating new productive opportunities. The language of opportunities is not contrasted with that of resources, but instilled in it with a view to subordinating it. In other words, the logic of compensation needs to be pervaded (and not substituted as neoliberal policies would have it) by that of investment. Thus the discourse of social investment, especially in human and social capital, is to replace the 'tax and spend' tendency of the Keynesian welfare state. Hence, the Third Way presents itself as the golden medium between the old social democratic recipes (focusing exclusively on resources) and the neoliberal ready-made solutions (concentrating strictly on opportunities). As such, it claims to be the only policy programme to successfully combine resources and opportunities. However, this view is misleading, in that it too readily assumes that the previous period of the conventional welfare state was one of individual irresponsibility and reluctance towards risk-taking. Thus, the cash welfare state is presented as one of the main reasons accounting for individual passivity, and for current low employment rates. This interpretation is in sharp contradiction with the very rationale of the conventional welfare state as presented earlier: aiming at redistributing resources (in order to provide people outside the labour market with decent living standards), it was not concerned with creating opportunities for beneficiaries, which was achieved mainly via macroeconomic policies. Recognising this division of labour within the Keynesian welfare state leads to the adoption of another interpretation of the so-called 'dependency' phenomenon: it is not the passivity of welfare, but the abandonment of the previous mechanism mobilised for creating opportunities (Keynesian demand-side policies) that lies at the very core of the present unemployment or inactivity problem. In other words, if people do not work, it is not because they prefer to stay on benefits, but because full employment as a macroeconomic objective has been mostly abandoned (for evidence of the present trend towards promoting flexible market solutions instead of investing in jobs, see, for instance, Strath, 2000). Such a conception carries with it a radically different diagnosis of unemployment and inactivity, and suggests other remedies: the main issue at stake is not how to push reluctant people back into work, but how to create or restore the conditions for full and valuable employment. Indeed, unemployment can be interpreted either as a matter of individual responsibility, or as a social concern where policies are mobilised in the perspective of full employment. Neoliberal and Third Way policies alike choose the first option, thereby insisting on the need to moralise individual unemployed and inactive people.

The European Employment Strategy (EES) takes for granted the same postulates: (a) job creation is first and foremost a market responsibility (guideline [henceforward GL] 2 of its latest version); (b) non-work is to be tackled via thorough revisions of the cash welfare state as well as the promotion of active labour market programmes (GL8). It equally advocates the abandonment of Keynesian demand-side policies and the revision of the benefit systems in order to eradicate welfare or dependency traps. The EES also calls for the setting up of servicing states, which entitle individuals to tailor-made interventions aimed at improving their employability. These can take the form of training, opportunities to gain work experience, socially useful activities or work. In this perspective, social policy is envisaged as a tool to improve the ability to gain access to the labour market rather than to protect individuals from the market (for evidence of the shift from decommodification to recommodification as a rationale of the welfare state, see, for instance, Esping-Andersen, 1999). Current social policy is aimed at equalising, as much as possible, the starting positions of individuals on the market. To this end, public investments in training and education, in services to families and infrastructure for communities, are considerably increased. Thus, the EES endorses – as do most national social protection systems – the language of equality of opportunities. In a capability perspective, the key issue is, then, the way to define valuable opportunities: what do the EES and other defenders of the active welfare state mean when they speak of equality of opportunity?

Human capital approaches versus capabilities

In the rhetoric of the active welfare state, opportunities are assimilated into employability, but their upgrading is pursued in very diverse ways by neoliberals and Third Way partisans. The former see the flexibilisation of labour costs as the way to improve employability and favour job creation. This is classically captured by the insider/outsider dilemma (Lindbeck and Snower, 1988), which identifies the cause of unemployment in the insufficient differential of incomes between work and non-work, resulting in dependency traps for unemployed and inactive people. The lack of individual goodwill is the main cause of unemployment and this ought to be reformed by making the option of exiting the labour market much less attractive. By contrast, Third Way defenders see the development of competencies as the condition for increasing both employability and employment. Following Layard and Nickell's conception (1991), they assume that a competitive working-age population will result in a more dynamic and inclusive economy.

Despite these differences, the 'making work pay' logic is explicitly advanced in both conceptions. Either by lowering labour costs for the potential employer, or by training the jobseeker with a view to increasing her market value, the aim remains one and the same: make the inactive and the unemployed more marketable. In both cases, opportunity is envisaged relative to the yardstick of the market, and the welfare state is called to produce attractive commodities that can find their way on the labour market, by furthering the individual adaptation to the requisites and expectations of the labour market. This translates into a focus on supply-side egalitarianism, as Streeck (1999) calls it, the aim of which is not to equalise capabilities or real freedoms to choose one's way of living and working, but to improve marketability and ability to compete on the labour market. In this respect, neoliberal and Third Way policies share common views, far from the logic of capabilities that promotes a different view of work as a utility and a way to realise oneself. In the capability framework, the promotion of employment quality is the key political challenge, which lies very far from the 'making work pay' logic endorsed by neoliberal and Third Way perspectives alike.

Despite its generous intentions in terms of social cohesion, the ESM also develops a restrictive conception of opportunities: by seeking to revise the benefit systems and their supposed tendency to promote laziness and dependency (GL8), it explicitly endorses the view of the welfare state as a factor of passivity; and by focusing on employability and lifelong training both for inactive and unemployed (GL1 and 4), it clearly adopts a strategy in line with supply-side egalitarianism.[2] By contrast with the previous 'resourcist' model of the cash welfare state, the ESM (just like neoliberal and Third Way policies) focuses on the development of opportunities at the micro level (by concentrating on the need to reform both the will and the capacities of jobseekers), while at the same time leaving the task of creating macroeconomic opportunities to market actors. In contrast with Sen's conception that calls for an adequate equilibrium between macro and micro programmes (in Sen's words, between individual and social factors of conversion), the ESM puts much more weight on the transformation of the individuals than on that of the labour market. In this perspective, investment in human capital is envisaged as essential if the European Union (EU) is to become the most competitive knowledge economy. GL1 insists on 'active and preventative measures for the unemployed and the inactive' (EU, 2003, p 6). Emphasis is placed upon the need to 'offer jobseekers access to effective and efficient measures to enhance their employability and chances of integration, with special attention to people facing the greatest difficulties in the labour market' (EU, 2003, p 6). GL3 and 4 respectively strive to 'address change and promote adaptability and mobility in the labour market' and to 'promote development of human capital and lifelong learning' (EU, 2003, pp 6-7). The workers' competitive employability in a context of global change is the key objective of the EES. Productive work features as the centrepiece, and all forms of non-work (that is, all activities outside the labour market) are interpreted as inferior functionings. Thus, the EES endorses a specific view of the 'equality of opportunities' discourse, which carries with it a biased definition of opportunities envisaged as strictly instrumental to economic productivity on the labour market.

In this context, the threat of disincentives within social security mechanisms is increasingly perceived, leading to in-depth and constant revision of benefit systems in order to unveil possible inactivity or unemployment traps and transform the system into a more employment-friendly one. The first Kok Report (European Commission, 2004) testifies to this move: by focusing on the necessity to make work pay in financial terms (by reducing the amounts of benefits relative to wages), to reinforce active labour market policies, to promote active ageing and to increase female activity rates, it introduces a new balance between decommodification and recommodification concerns. In other word, decommodification is legitimate only insofar as it actively promotes recommodification. This goes along with a focus on quick labour market reintegration, on the explicit ground that a bad job is better than no job at all, since it may, it is claimed, open up higher professional prospects. This postulate concerning the superiority of low-quality jobs vis-à-vis all forms of non-work tends to undermine concerns connected with the regulation of the labour market. Indeed, the language of the EES sees work as a commodity, the marketability of which is to be improved via financial incentives and training programmes in order to increase the employment rates. In this perspective, the ambition to pursue macro quantitative targets – the overall employment rate of 70%, the female rate of 60% and the rate of 50% for older workers to be reached by 2010 – prevails over the issue of the quality of the opportunities offered to the individuals concerned. Such policies thus regard persons as means towards macro purposes, while the capability approach sees macroeconomic stability and prosperity as an instrument in the perspective of human flourishing.

In all these respects, the EES is very much in line with approaches centred on capital fructification, and sharply contrasts with the capability framework. What ultimately matters in the EES is not the individuals' real freedom, but their ability to process capital in order to generate further capital. As such, the rhetoric around the ESM features as a capitalistic discourse, in which the concern for the enhancement of human freedom has a subordinate position. Esping-Andersen and colleagues' report to the Belgian Presidency in 2002 (Esping-Andersen et al, 2003) explicitly endorses such a view centred on capital growth, when they recommend a social investment strategy with the ambition to adapt individuals and society in order to increase competitiveness and better cope in the new knowledge economy. In Finlayson's words, this amounts to promoting an ideal vision of the actor as 'a reflexive individual who regards him/herself as a form of capital to be processed, refined and invested, and who does this within the context of an obligation to the community to be productive' (2003, p 166, quoted in Lister, 2004).

Whatever the national diversities in the implementation rhythm, the appeal to a social investment strategy has defined a kind of common normative framework with deep-rooted consequences in the evolution of social policies. The EU, with its rhetoric of an ESM, plays a significant part in the dissemination of this normative framework. However, when assessed against this yardstick, the ESM displays its one-sidedness in at least three respects: (a) beyond a certain limit (that is, over the poverty threshold), social protection is interpreted as a factor generating dependency; (b) improving opportunity is identified with increasing individuals' marketability; and (c) approaches centred on human and social capital and the growth of output per head prevail over the concern for capabilities and real freedoms. This threefold bias has a significant impact on the way to define the target groups of the welfare state, as the next paragraph will make clear.

Who is to be helped? From categories to individuals

As mentioned earlier, the aim of the conventional welfare state is to compensate for income losses resulting from the occurrence of predefined social risks. An actuarial calculus allows determination of the amount of compensation to be offered via social insurance mechanisms. Individual characteristics do not intervene in this calculus, and it is the overall cost for society and the wage percentage to be paid in order to cover such expenses that matter. Therefore, the conventional welfare state is not interested in individual characteristics such as adequate moral behaviour, or biological working capacity. This approach is rooted in the use of categories (unemployed people, ill people, disabled people, and so forth), and human beings fulfilling the eligibility criteria for membership of these categories are entitled to cash benefits, whatever their ethical behaviour or degree of responsibility in the occurrence of the social risk. Such a categorical approach to social security prevents any arbitrary decision by the holders of public authority; it keeps the benefit recipients out of the grip of the welfare officers, but at the same time it makes impossible the design of tailor-made programmes in their favour.

By contrast, neoliberal and Third Way social policies focusing on opportunities place individual characteristics at the very centre of public action. While members of risk categories used to receive compensating resources whatever their specific behaviour, beliefs, expectations, wishes, and so forth, individual beneficiaries of 'equal opportunities' policies are required to provide much more data about personal behaviour, competencies and beliefs. The threat of undue intrusion into the private sphere is exacerbated in this framework. With the entry of individual characteristics into the field of social policies, the ambivalence of public action is reinforced. Does this transformation contribute to the increase of the recipients' capability for work? Or is it a way to compel them into exogenously determined behaviour? In such an individualised pattern, the criteria used by local welfare agents in order to assess individuals are key: to what extent do these criteria allow individual expectations and wishes to be taken into account? To what extent do they require that they be shaped according to publicly designed targets?

Answers to these questions very much depend on existing institutional configurations, which vary both along country and social security branches. Male unemployed people under the age of 50 are usually submitted to the most stringent requirements. In Denmark, activation was introduced in the mid-1990s, since when the constraints imposed on jobseekers have been constantly stepped up. A recent reform has introduced the obligation to accept any reasonable job from the very first day of unemployment, thus exacerbating the requirements of mobility in terms of wages, qualification and geographical settlement. However, the services provided to the Danish unemployed also include enabling interventions. Empirical evaluation studies of the Danish employment policies indeed show that compulsive elements are dominated by the deep-rooted values of citizenship, requiring that all recipients be treated as citizens in their own right. In the UK, workfare has a longer tradition. The years of Conservative government coincided with the increase of conditionality, the tightening of controls and the focus on moralising jobseekers' behaviours, with hardening sanctions for non-compliance. The New Labour government introduced enabling elements such as training and work experience, but without suppressing the workfare dimension attached to the previous mechanisms. After a one-year spell, participation in the New Deal programmes is mandatory for all young and long-term unemployed people. In Germany, yet another method prevails. Active labour market policies, although explicitly mentioned in legal provisions for a very long time, were rather loosely implemented until the mid-1990s. The Hartz Commission has recently introduced more stringent requirements for unemployed people, including benefit reduction and increased pressure on all persons able to work. There are also elements of empowerment, but they are increasingly subordinated to quick reintegration to the labour market (Dingeldey, 2004). In most countries, equivalent examples can be found with increasing pressure being put on male unemployed people under the age of 50, and especially on young people. The EES shares the same concern, with the most compelling and clear-cut policies focusing on young and long-term unemployed people (GL1). In both cases, the active welfare state is connected with individualised mandatory programmes aimed at promoting rapid reincorporation into the labour market.

Old and disabled people, due to their reduced capacity to work, enjoy softer eligibility criteria and undergo fewer constraints to actively participate. After retirement age (which ranges between 60 and 67 in the EU), the legitimacy of inactivity is widely recognised. Many member states have extended this period of legitimate inactivity with the creation of early retirement programmes: people over a certain age (roughly 55) are entitled to unconditional benefits, bridging the gap until the retirement age. The present focus on active ageing, of which the EU is an active promoter (GL5 of the EES), has deep-rooted consequences for pension policies, which take two main pathways: (a) contesting ageing workers' entitlement to early retirement programmes; and (b) striving to postpone the retirement age. Furthermore, the emphasis on active or successful ageing coincides with a new way to envisage old age. Receipt of a pension is no longer deemed to constitute entitlement to rest and guaranteed consumption, for these years are regarded as a period of active participation.[3]

In line with the EES, most EU countries are currently seeking to abrogate early exit schemes and design financial incentives for employers who choose to keep their older workers. The 'making work pay' logic underlying these reforms sometimes also implies the setting up of training programmes for senior workers. In Sweden, the work ethic is deep-rooted, and the early exit schemes introduced at the beginning of the 1990s (as a collectively agreed way to deal with massive dismissals) were soon perceived as problematic. As a result, three reforms were introduced into the pension system: (a) the restriction of early retirement and disability schemes (henceforth accessible only if strict medical criteria are met); (b) the introduction of a more flexible retirement age (every worker being allowed to retire between the ages of 61 and 70 since the 1999 reform, with the period of contributions determining the amount of pension paid); and (c) the setting up of active policies especially targeted at ageing long-term unemployed persons between the ages of 55 and 64 (a 2002 Bill created training programmes and protected jobs financed by the state in favour of this population). Active ageing is promoted in Sweden via the use of incentives aiming to increase the financial attractiveness of work and with a view to enhancing older workers' capacity to be socially useful. As a result, productive and remunerative work features as a more valuable and lucrative alternative than compensated inactivity for older workers (Mandin, 2004). In the UK, early exit schemes have always been the exception (the only one, the Job Release Scheme, was ended as early as 1988). During the Conservative period, the problems linked to ageing workers' low employment rates were mainly tackled via financial incentives encouraging jobseekers to accept low-paid jobs. By contrast, the Blair administration introduced two other ways to promote active ageing: the development of lifelong learning in order to prevent older workers' long-term exclusion from the labour market (that is, the New Deal 50+); and the increased flexibility of the pension system, so that most workers aged 65+ have to work in order to be effectively protected against poverty. In practice, however, active ageing is mainly promoted via the reduction of cash benefits (with the aim of eradicating dependency traps). The poor success of UK training programmes until now is evidence of the difficulties encountered when it comes to promoting work not only as a more lucrative option, but also as a more attractive and valuable opportunity. Continental countries face still higher obstacles when striving to set up programmes in favour of active ageing. Early retirement is increasingly turned into a more expensive option (for instance, in Germany where incentives are being introduced to encourage older workers' participation in the labour market, or in France where many early exit programmes are being ended), but no corresponding active labour market policy is being set up in favour of older people. Thus, if inactive ageing is being discouraged everywhere, individualised social policies are envisaged as options or incentives rather than constraints imposed on ageing workers. GL5 of the EES encompasses all these trends: the main focus is on eliminating incentives to inactivity, but training programmes as well as labour market flexibility are also mentioned.

The evolution of disability insurance follows similar lines. During the golden age of welfare, the definition of disability was stretched in order to encompass such situations as job unavailability or obsolescence of competencies. By contrast, the rhetoric of activation has put more pressure on the beneficiaries of such extended disability, especially on partially disabled people. The link between disability and biological capacity to work has been considerably reinforced by the tendency towards activation, and stricter eligibility conditions as well as behavioural requirements are increasingly imposed on benefit recipients in the field of disability. As Mabbett (2004) shows, the European Commission is a strong promoter of active disability. But the use of constraints is advocated only in cases of social disability (when disability is due to social causes): if physical or mental causes account for disability, then the new active programmes are offered as options.

Diversity is still greater when it comes to reconciling work and family life. Three gendered regimes are identified by Orloff (2002): (a) the 'dual-earner' model where extensive public services with generous transfers are provided to families, thus resulting in an extensive degree of defamilialisation and high female employment rates (corresponding to the Scandinavian countries); (b) the 'general family support' regime with moderate transfers and tax breaks for housewives, deficient public services and, consequently, little defamilialisation and low employment rates (mostly in Continental countries); and (c) the 'market-oriented model' where few public services go hand in hand with residual transfers and quite a high degree of defamilialisation, mostly achieved via market mechanisms. This results in a significant diversity of the policy tools used to promote female participation, with different mixes of constraints and opportunities, and variable degrees of pressure put on lone mothers and on inactive women to make a rapid return to the labour market (Bonvin, 2004). In this field, the EES clearly advocates the adoption of the 'dual-earner' family with extensive child care services and reinforcement of the trend towards female commodification. GL6 puts women on the same footing as men, and the objective of providing child care for 90% of children between three years old and school age and for 33% of children under three is clearly envisaged as an efficient way to increase employment rates. As a matter of fact, the whole EES in favour of women is subordinated to achieving the overall and female employment rate targets. Thus, the conditions for female activation are created with a quantitative purpose, in which the issue of employment quality features as secondary.

Hence, the mix of constraints and opportunities is quite different depending on category of population and national institutional specificities. In this field, the EES consistently advocates activation for all categories of the working-age population. GL5 to 7 seek to 'increase labour supply and promote active ageing', along with 'gender equality' (interpreted in terms of equal access to commodification on the labour market), and to 'promote the integration of and combat discrimination against people at a disadvantage in the labour market' (EU, 2003, p 7). The principal focus in each instance is on the employability and recommodification of older people, women and the most disadvantaged. The rhetoric of opportunities prevails for ageing people, as well as for physically and mentally disabled persons, whereas non-disabled unemployed people under the age of 50 are facing more stringent pressures. Despite this difference, the recommendation is one and the same for all categories: inactivity and unemployment are to be made costly options in order to increase the comparative attractiveness of work. The line of reasoning underlying the EES is the following: if people are granted freedom of choice, they will choose inactivity since, it is claimed, work is a disutility. An undisputed postulate lies at the core of the ESM: the only way to increase employment rates is to set up an adequate system of financial incentives in order to persuade unemployed and inactive people to enter the labour market. As a consequence, the alternative view – the claim that making work truly attractive and valuable in terms of human fulfilment could well be the best way to increase employment rates – is not even debated.

The ESM and capability for voice

Conventional welfare relies on a centralised pattern of public action. Categories of social risk are defined by central political bodies with the help of central administrations, and local civil servants are then in charge of implementing these directives. The issue of redistribution of cash resources is regarded as a mechanical device where human discernment plays very little part. Local welfare agents' initiatives are constrained in order to avoid arbitrariness in decision-making. In such a model, it is no wonder that the main tools to bring about reform are lobbying and pressure put on the central political and administrative bodies in order to modify the level and duration of benefits provided via the cash welfare state. This has been coined the age of neo-corporatism, when trades unions and the political Left were uniting their forces in order to impose their view on decision-making parliamentary bodies. In the academic sphere, this was the golden age of 'power–resource theories' explaining the diversity between welfare states via the varying ability of trade unions and political leaders of the Left to impact on welfare design (see, for instance, Korpi, 1983).

Neoliberals and Third Way partisans contest this centralised mode of government and insist on the need to modernise public services. To this end, they recommend setting up local partnerships between public and private actors, which induce a twofold transformation in terms of governance: first, the mobilisation of private and civil society actors in the pursuit of publicly designed targets; and second, a new balance within the public sector itself between central and local actors, giving the latter more autonomy and decision-making power in their daily action. Under such conditions, the external technocratic state imposing its objectives from the outside is called to give way to other views of public action where the content of public policies is to a larger extent defined in context (in line with the situated state described in Storper and Salais, 1997). The local actors' ability to voice their concerns becomes key in this model, that is, the extent to which they are able to make their point of view count in the course of public action (Bohman, 1996).

The new mode of governance relying on local partnerships requires a significant transformation of the part played by the central level in the policy process. However, it does not coincide with a retreat of the central state (as neoliberals would have it in order to pave the way for market solutions), but with the designing of new patterns of public action along the so-called New Public Management (NPM) principles. In this perspective, the state retains a key role in the course of public action, in that it is responsible for monitoring the whole process and checking its efficiency via the use of new managerial techniques such as performance indicators, benchmarking practices, budget envelopes, and the like. This raises many problems in terms of capability for voice, especially when the directives elicited by the central level compel local actors into specific modes of intervention, and prevent the design and implementation of tailor-made programmes at a situated level. In such cases, NPM guidelines feature as a refinement of the old technocratic logic rather than as a new pattern of situated public action.

Empirical evidence shows that most EU countries have recently adopted such a managerialist mode of governance of their public employment services, where the adoption of goals, objectives, performance indicators, and so forth, aim at empowering local actors and/or shaping their practices. In 2000, 10 of the EU15 member states mobilised management by objectives in their employment services (Mosley et al, 2000). The same mode of governance can be observed in all these public offices and is based on a two-step procedure: (a) ex ante setting goals, operational objectives and quantitative performance targets; and (b) measuring and reporting the actual level of performance against these predefined objectives. In three countries, namely the Netherlands, Sweden and the UK, the issue of decentralisation (and of enhancing local actors' capability for voice) plays no role whatsoever in the decision to introduce such management techniques, which are envisaged as tools for improving the efficiency of central steering. Other countries, such as Denmark, use them with a view to promoting a more participatory model of management. Regionalisation is a key feature of the 1994 Danish reform of employment services, with the setting up of actual operational targets at the regional level. However, the definition of overall goals and objectives remains a national prerogative. In the UK, the introduction of management by objectives is explicitly meant to tighten the relationship between the ministerial authorities and the public employment service. The recent setting up of Jobcentre Plus, where placement and benefit administration are merged, clearly aims at reinforcing the efficiency of the public employment service in implementing the directives received from the government. In

Germany, the modernisation of public services on the labour market, advocated by the Hartz Commission, is achieved via the setting up of new public employment offices to a large extent modelled on the British Jobcentres Plus with their focus on efficiency (Finn and Knuth, 2004). In all these countries (although belonging to different welfare regimes), the adoption of managerialist modes of governance coincides with an increasing focus on local actors' responsibility together with a reinforced state control and monitoring of the local actors' behaviours. Empirical studies evidence the significant gap between NPM discourses (encouraging individual initiatives) and actual practices at the local level: whereas NPM rhetoric carries with it the promise of more autonomy for local actors, their actual margin of manoeuvre is strictly limited by their subordination to performance targets and their budgetary dependency (local public employment services not abiding by the fixed targets risk losing part of their allocated budget), all the more so in that such reforms of the modes of governance are most often driven by the concern to rationalise the use of public money (Giauque, 2004).

The increasing tendency to introduce performance targets in order to guide and control the action of the public employment services acts as a powerful obstacle impeding, to a significant extent, local agents' capability for voice. Indeed, centrally designed objectives may impose behaviours that will not necessarily translate into better service delivery, insofar as they encourage 'making a good showing on the record as an end-in-itself' (Blau, 1963, quoted in Wright, 2001, p 247). When they are internalised by all actors involved in social integration policies, recipients and civil officers alike, these performance targets shape wishes, expectations, and so on, into adaptive preferences. As a consequence, 'Staff make efforts to meet targets but these efforts are not necessarily of the kind intended by those who design the target' (Wright, 2001, p 247). Even if local actors do their best to help the neediest, performance targets established at the national level are often self-defeating instruments, in that they prevent the achievement of the very objective of the active labour market policies, that is, quick and long-lasting professional integration. The everyday work of the local welfare officer is thus locked within the difficulty of making their quantitative mission consistent with their real work.

As empirical evidence illustrates, such NPM approaches are very much in line with classical top-down procedures: the main change consists of arousing local agents' responsibility and motivation in order to reach the centrally designed targets. As such, they do not fulfil the promises of the new patterns of situated public action. And, just like all top-down processes, they often produce local resistance to the central directives (for instance, by cheating on the indicators) or meaningless ritual compliance. Indeed, these new modes of governance tend to reproduce the same disconnection between central directives and actual local practices that can be observed in all authoritarian frameworks such as the Weberian bureaucratic iron cage or the Taylorian firm.

The implementation of the EES follows similar lines. It is being advanced through the so-called Open Method of Coordination (OMC), which represents an importation of the managerialist doctrine (Clarke and Newman, 1997) within EU governance modes, by which timetables are fixed, indicators established in order to measure progress, best practices identified, specific targets set, periodic monitoring and evaluation instituted, and so on. Local or national initiatives may flourish, provided they fit within this general framework. Again, attitudes of ritual compliance can be observed at the national level, where the writing of the National Action Plan for Employment often looks like a show of goodwill on the indicators, bearing little relationship with actual practices. In the present state of the OMC, the use of managerialist principles contributes to such disconnection between the EU, national and local level, and acts as an obstacle preventing reflexive public action. The democratic deficit observed in the arenas where objectives and quantitative targets are fixed (which is well documented in the case of the EU – see, for instance, Salais et al, 2002; Zeitlin, 2004) is hardly surprising under such circumstances. The technocratic way of designing targets and indicators accounts to a large extent for the insufficient involvement of social and civil actors in the OMC processes. Indeed, if the designing process is confiscated by groups of experts, it implies that the local actors' margin for manoeuvre and capability for voice is significantly reduced by the requirements of technical compliance with predefined objectives. If such is the case, it is most doubtful whether EU slogans like the 'principle of subsidiarity' or the 'Open Method of Coordination' will really pave the way towards genuinely reflexive policy-making. At the time of writing, the impact of the ESM in terms of capability for voice can be assessed as, at best, ambivalent. Indeed, it is still very unclear whether the fashionable appeal to governance contained in the OMC really makes a difference vis-à-vis conventional government and promotes local actors' capability for action, or whether it is rather a subtle way of confirming technocracy and government in their prerogatives.

Conclusion

The ESM presents itself as distinct from the United States (US) model in at least three respects: the connection between economic prosperity and social cohesion, the focus on social dialogue and coordinated collective bargaining, and a concern for more equal wage and income redistribution (Ferrera et al, 2001). In substantial terms, the ESM supports a harmonious combination of economic and social objectives, while at a procedural level it calls for the active involvement of social and civil actors alike. At the level of principles or objectives, the ESM is perfectly in line with the capability approach, but what actual policies and modes of operation are mobilised in order to make these good intentions come true? This chapter has pointed out serious shortcomings of the ESM in two respects:

- In terms of capability for work, the ESM combines a strong focus on increasing the overall employment rates (regarding work as the most valuable functioning, irrespective of the issues connected with employment quality) with a clear preference for supply-side programmes concentrated on upgrading human capital and eradicating dependency traps. Such a view is in sharp contrast with the capability approach and its endorsement of real freedom to work (rooted in a conception of valuable work as an essential part of human fulfilment).
- In terms of capability for voice, technocratic modes of governance co-exist with measures favouring local action: whereas the former imply regular monitoring processes, the latter very much depend on local actors' goodwill and capacity for initiative. In the present state of affairs, the managerialist modes of operation of the OMC look more like a refinement of the old technocratic recipes than a new pattern of situated public action.

Despite generous intentions, the policy tools used to implement the ESM result in significant failures when confronted with the capability framework. In our view, the translation into reality of the good intentions displayed by the ESM calls for a questioning of its threefold normative bias in favour of: (a) supply-side programmes (versus demand-side policies); (b) a very restrictive view of opportunity as productive work (versus capabilities); and (c) technocratic modes of governance (versus situated and reflexive public action).

Notes

[1] The capability approach does not entail that everybody is entitled to be fully capable, that is to be absolutely free from all constraints and limitations. Quite differently, it calls for the equalisation of capabilities, in other words, each and every member of society should have the same capability set. The objective pursued is not absolute freedom, but equal capability.

[2] Precise quantitative targets and monitoring processes are set up in this field of supply-side programmes (see Salais, this volume). By contrast, the regulatory action on the labour market is left to market actors and entrepreneurs (for job creation – GL2) and to social partners (when it comes to the issues of security and quality of employment), thus making such issues very much dependent on their goodwill.

[3] This topic has gained prominence with the emergence of the so-called 'third age'.

References

Bohman, J. (1996) *Public deliberation, pluralism, complexity and democracy*, Boston, MA: MIT Press.

Bonvin, J.-M. (2004) 'The rhetoric of activation and its effects on the definition of the target groups of social integration policies', in Serrano Pascual, A. (ed) *Are activation policies converging in Europe?*, Brussels: ETUI, pp 101-27.

Clarke, J. and Newman, J. (1997) *The managerialist state*, London: Sage Publications.

Dingeldey, I. (2004) 'Welfare state transformation between 'workfare' and an 'enabling' state', Paper presented to the ESPAnet conference, Oxford, UK, 9-11 September.

Esping-Andersen, G. (1990) *The three worlds of welfare capitalism*, Princeton, NJ: Princeton University Press.

Esping-Andersen, G. (1999) *Social foundations of post-industrial economies*, Oxford: Oxford University Press.

Esping-Andersen, G., Gallie, D., Hemerijk, A., Myles, A. (2003) *Why we need a new welfare state?*, Oxford: Oxford University Press.

European Commission (2004) *Jobs, jobs, jobs – Creating more employment in Europe*, Luxembourg: Office for Official Publications of the European Communities.

EU (European Union) (2003), Council Decision of 22 July 2003 on guidelines for the employment policies of member States, *Official Journal of the European Union*.

Ferrera, M., Hemerijk, A. and Rhodes, M. (2001) *The future of social Europe*, Lisbon: Celta Editora.

Finn, D. and Knuth, M. (2004) 'One stop? Joining up employment assistance and benefit administration in Britain and Germany', Paper presented to the ESPAnet conference, Oxford, UK, 9-11 September.

Giauque, D. (2004) *La bureaucratie libérale*, Paris: L'Harmattan.

Giddens, A. (1998) *The third way*, Bristol: The Policy Press.

Korpi, W. (1983) *Democratic class struggle*, London: Routledge.

Layard, R. and Nickell, S. (1991) *Unemployment, macroeconomic performance and the labour market*, Oxford: Oxford University Press.

Lindbeck, A. and Snower, D. (1988) *The insider-outsider theory of employment and unemployment*, Cambridge, MA: MIT Press.

Lister, R. (2004) 'Towards a social investment state?', Paper presented to the RC19 annual conference, Paris, 2-4 September.

Mabbett, D. (2004) 'Learning by numbers: the role of indicators in the social inclusion process', Paper presented to the ESPAnet conference, Oxford, UK, 9-11 September.

Mandin, C. (2004) 'Active ageing in Europe', Paper presented to the ESPAnet conference, Oxford, UK, 9-11 September.

Mosley, H., Schütz, H. and Breyer, N. (2000) *Operational objectives and performance indicators in European public employment services*, Report prepared for the European Commission, Berlin: WZB.

Orloff, A. (2002) *Women's employment and welfare regimes*, Social Policy and Development Programme Paper no 12, Geneva: UNRISD.

Salais, R., Raveaud, G. and Grégoire, M. (2002) 'L'évaluation de l'impact de la stratégie européenne pour l'emploi', *Etude pour la DARES*, Paris: IDHE.

Sen, A. (1992) *Inequality reexamined*, Oxford: Oxford University Press.

Sen, A. (1999) *Development as freedom*, Oxford: Oxford University Press.

Storper, M. and Salais, R. (1997) *Worlds of production*, Cambridge, MA: Harvard University Press.

Strath, B. (ed) (2000) *After full employment*, Brussels: PIE-Lang.

Streeck, W. (1999) 'Competitive solidarity: rethinking the European Social Model', Paper presented to the annual meeting of the Society for the Advancement of Socio-Economics, Madison, US, 8-11 June.

Wright, S. (2001) 'Activating the unemployed: the street-level implementation of UK policy', in J. Clasen (ed) *What future for social security?*, Dordrecht: Kluwer Law International, pp 235-50.

Zeitlin, J. (2004) 'The Open Method of Coordination in action: the European employment and social inclusion strategies', Paper presented to the conference: 'The EES: discussion and institutionalisation', Brussels, 30-31 August.

TEN

Social dialogue as a regulatory mode of the ESM: some empirical evidence from the new member states

Céline Lafoucriere and Roy Green

Introduction

Jepsen and Serrano Pascual (2005, p 1) explain that the term 'European Social Model' (ESM) is increasingly used within the European Union (EU) as a 'catchword describing the European experience of simultaneously promoting sustainable economic growth and social cohesion'. However, the vague nature of this concept becomes apparent as soon as one focuses on the question of its definition. As part of the overall research task undertaken in this book, this chapter focuses on establishing social dialogue as an intrinsic regulatory tool of the ESM. Developed in the last few decades and strengthened in the 1980s and 1990s by the European institutions in collaboration with the member states, social partners have increasingly been given a crucial role in the European process of 'deregulation' with a view to 're-regulation' in order to achieve a viable and well-functioning level of 'concerted regulation'. This principle of concerted regulation aims to involve all actors from all sections of the spectrum in order to lighten the weight of government legislation, which has proven rather inefficient for long-term viable employment solutions in the past, and to give more importance to social dialogue and collective bargaining, the latter being better suited to finding appropriate long-term solutions to each sector and/or plant. This rather young process within the EU15 had still to prove its worth before the latest enlargement process took place, in May 2004. The question raised in this chapter is whether social partnership structures, in the new member states, are ready to receive the ESM and respond to its demands. The focus will be, first, on their organisational models, but also on the different countries' economic markets, and in so doing will question the suitability of the ESM for these new members who carry strongly different traditions and historical backgrounds and whose future economic and social interests may also accordingly be rather different. Second, the potential threats that these new member states represent for the future of European social dialogue will be pointed out and, as such, for the ESM as a whole.

The ESM or Concerted Regulation Model

The literature on the 'varieties of capitalism' demonstrates that the European countries have long opted for a different economic model than the one observed in the United States (US) (Soskice and Hall, 2003). Although the EU chose to de-regulate its markets further, with the Cardiff Process that started in 1998, its goals are quite different from those of the dominant model of laissez-faire capitalism (Regini, 2003). Having reached a consensus on the fact that heavy government regulations do weigh on European markets, slowing down good productivity and competitiveness levels as demonstrated in the last 20 years, the EU, in 1997 at the Luxembourg Summit, set in motion an overall reform process. Described as a three-level process, the so-called European Employment Pact (EEP) aims to reform labour markets, with its European Employment Strategy (1997), to restructure product and capital markets, via the Cardiff Process (1998), and to develop a macroeconomic dialogue as established in the Cologne Process (1999). These three processes establish what is believed to be the basis for the ESM in the sense that it focuses less on finding common solutions to common problems than on providing common tools to tackle similar European-wide problems, such as high rates of unemployment and changing methods of work, thereby seeking to provide an alternative option to the initial two respectively found in countries of the EU and the US.

This model, which the authors choose to call the 'Concerted Regulation Model' (CRM), focuses more on 'process' than on 'content' and represents a move away from heavy general government legislation, insofar as it provides only a lowest common denominator for all sectors of the economy, in order to achieve a more appropriate sector-/plant-based concerted regulation. Without discarding issues of content, it is in the issues of process that the greatest divide between the US and the European model can be found to lie. As opposed to the US concept of wide deregulation of social policy, which consists of making labour markets more flexible by abolishing employment regulations and liberalising wage-setting, which will then be determined by the market itself, the CRM aims at re-regulating its labour market at different levels (Green and Lafoucriere, 2004). Although it shares the same targets of high productivity and competitiveness, the CRM differs strongly from the US model of labour market flexibility and deregulation, insofar as it focuses on a constantly evolving balance of economic dynamism and social protection. To this end, the CRM aims at triggering a process of competition and deregulation at the national level but with a view to integrating and re-regulating at all other possible levels, thereby ensuring the participation of all social forces, including wider involvement of workers (Green and Lafoucriere, 2004).

The element just described establishes what the authors believe to be one of the intrinsic regulatory pillars of the CRM. The principle of re-regulation, to be efficient, must involve different partners and establish strong and coherent social partnerships. The social partners are thus given a key role in establishing the CRM.

Why is social partnership intrinsic to the ESM or CRM?

The last few decades since the 1970s have shown that productivity growth and high levels of competitiveness could not be achieved in the EU without being accompanied by effective social policies. Late industrial developments and changing needs of the labour market have also raised the issue of workers' participation. Moves towards a knowledge-based society (KBS) have changed the structure of labour markets and workplaces. The reduction of working time, growing number of atypical contracts, as well as the increasing dichotomy between high- and low-productivity jobs, have changed traditional labour values. Overall, and as mentioned previously, the EU has come to realise that government legislation no longer represents a satisfactory option; and if space is now needed for customisation of the labour market, space is also needed for the customisation of social decisions to different sectors and activities, thus entailing the intrinsic need for collective bargaining and social partnerships at large (Green and Lafoucriere, 2004). The CRM, therefore, is based on a progressive realisation, by the member states as well as the European institutions, that:

> Social dialogue does not *supplement* but *complements* classical parliamentary democracy. Allowing large groups in society to participate in the policy formulation and decision-

making processes regarding economic and social policy can strengthen and consolidate traditional policy mechanisms. Social dialogue is *flexible*: partners may meet whenever they deem it necessary. But it may also be *strategic*: aimed at securing long-term rather than short-term gains. (Richly and Pritzer, 2003, p 2, emphasis added)

The concept of 'long-term solutions' is crucial to the development of social partnership within the context of the CRM. Considered to be closer and more present at sectoral and plant levels, social partners have a better understanding of the needs of each sector/plant. The developing use of collective agreements should therefore aim at slowly complementing government legislation, which will in turn become increasingly lighter and aimed at ensuring minimum standards only.

As Jepsen and Serrano Pascual (2005) note, there are strong structural and organisational differences between European economic policy reflected in the European Monetary Union, which takes a closely monitored and obligatory format, and European social policy reflected in the European Employment Strategy (EES), which is only a guidance process, but which already sends strong messages for the creation of European-wide social partnerships, including in what concerns the more sensitive macroeconomic questions. The Lisbon Summit, held in 2000, strengthened this position by stating that:

As well as preserving macro-economic stability and stimulating growth and employment, macro-economic policies should foster the transition towards a knowledge-based economy, which implies an enhanced role for structural policies. The macro-economic dialogue under the Cologne process must create a relationship of trust between *all* the actors involved in order to have a proper understanding of each other's positions and constraints. The opportunity provided by growth must be used to pursue fiscal consolidation more actively and to improve the quality and sustainability of public finances. (European Council, 2000, para 22, emphasis added)

While setting European economic objectives for the coming years, the Council recognised the involvement of all actors as a driving force behind successful and effective economic reform, and as intrinsic to economic and social progress for the whole Community. Crucially the Cologne Process offers access to the macroeconomic dialogue to social partners for the first time in the history of the EU. Essentially, it established the ESM as a key competitive advantage of the EU in policy terms. By the same token, it is crucial to understand that the social model sees the economy

> ... as embedded in the social structure and as depending on that structure for its capacity to operate effectively.... It sees a need for the active cooperation of workers in the work process ... and it recognizes the importance of institutions and the role they play in creating a framework in which a market operates, in mediating the relationship between the economy and society, and in reconciling economic efficiency with other social goals. (Osterman et al, 2001, pp 3-4)

The above concept is intrinsic to the success of the CRM. Economic and social policy must be envisaged as interdependent. As a reflection of this it is important to bear in mind that the role of social partners has shifted from income policy to greater flexibility of the labour market: greater employment, less rigidity and the ability to create new jobs; as well as reforms of labour markets and, to some extent, participation in reforms of the social security systems, although the latter two objectives are much more difficult and complex to achieve by concerted means than are traditional income policies, for example. One condition is, however, crucial to the efficiency of a European CRM: for it to be permeable to pressures and achieve a high degree of stability the involvement of various social groups in decision-making must be seen less as slowing down the decision-making process than as ensuring the success of the decisions taken. As Regini (2003) explained, it is precisely in the trade-off between a slower decision-making process and the greater likelihood of the successful implementation of its input, that the challenge between the different models of economic regulation is located today. The latter development has been highly difficult to achieve, as has been seen since the early 1980s in the 'old' EU15, and will certainly prove even more complicated in the new EU25.

EES demands for social dialogue

According to a recent International Labour Organisation definition:

> ... social dialogue represents all types of negotiation, consultation and information sharing among representatives of governments, social partners or between social partners on issues of common interest relating to economic and social policy. (Richly and Pritzer, 2003, p 2)

The above definition comprises the very sensitive issues that still surround the concept and definition of 'social dialogue' today. In the industrial relations domain, consultations and negotiations are generally conducted between the parties independently of relations with the state, even in the public sector. In the domain of social dialogue, however, the state (or supra-state) establishes the conditions and topics for consultation and negotiation and incorporates the outcomes into its action (Winterton and Strandberg, 2004). It is in the latter sense, albeit evolving towards the former, that social dialogue is envisaged in the ESM. Guided by the member states and the European institutions (supra-state), the social partners are asked to negotiate among themselves, thereby acquiring enough experience and awareness to slowly become independent. As Richly and Pritzer (2003) note, social dialogue is an idea that is neither politically nor ideologically neutral. This raises some crucial questions for the new member states. Considering their historical backgrounds and political traditions, social dialogue may be thought to impinge on the role of governments in the new member states. Equally it might be feared that social dialogue will be seen as incompatible with the notion of an efficient market economy, while it is already considered, within the ESM, to contribute not only to the resolution of conflicts but also to improving productivity and competitiveness, as well as developing social and economic policies. As Bercusson et al (1996) explain, the value of social dialogue as an instrument for social and labour regulation within the EU depends upon the effectiveness of social partner representative organisations within the member states. In the new member states the fear is that employers' associations are insufficiently developed and/or that labour organisations have not yet sufficiently evolved in terms of independence from the state, thereby threatening the future of the ESM as a whole.

The demands of the EES on social dialogue are particularly important. The four old pillars of the strategy, which are still clearly reflected today in the new guidelines, all call on social partners to play a strongly innovative and independent role. Although the EES is considered to be a guidance process, having adopted a non-obligatory format, the notion of social dialogue within it is of much greater importance than it might seem. As Vaughan-Whitehead (2003) explains, social dialogue is part of the *acquis* in a horizontal manner. The formal need to consult with social partners is present in the texts of several directives, in which are included references to the principle of workers' consultation:

> The directive on European Works Council provides an instrument for social dialogue and workers' representation across borders and is particularly relevant in view of prospective European Union enlargement and intensified capital movement in an enlarged Europe. (Vaughan-Whitehead, 2003, p 280)

However, it is crucial to remark on the fact that social dialogue is also part of the institutional *acquis*. Article 138 creates an obligation to consult social partners on most legal provisions that the European Community intends to adopt. Furthermore, and if they so wish, social partners may choose to interrupt the legislative process, by initiating negotiations, for the purpose of reaching agreements. The autonomy enjoyed by the social partners in initiating the process to start negotiations between themselves clearly highlights the fact that social dialogue has become a real 'driving force' behind European social and economic progress. The EES, the employment title of the Amsterdam Treaty, and the Lisbon Strategy, clearly offer new opportunities for social partners' actions.

> All these institutionalised forms of social dialogue represent unavoidable mechanisms of social progress which must be taken into account by the applicant countries and integrated in their national systems and structures. Much is therefore at stake for the social partners of applicant countries. (Vaughan-Whitehead, 2003, 237)

To the above end, social partners have important work to do in most of the new member states to ensure that genuine structures of social partnership develop. It is in order to corroborate these essential elements of the ESM *or* CRM that the following section concentrates on collecting and analysing empirical data in different new member states and on evaluating the current state of the social dialogue situation in these countries, and for the new EU25.

Social dialogue in the new member states: the state of play

Predominance of tripartism

Although social dialogue has strong historical roots in the new member states, insofar as collective bargaining developed well before Communism, its structures today are ambivalent. Following the collapse of Communism, in 1989, and in the rush for decentralisation and establishment of proper market economies, all new policies were directed by government alone and did not seem to lead to the democratisation of the decision-making process. Critically, strong tripartite structures were developed in the following years in order to proceed to an ambiguous process of 'mutual legitimisation' of trades unions and governments. Old Communist trades unions, as well as new trades unions, found themselves in dire need of re-legitimisation or legitimisation (Vaughan-Whitehead, 2003) and thus welcomed the new government call for tripartism. Cooperation with the state was seen as a safe way to ensure their role in the new society, thereby attracting new members and ensuring representativeness. By the same token, new governments also used this newly found collaboration in order to heighten their legitimacy among their populations (Lafoucriere, 2004). Since the underground trades union movements had been highly active against the old regime, their cooperation with the new governments was to help the latter's credibility among the younger population. This process of mutual recognition can generally be seen as the historical root of the supremacy of tripartism in the new member states. As shown in Table 10.1, all new member states have developed a tripartite main body dealing with social and economic issues. Although representation and legal status vary across the board, these bodies are fairly well organised and meet on a regular basis. However, two main issues arise from an overall collection of empirical data. First, the insufficient participation, on a day-to-day basis, of social partners in these platforms is striking. Across-the-board individual interviews with social partners and government representatives have highlighted the fact that, in countries where these institutions are regulated by tripartite agreements with no legal basis, social partners display a pronounced tendency to stay away from meetings. This is the case in Latvia, Lithuania, Czech Republic, Hungary, Malta and Cyprus. The data collected seem to highlight a wide lack of specific technical expertise among social partners, which could explain their absence from some of these meetings (Zeman, 2004). Others have also claimed that, in countries where trades unions are ideologically divided, such meetings tend to become platforms for argument between them, therefore not leading to any concrete actions and/or decisions that would involve agreement from the trades union representatives. This is particularly the case in Malta (Lafoucriere and Zammit, 2005).

Many of the interviews bring to light the fact that social partners are encouraged by their governments to believe that these platforms provide a sound basis for information and consultation, and fear that the creation of autonomous social dialogue platforms might be seen

Table 10.1: Structure and legal basis of national tripartite councils in the new member states

Country	Designation	Employers' representatives	Trade union representatives	Legal basis
Estonia	Social and Economic Council	1	2	Law 1998
Latvia	National Tripartite Co-operation Council	1	1	Tripartite agreement 1998
Lithuania	Tripartite Council	2	4	Tripartite agreement 1995
Poland	Tripartite Commission for Social and Economic Issues	4	9	Law 2001
Czech Republic	Council for Economic and Social Agreement	2	2	Tripartite agreement 1997
Slovakia	Tripartite Economic and Social Concertation Council	1	1	Law 1999
Hungary	National Interest Reconciliation Council	9	6	Tripartite agreement 2002
Slovenia	National Economic and Social Council	5	5	Agreement 1994 – special law in preparation
Malta	Maltese Council for Social and Economic Development	2	2	Tripartite agreement 1998
Cyprus	Labour and Economic Advisory Board	2	2	Tripartite agreement 1974

Sources: Kohl and Platzer (2004); Lafoucriere and Zammit (2005)

not only as a betrayal of their government but also as jeopardising their participation in these platforms, which they often regard as a 'privilege' (Lafoucriere, 2004). It therefore appears evident that the continuing dominance of the state explains the success of tripartism:

> Moreover in the wake of the collapse of the communist regimes there was no real culture and practice of autonomous industrial relations, and the prevalence of the state in all economic and social matters was such that this form of dialogue became a natural and inherited form of policy-making democratisation after decades of centralisation and totalitarianism. (Vaughan–Whitehead, 2003, p 34)

Although some of these structures have evolved over time, most seem to remain within the same format. Tripartism still rules across the board and raises the question of state predominance in the new member states, contrasting strongly with the process of decentralisation of the decision-making process put forward by the ESM, in Western Europe. In order to fully understand the reasons behind such a situation several other aspects must be highlighted.

Ideologically divided trades unions

Although trade union membership rates are, in some cases, much higher in the new than in some of the old members, trades unions tend to remain relatively weak across the region (see Table 10.2 later in this chapter). Their weakness can be described as lying at two different levels: first, their lack of autonomous action and, second, their relatively low influence on national government policy.

The ideological divide between trades unions, which can prevent a lack of autonomous social dialogue and action, is crucially prominent among the southern members. It is interesting to note that this is a striking feature in two of the new members which have the highest union density. The UK bipolarisation model appears to have left some strong stigmata in Cyprus and Malta. In these two new members, both of which were occupied by the UK for quite some time albeit to differing degrees, the social partnership model adopted at that time continues to weigh heavily on today's situation and may have even stronger consequences on the future of the EU's social dialogue format. It is crucial to note that in the case of Malta and Cyprus there are no central organisations to bring all trades unions together under a single umbrella.

In both countries two strong federations bring together different trades unions, which tend to be organised by industry rather than by occupation. In Cyprus, the Cyprus Workers' Confederation (SEK) and Pancypriot Federation of Labour (PEO) are the two strongest federations, sharing the top rank according to economic and sectoral changes. The situation is similar in Malta, where the General Workers' Union (GWU) membership rate closely models that of the Confederation of Malta Trade Unions (CMTU). However, and according to the different interviews carried out, there is very little hope for the creation of a general confederation of unions that would bring them all together under a single umbrella, thereby lending them greater power in a context of social dialogue. By way of illustration, John Monks' last visit to Malta, in June 2004, in an effort to encourage the creation of a Trade Union Confederation (TUC), following a similar model to the one found in the UK, provoked some avid reactions. The merger that existed in the 1970s between the GWU and the national Labour Party, in power at that time, seems to remain the most recurrent theme and cause for vigorous opposition to any cooperation between the unions. The old ideological divide very obviously still prevents trades unions from uniting their efforts and gaining sufficient weight to collectively and autonomously bargain with the employers' organisations. Crucially, and as will be explained further, the virtual absence of employers' organisations does not stimulate trades unions to organise further.

Of course it is essential to note that these two southern members have a very different historical and social dialogue background from all other Central and Eastern European members, and notably the Baltic countries, which formed the three USSR satellites during the Communist era. The independence of Latvia, Lithuania and Estonia was followed, in each case, by a certain vacuum of social partners' cooperation conditioned by the political and economic situation as well as the social situation brought about by Soviet domination. When, at the beginning of the 1990s, the first social partner institutions were established, the situation remained particularly difficult for the social partners. The concepts of trades unions, collective bargaining and workers' involvement were still regarded as elements of the former socialist production management system and thus unsuitable for a well-functioning market economy. Deepening this lack of legitimacy, trades unions in these countries also seem to remain extremely divided between the old and the new 'socialist ideal', making social partnership a rather complicated exercise. Low membership rates are a reflection of this lack of organisation and cohesion among trades unions and have manifestly left ample space for government action. One illustration of this would be the measures taken by these governments to abolish the centralised trade union membership fee, thereby restricting trades unions' influence on social and economic processes, in particular with the aim of reducing financial income and thereby also reducing possibilities of organising strike action.

In the Baltic countries, confrontational attitudes seem to prevail between government and trades unions, as well as between trades unions themselves, and, typically, between employers and trades unions (Gruzevskis and Blaziene, 2005), allowing platforms of a tripartite nature to proliferate.

This lack of cohesion and agreement between trades unions, across the board, has permitted wide top-down social dialogue developments to take place. This has two major consequences:

- First, national organisations tend to be much more developed and better organised than local and/or enterprise-level organisations, directly affecting sectoral dialogue, which remains virtually non-existent.
- Second, this situation has resulted in different agreements being modelled on existing legislation. This was the case, for example, in Lithuania where the first tripartite council was established on the basis of the provisions contained in the 'unemployment support legislation' (Gruzevskis and Blaziene, 2005).

The ideological divide between trades unions, and thus their lack of organisation, leaves considerable space for government action and does not correspond to the overall process of a decentralisation of decision-making, which is witnessed in Western Europe and which is stimulated by the ESM. Paradoxically, it is important to note that the high rates of union density witnessed in Cyprus and Malta do not actually appear to give trades unions much more influence on government and/or weight to bargain autonomously.

Crucially, it is also important to note that union membership rates have been declining across the board in the region. Although some of the reasons behind this decline are more structural and economic than anything else, some of the responsibility does lie with the trades unions themselves. The compulsory membership fee having been replaced by a more voluntaristic democratic model of membership, trades unions saw their membership decline. Combined with a wide restructuring process, which took place in the early 1990s, and the diminution of the public sector, which led to the creation of a majority of small- and medium-sized enterprises in which trades unions are finding it very difficult to gain representation, the union density has taken a hard blow. However, the lack of organisation in central trades union organisations and the ideological gap between different national trades union organisations have not helped their credibility and legitimisation among potential new members. This is strikingly the case in Poland, where trades unions are known to be experiencing a deep crisis of legitimacy (Kozek, 2004). This same situation seems to be present in all new member states, placing government legislation at an advantage. However, it is only fair to note that the prevalent lack of employers' organisations hardly encourages trades unions to organise further.

Employers' striking absence

Representing the 'new breed' in the Central and Eastern European region, employers remained fairly badly organised until today. Three reasons seem to emerge from the data collected:

- First, and as already mentioned, employers are new actors in the previously centralised region and therefore still have to organise themselves into viable organisations.
- Second, most of the employers in the region tend to be foreign investors who have no interest in organising at the national level and tend to apply their own national social organisation format, if that.
- Third, and recurrently, employers express no wish to organise in tighter umbrella institutions that would enable them to act autonomously with trades unions.

To judge from the numerous interviews, employers recurrently seem to follow the same line of action in the sense that the current situation seems to suit them perfectly. Employers, who are well aware of their influence and power on government economic policy, clearly favour tripartite consultation as against bipartite autonomous action. Sectoral-level bargaining, in particular, is not portrayed as a desirable option for the employers (Cziria, 2005; Lafoucriere and Zammit, 2005; Ozola, 2005). Having obtained suitable recognition through solid government legislation, employers do not wish to enter a more flexible form of bargaining within which they see themselves as the losing partner.

Further to this, it is important to note that in most of the new member states there is no legislation that specifically regulates the behaviour of employers. Although most are now in the process of designing such legislation, as is the case in Estonia, such an observation demonstrates the great freedom with which employers are currently able to evolve.

The lack of employers' organisations tends, however, to cause more problems on a representation basis. This is strikingly the case in Hungary, where the large number of employers' organisations, as well as trades unions, means that representation on tripartite boards, as is notably the case on the Mixed European Union–Hungarian Consultative Committee, has to take place on a rotating basis (Galgoczi, 2004). However, it must be mentioned, as explained by Galgoczi, that Hungarian government tradition has always been seen to favour employers over trades unions in the consultative process. Employers therefore hardly seem to suffer greatly as a result of their own lack of organisation. The general trend to over-legislate industrial relations, in contrast with lighter legislation of labour, in the region appears to satisfy employers more than trades unions. This tendency prevents voluntaristic social dialogue and gives industrial relations more of an obligatory format, leaving some of the crucial issues, such as sectoral collective bargaining, to fall by the wayside. This could, however, become the cause of greater problems and challenges for the future of the ESM, in its concerted regulatory format. More and better organisation is needed on the part of both trades unions and employers in order to further democratise systems of industrial relations and achieve viable levels of autonomous social dialogue as well as collective bargaining.

An ambiguous start for bipartite autonomous social dialogue

Despite a number of achievements in promoting social Europe within the latest enlargement process, such as the adoption of all chapter 13 directives of the *acquis*, not much has been done in practice to promote the development of autonomous social dialogue in the new member states. This could be seen as a weakness on the part of the European institutions, although it could be argued that this is mostly a spillover effect of several old member states having repeatedly tried to undermine social rights in the belief that they would be costly for enterprises and lead to excessively rigid labour markets (Vaughan-Whitehead, 2003). There are those, however, who are ready to accept that social matters should be attended to, but only after economic growth has been ensured. As highlighted by Vaughan-Whitehead (2003), it is in this spirit that many analysts have challenged the coherence and viability of a common social model that is seen as contradicting the current logic of international economic competition and globalisation. This is mainly the case of the followers of Adam Smith who have been actively discrediting European social policy since the early 1970s. Taking this issue further, they draw attention to the fact that this trend, which has obviously already had some effect on the latest enlargement process, presents an imminent danger for the future of the ESM, as it may become the dominant trend in the EU25. Although the Lisbon Strategy's aims are centred on demonstrating the intrinsic link between economic performance and social progress, and on presenting social progress by the social partners as a production factor, the message does not appear to have been made extremely clear to the-then candidate countries, although one section of the social agenda of the Nice Summit did identify, among the main common challenges, the need to make a 'success of enlargement in the social field'. However, and if one agrees on the need for strong autonomous social dialogue to be developed in all member states, it is striking to see that the only criteria that candidate countries had to fulfil for accession were the Copenhagen criteria, which include:

- the establishment of democratic principles and structures;
- development of a functioning market economy; and
- acceptance and transposition into national law of the whole EU legal *acquis*.

Although the social *acquis* clearly stating the need for a predominant role of social partners was part of it, not enough emphasis was applied to these issues and these measures, like many others, although adopted in national legislation, were not applied and implemented at a practical level, as is reflected in the empirical findings. When this is combined with a rather timid and ambiguous message from European institutions to the new member states on the crucial need to develop autonomous social dialogue further, in order to consolidate the ESM, this could represent an imminent danger for the future of the ESM or CRM. As explained by Vaughan-Whitehead, the economies of many Central and Eastern European countries are already dominated by deregulation and neoliberal theories. The advisory work of international monetary institutions, combined with the emergence of a new generation of political leaders with a strong willingness to do everything possible to promote real capitalist economies, has already had a major impact.

This only serves to emphasise even further the difficulty of persuading these countries of the virtues of the ESM.

As mentioned above, the new member states' trades unions and employers' associations, whether reformed or newly created, have struggled to gain legitimacy and institutional effectiveness and have recently suffered a further decline in membership (Kocsis, 2000). In four of the new members – Lithuania, Hungary, Poland and Estonia – less than 20% of the workforce is organised. This has led to serious organisational difficulties, which have led in turn to the increasing weakness and fragmentation, with the exception of Slovenia, of trades unions at company level (Kohl and Platzer, 2003). This negative evolution, combined with a generally badly organised employers' movement, did not have the effect of strengthening autonomous bipartite social dialogue. In the new member states, employer organisations are estimated to have affiliated 30-40% of industrial firms but less than 5% of all firms, representing as little as 15% in employment terms in Poland for example (Lado and Vaughan-Whitehead, 2003). Taking the coverage of collective bargaining as an indicator of the scope and significance of autonomous social dialogue, in most new member states only a minority of workers are covered by collective agreements. In Latvia and Lithuania the figure is 20% of workers. Overall, Lado and Vaughan-Whitehead (2003) estimate that 70-75% of employees in the central and eastern regions are not covered by collective bargaining. Slovenia is an exception with 98% of workers covered (see Table 10.2). As Winterton and Strandberg (2004) highlight, this special case is explained by bargaining arrangements that closely resemble those of the Austrian system, where membership of the Chamber of Commerce is obligatory for all enterprises.

As a result of these structural weaknesses of social partners' organisations, sectoral bargaining is particularly underdeveloped in the new member states. This is particularly due to the level of organisational fragmentation or simply because they are not authorised to conclude binding agreements (Ghellab and Vaughan-Whitehead, 2003).

From Table 10.2 it can be observed that the scant use of collective agreements is undeniably linked to the lack of organisational efforts of both trades unions and employers' associations. This is the case in Poland, Estonia, Latvia and Lithuania. A certain degree of inflexibility of extension of collective agreements also seems to be reflected in the low organisational density of social partners. However, it is crucial to note that, while one of the new members can be found in the top rank of collective agreements with values of more than 90%, most can be found in the lower ranking sections together with the UK and Ireland – with a predominance of collective bargaining coverage of less than 50%, and even lower than 20% in three of the new members.

Extension of collective agreements to other sectors is also a crucial element of the further development of collective bargaining. If national rules and regulations allow for such extension practices to be applied, then social partners' low organisational rates do not have such an impact on coverage by collective agreement. However, it is in countries with the lowest rates of organisational density that one finds most inflexibility in the possibility of extending collective agreements to other sectors.

Leaving aside the exceptional Slovene case, Table 10.3 demonstrates that a large majority of new members share rates of collective agreements similar to the European Anglo-Saxon model. These include Slovakia, the Czech Republic, Poland, Hungary, Estonia, Latvia and Lithuania.

Table 10.2: Organisational density and coverage by collective agreements in the EU

Country	Union density	Employers organisational density	Coverage by collective agreements	Extension of collective agreements
Finland	72	60	98	Customary
Austria	40	75	98	Customary
Slovenia	42	45	98	All collective agreements
Sweden	80	80	95	In some cases
France	9	60	95	Customary
Belgium	55	60	90	Customary
Italy	36	40	90	Customary for pay
Greece	30	40	90	Customary
Denmark	80	50	80	Not formally
Portugal	25	60	80	Customary
Spain	18	50	80	Frequent
Netherlands	28	45	78	Frequent
Germany	30	60	75	In some branches
Slovakia	35	50	48	Possible
Ireland	45	40	45	On occasions
Hungary	25	40	42	Rare
UK	29	40	36	No
Czech Republic	30	35	35	More frequent since 2000
Poland	18	20	30	Possible from 2000
Estonia	15	30	20	Possible from 2000
Latvia	20	30	20	Possible from 2002
Lithuania	14	20	13	No

Sources: Lado and Vaughan-Whitehead (2003); Kohl and Platzer (2003, 2004); Lafoucriere (2004); Lafoucriere and Zammit (2005)

Table 10.3: Towards a typology of autonomous bipartite social dialogue and collective bargaining

Categories	Rates of collective agreements and extension possibilities
Continental EU13	Between 75% and 98%, reflecting frequent extension of collective agreements
Anglo-Saxon EU2 (UK and Ireland)	Between 36% and 45%, reflecting rare extension of collective agreements
Mediterranean type (Malta/Cyprus)	Between 60% and 70%, reflecting frequent extension of collective agreements
Eastern type (Slovenia/Slovakia)	Between 48% and 98%, reflecting frequent extension of collective bargaining
Central-Eastern type (Czech Republic/ Poland/Hungary)	Between 30% and 42%, reflecting possible extension of collective agreements
Baltic type (Estonia/Latvia/Lithuania)	Below 20%, reflecting strong inflexibility in extension of collective agreements

The pre-enlargement fears that the momentum gained by autonomous social dialogue, both at European and national levels, might be lost against predominant trends towards purely capitalist economies seem to have become a reality. More critically Table 10.3 clearly demonstrates that the underrepresented Anglo-Saxon model of deregulation, within the EU, now seems to have acquired a substantial number of 'working partners'. This may pose great threats to the future of the ESM in its concerted regulatory form.

Concluding remarks

In response to the first hypothesis and in the light of empirical findings, it appears increasingly urgent that the EU should provide a general definition of the concept of 'autonomous social dialogue' and clearly explain the need for 'collective agreements'. It is essential that these concepts be given a legitimate place within the ESM so that they are increasingly conceived of as means of ensuring the success of the decision-making process rather than slowing it down. In countries where there is no inherent culture of autonomous social dialogue these principles might turn out to be more difficult to implement than in the old EU15. It is for these reasons that the authors recommend that the European institutions adopt a stronger stance in relation to the concept of social dialogue. This essential pillar of the ESM must clearly be highlighted as being intrinsic to its functioning as well as being *the* key competitive advantage behind Europe's long-term successful economic and social development. The predominance of tripartism, which reflects the dominance of the state in most of the new member countries, should be considered as unacceptable for the ESM. As a consequence of this, it is clear that the new members' social partners are clearly not ready to respond to the ESM's demands. For this there are two reasons: first, they are not organised well enough to have sufficient autonomous weight; second, and probably more crucially, the EES does not seem to be a totally well-suited answer to the labour market and employment challenges encountered in these countries. The authors therefore believe that a crucial overall review both of a European-level social dialogue definition and of a more flexible EES should be considered in order to enable the new members to take the requisite resolutions. In the absence of such a process, and as demonstrated above, there exists a strong risk that the Anglo-Saxon model, having found new partners, will become prevalent within the EU and thereby discredit the rather fragile ESM.

References

Bercusson, B., Deakin, S., Koistinen, Y., Kravaritou, U., Mückenberger, A., Supiot, A. and Veneziani, B. (eds) (1996) *A manifesto for a social Europe*, Brussels: ETUI.

Cziria, L. (2005) 'The role of social dialogue in Slovakia's accession to the European Union', in C. Lafoucriere and L. Magnusson (eds) *The enlargement of Social Europe: The role of social partners in the European Employment Strategy, part II,* Brussels: ETUI, pp 149-202.

European Council (2000) *Presidency conclusions*, Lisbon European Council 23 and 24 March, Brussels: European Council.

Galgoczi, B. (2004) 'The implementation of the EES in the context of accession and candidate countries', in B. Galgoczi, C. Lafoucriere and L. Magnusson (eds) *The enlargement of Social Europe: The role of social partners in the European Employment Strategy*, Brussels: ETUI, pp 77-94.

Galgoczi, B., Lafoucriere, C. and Magnusson, L. (eds) (2004) *The enlargement of Social Europe: The role of social partners in the European Employment Strategy*, Brussels: ETUI.

Ghellab, Y. and Vaughan-Whitehead, D. (eds) (2003) *Sectoral social dialogue in future EU member states: The weakest link*, Geneva: ILO.

Green, R. and Lafoucriere, C. (2004) 'The European Social Model and globalisation', Paper presented at the Irish Academy of Management, Dublin, 1-3 September.

Gruzevskis, B. and Blaziene, I. (2005) 'EES implementation promoting the development of social dialogue in Lithuania', in C. Lafoucriere and L. Magnusson (eds) *The enlargement of Social Europe: The role of social partners in the European Employment Strategy, part II*, Brussels: ETUI, pp 61-100.

Jepsen, M. and Serrano Pascual, A. (2005) 'The European Social Model: an exercise in deconstruction', *Journal of European Social Policy*, vol 15, no 3, pp 231-45.

Kocsis, G. (2000) 'Industrial relations in Central and Eastern Europe in the perspective of European Union enlargement', *South-East Europe Review for Labour and Social Affairs*, vol 3, no 1, pp 9-20.

Kohl, H. and Platzer, H.W. (2003) 'Labour relations in Central and Eastern Europea and the European Social Model', *Transfer*, vol 9, no 1, pp 11-30.

Kohl, H. and Platzer, H. W. (2004) *Industrial relations in Central and Eastern Europe: Transformation and integration*, Brussels: ETUI.

Kozek, W. (2004) 'How far into implementation? Social dialogue in Poland for participation in the EES', in B. Galgoczi, C. Lafoucriere and L. Magnusson (eds) *The enlargement of Social Europe: The role of social partners in the European Employment Strategy*, Brussels: ETUI, pp 301-44.

Lado, M. and Vaughan-Whitehead, D. (2003) 'Social dialogue in candidate countries: what for?', *Transfer*, vol 9, no 1, pp 64-87.

Lafoucriere, C. (2004) 'Social dialogue in Cyprus: a reliable model threatened by European Union accession?', in B. Galgoczi, C. Lafoucriere and L. Magnusson (eds) *The enlargement of Social Europe: The role of social partners in the European Employment Strategy*, Brussels: ETUI, pp 157-201.

Lafoucriere, C. and Zammit, E. (2005) 'Social dialogue in Malta: a model threatened by ideological divide', in C. Lafoucriere and L. Magnusson (eds) *The enlargement of Social Europe: The role of social partners in the European Employment Strategy, part II*, Brussels: ETUI, pp 101-48.

Osterman, P., Kochan, T., Locke, R. and Piore, M. (2001) *Working in America: Blueprint for the new labor market*, Cambridge: MIT Press.

Ozola, I. (2005) 'Social dialogue in Latvia: a challenge for the social partners', in C. Lafoucriere and L. Magnusson (eds) *The enlargement of social Europe: The role of social partners in the European Employment Strategy, part II*, Brussels: ETUI, pp 25-60.

Regini, M. (2003) 'Tripartite concertation and varieties of capitalism', *European Journal of Industrial Relations*, vol 9, no 3, pp 251-63.

Richly, L. and Pritzer, R. (2003) *Social dialogue at national level in the EU accession countries*, Working Paper, Geneva: ILO.

Soskice, D. and Hall, P. A. (eds) (2003) *Varieties of capitalism: The institutional foundations of comparative advantage*, Oxford: Oxford University Press.

Vaughan-Whitehead, D. (2003) *EU enlargement versus Social Europe? The uncertain future of the European Social Model*, Cheltenham: Edward Elgar Publishing.

Winterton, J. and Strandberg, T. (2004) 'European social dialogue: an evaluation and critical assessment', in B. Galgoczi, C. Lafoucriere and L. Magnusson (eds) *The enlargement of Social Europe: The role of social partners in the European Employment Strategy*, Brussels: ETUI, pp 21-76.

Zeman, F. (2004) 'The EES challenges and prospects for the social partners in the Czech republic', in B. Galgoczi, C. Lafoucriere and L. Magnusson (eds) *The enlargement of Social Europe: The role of social partners in the European Employment Strategy*, Brussels: ETUI, pp 135-56.

Index

Page numbers in *italic* refer to tables or figures.